Painting with Light

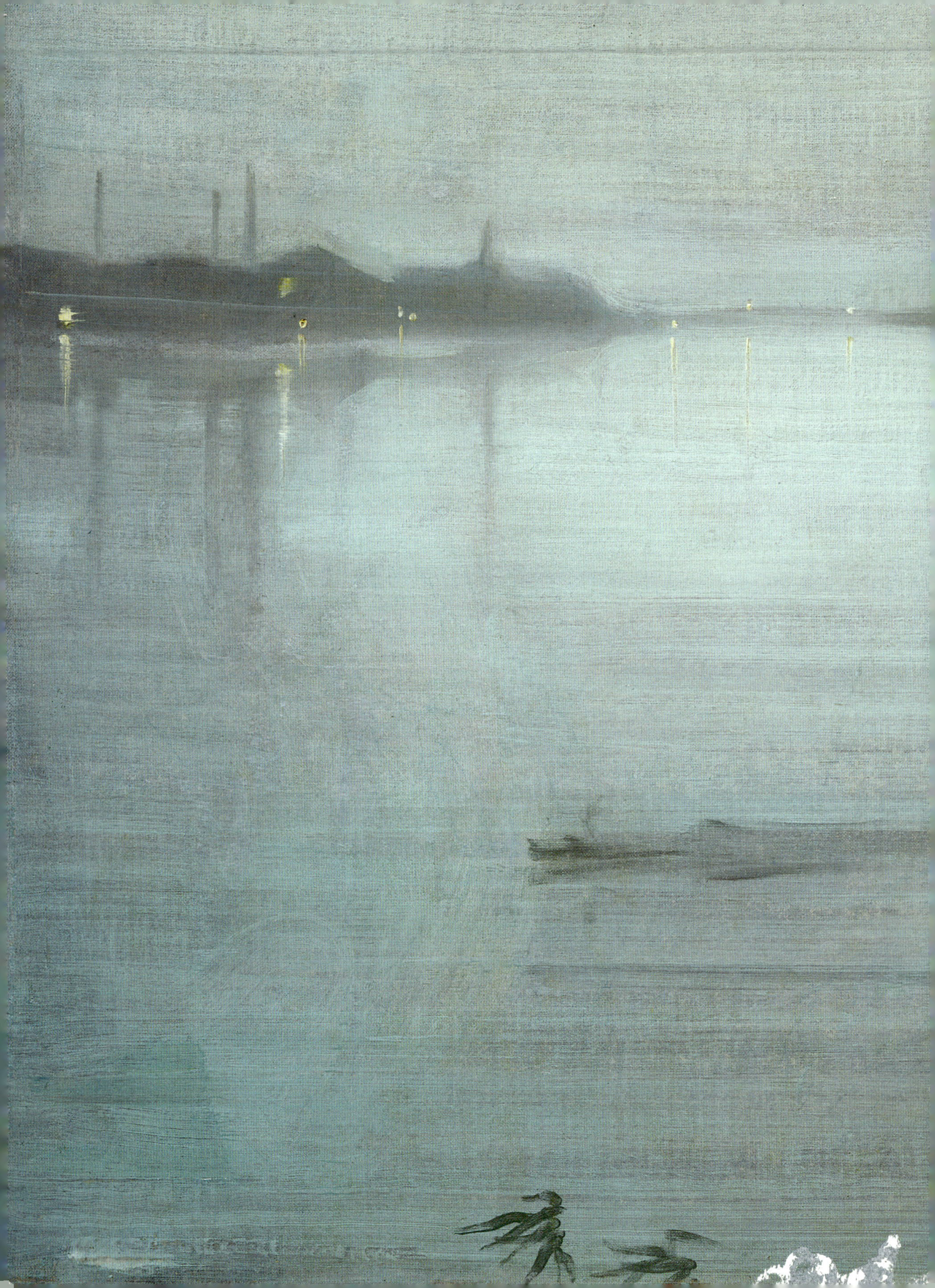

Painting with Light

Art and Photography from the Pre-Raphaelites to the modern age

Carol Jacobi and Hope Kingsley
with contributions by Elizabeth Jacklin

Tate Publishing

First published 2016 by order of the Tate Trustees
by Tate Publishing, a division of Tate Enterprises Ltd,
Millbank, London SW1P 4RG
www.tate.org.uk/publishing

on the occasion of the exhibition
Painting with Light: Art and Photography from the Pre-Raphaelites to the modern age

Tate Britain, London
11 May – 25 September 2016

Supported by Tate Patrons

A catalogue record for this book is available from the British Library

ISBN 978 1 84976 402 5
Distributed in the United States and Canada by ABRAMS, New York

Library of Congress Control Number: 2016932039

Designed by Maggi Smith, Sixism Ltd
Colour reproduction by DL Imaging, Ltd, London
Printed and bound in Italy by Pigini

Front cover:
Mina Keene, *Decorative Study* c.1906 (detail, no.117)

Back cover:
Dante Gabriel Rossetti, *Proserpine* 1874 (detail, no.114)

Frontispiece:
James Abbott McNeill Whistler,
Nocturne: Blue and Silver – Cremorne Lights 1872 (detail, no.83)

Measurements of artworks are given in centimetres, height before width

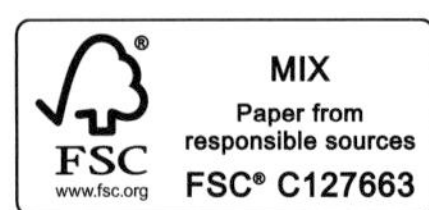

CJ – Carol Jacobi
EJ – Elizabeth Jacklin
HK – Hope Kingsley

Contents

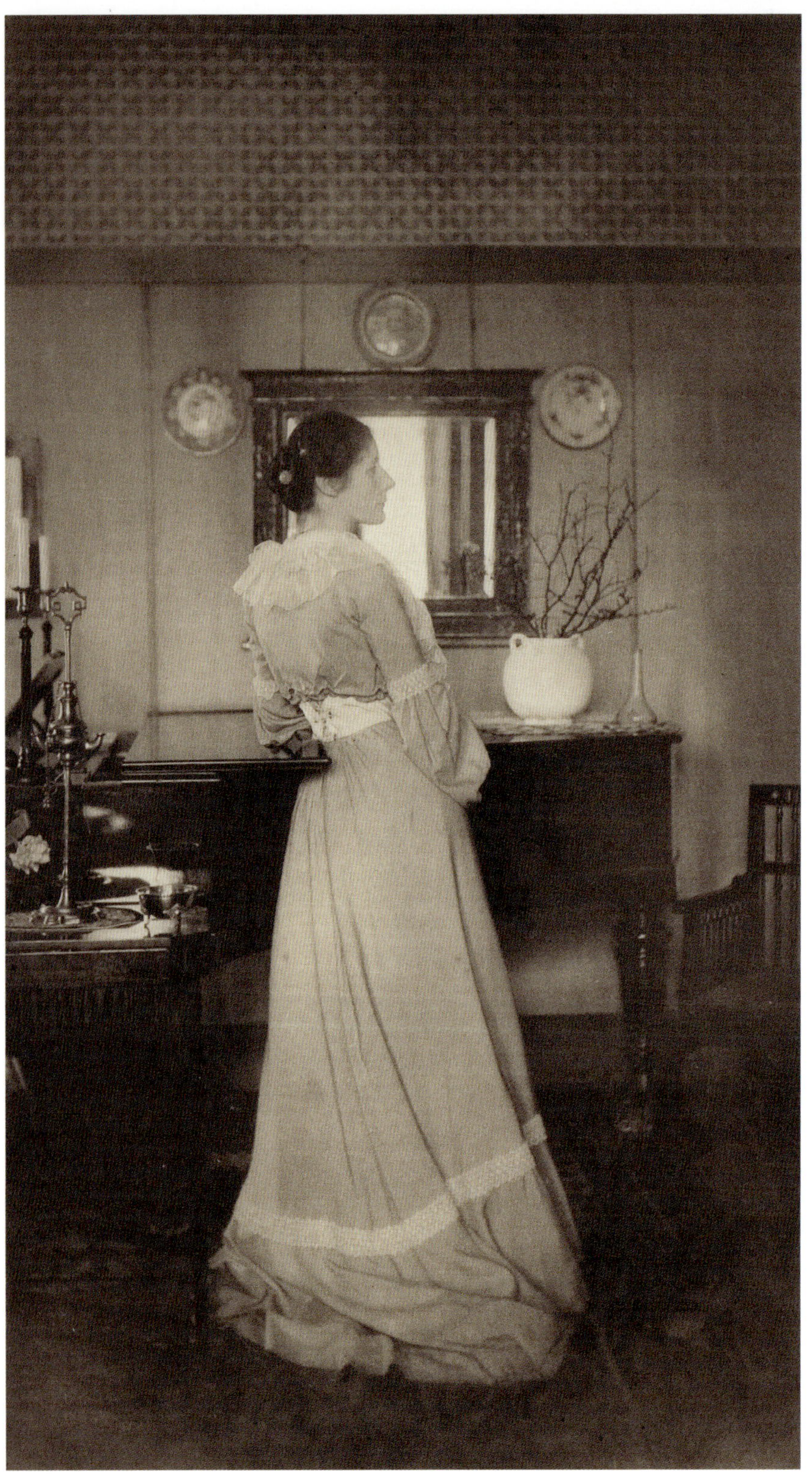

1 James Craig Annan
Mrs D.Y. Cameron
(Jeanie Ure Maclaurin [sic])
c.1897–1900
Photogravure on paper 21.6 x 12.3
Private collection

Annan's study shows David Young Cameron's wife Jeanie Ure Maclaurin in their Glasgow home, sparely decorated with Japanese objets d'art. The Camerons were both artists, he a respected artist-etcher of the Glasgow School (see pp.98–9), while she made complex designs in embroidery.

Photography as Art

Hope Kingsley

In 1902 the art critic D.S. MacColl returned to his desk during the dog days of summer to discover that, for lack of anything more interesting to discuss, the topic had arisen: 'Is photography an art?' He ranked the debate and the medium among the 'lesser diversions [that] fill in the off-seasons ... When the football and cricket celebrations are not in full swing, leap-frog, marbles and rounders steal punctually in. So in the galleries; between summer and winter there are minor sports.'[1]

MacColl would become Keeper of the Tate Gallery, and his prejudices were instructive: 'No one ... who thinks about it, denies that photography is an art in various degrees of fineness.'[2] But the medium did not allow the range of creative intervention that would make it a fully fledged art form. For much of photography's short history its practitioners and their advocates had largely concurred, tending to drop the 'fine' and limit their aspirations to an 'art' that might be ranked as a skill or a craft. In this way they sidestepped the thorny issue of how much artistic self-determination was possible while remaining so dependent on the mechanisms of the camera, chemistry and the stubborn presence, in front of the lens, of material reality.

Photographs share a simple consonance with other works of visual art in the formal components of a picture – composition and framing, attention to areas of light and shadow, and image resolution in distinctness or diffusion. The photographer might modify these elements, using light to give emphasis, so that certain parts of the scene – the sitter's face and hands in portraits by D.O. Hill and Robert Adamson (nos.3, 5), for instance – come forward out of a dark background. Twenty years later, Julia Margaret Cameron used a similar approach, along with selective focus and close framing of the subject, to give psychological intensity to her portraits (no.64).

There were also practical reasons for these choices, largely to do with shortening the slow exposure time of mid-nineteenth-century photographic materials. Hill and Adamson photographed out of doors in strong daylight, where the bright highlights registered quickly while the background fell into darkness. Cameron reduced exposure time by opening up her lens aperture; this decreased the lens's depth of field, giving a narrow plane of focus and a concentrated power to the subject. Her contemporary, Clementina, Lady Hawarden, posed her daughters in the tall bright windows of her South Kensington flat and often used mirrors to bounce the light back, filling in the shadows (no.53).

A different and controversial method was exhibited a few years earlier. Henry Peach Robinson's combination prints (no.56) were composites built up from multiple negatives. Robinson insisted that he was using synthesis as a painter might, but many believed these 'patchwork' images undermined photography's crucial virtue, its ability to portray the natural world directly and truthfully, without an artist's mediation. Robinson protested that he was simply expanding his pictorial repertoire and compensating for the inadequacies of the technology: his lens could not accommodate the full field of view without losing image definition at the periphery, while also requiring a longer exposure time than was practicable for posed figures. Robinson's technical means might have been inadequate to his intentions, but his underlying premise was more persuasive; as a photographic artist, he could legitimately adopt an artist's manipulative devices: 'I believe that the time will come when photographs will be admired more for their invention than their execution.'[3] Robinson was right, and even his critics would use combination printing, albeit with more restraint, for years to come.

As the century developed, so did other possibilities. In the later 1880s Peter Henry Emerson and Thomas Goodall argued that their photographs matched a range of focus and indistinctness that was true to human vision, based on theories of physiological optics discussed by Goodall's fellow painters at the New English Art Club (no.89). Their photographs of the people and landscapes of the Norfolk Broads were initially printed in platinum, a process whose long, subtle tonal range perfectly suited the naturalist tonal values current in British impressionism. The aesthetics of those platinotypes – a matt finish and neutral image colour – were thought more elegant than the shiny coated surface and brown hues of albumen prints, the standard photographic print of the previous thirty years. And many still admired the earlier aesthetic of Hill and Adamson's salted paper prints, whose plain uncoated surface and sepia colour were praised for their resemblance to drawings. Such preferences were fiercely debated in the photographic press, as were issues of size, framing and presentation that might encourage an intimate viewing experience or provide an exhibition spectacle.

Photography was ever attentive to the inspirations of fine art, from Elizabeth, Lady Eastlake, famously seeing 'the spirit of Rembrandt ... revived' in the photographs of Hill and Adamson,[4] to Robinson walking the readers of his book, *Pictorial Effect in Photography* (1869), through the rooms of the National Gallery, pointing out inspirations and lessons from Van Dyck to Turner. Reviewers of Cameron's photographs understood them in the terms of old master painting; *Macmillan's Magazine* declared that 'the beauty of the heads in these photographs is the beauty of the highest art. We seem to be gazing upon so many Luinis, Leonardos, and Vandyckes [sic].'[5]

Emerson acknowledged the French predecessors of modern British painting, citing Jean-François Millet and Jules Bastien-Lepage in his *Naturalistic Photography for Students of the Art* (1889). It took him a few more years to embrace the influence of James Whistler, though that painter was a touchstone for Goodall and the New English Art Club. Whistler's art was increasingly cited by photographers; in 1897 the photographer Eustace Calland laid out the challenge and the possibilities: 'We may point to such qualities as extreme reticence and love of quiet and subtle effects, nature seen in new ways, new aspects without undue sacrifices, versatility, the tender fusion of tones ... as usefully affecting our practice.'[6] These elements might be couched in the terms of other visual arts or simply borrowed wholesale, as the photographer George Davison (no.95) observed in 1891: 'Photography has come late in the day. It would be difficult for it to avoid likeness to something that had preceded it.'[7]

Exhibitions were key to photography's public profile. The Photographic Society of London (later the Royal Photographic Society) set the bar from its inception, with an annual exhibition that was reviewed in the general press. In return, photographic journals detailed important art exhibitions such as those at the Royal Academy. That reciprocity increased in the 1890s, when periodicals like the *Amateur Photographer* regularly reviewed independent groups such as the New English Art Club, mirroring the coverage of the Photographic Salon of the Linked Ring Brotherhood in *The Studio* and the *Art Journal*. Those associations were seen as having similar aims and effects, as A.C.R. Carter wrote in 1900: 'Each has its origin in the high-mettled [sic] protest against convention; each holds its exhibitions in the same gallery [Dudley Gallery, London]; each has its strong leaven of stylists, irreconcilables, and zealots.'[8]

The Linked Ring had been formed in 1892 in secession from the Photographic Society, thought too much in thrall to commercial photographic interests. The Ring's international cohort, including Americans like Fred Holland Day (no.111) and Alvin Langdon Coburn (no.93), embraced an eclectic mix of ideas often termed 'pictorialism', defined by the *Amateur Photographer* as 'photographs which aimed at being pictures in the higher acceptation of the term, irrespective of, or to the subordination of, technical excellence'.[9] Great attention was paid to printmaking. The photomechanical process of photogravure tapped into the artisanal values of the fine print and allowed handwork on the plate. Direct processes like gum bichromate and gum platinum were even more malleable. Davison listed the aspects that were amenable to additive effort: 'colour of pigment or image, depth of printing, combination and modification, local or general, relative tone or emphasis', appealing to 'every photographer who has an artistic feeling to be satisfied'.[10]

A new opportunity arose in 1907 with the introduction of Lumière autochrome plates (p.108), which produced full-colour images on a glass plate in a single exposure. The following year, *The Studio*'s special issue on colour photography described autochromes as presenting the 'effect of a sharpened and acidulated nature, curiously tense and glittering, almost metallic'.[11] This was not an altogether pleasant sensation, though the entrancing shimmer of the grains of colour produced an 'odd quality – piquant, curious, staccato'.[12]

Some of this innovation arose from an effort to revitalise photography, returning its practice to the days before modern manufactured materials with their mass-produced homogeneity and predetermined results. There was a strong nostalgia for a time when photography was newly minted, as demonstrated by a remarkable display at the 1898 Exhibition of the Royal Photographic Society. The 'Historical Section' represented a rich array, from daguerreotype plates to early cameras and the very first photographic book, William Henry Fox Talbot's *The Pencil of Nature* (1844–6). Two volumes of calotypes by Hill and Adamson (though credited solely to Hill) were shown with forty-eight loose prints, among which was the portrait of William Etty illustrated here (no.5). Cameron was represented by fourteen photographs.

Hill and Cameron were already familiar from retrospective exhibitions and publications initiated by influential and effective advocates. Cameron's son, Henry Herschel Hay Cameron, was a professional photographer and a founding member of London's Camera Club and the Linked Ring. In 1889, ten years after his mother's death, he exhibited her work at the Camera Club and loaned prints for the production of photogravure plates in the October 1890 issue of *Sun Artists*. In his essay for that issue P.H. Emerson described Cameron's portraits as 'the only "old masters" photography has to boast of' and encouraged his readers to pay attention: 'Every photographer in the world will do well to hang in his studio such classical works ... that would teach him almost as much as reproductions of the great masters of portraiture – Titian, Velasquez, Holbein, Rembrandt, Gainsborough, and Whistler.'[13]

Pay attention they did: in 1913 Alfred Stieglitz published photogravures of six Cameron portraits in his influential New York journal *Camera Work*. Twenty-one gravures of Hill and Adamson photographs appeared in the 1905, 1909 and 1912 issues. The plates came from James Craig Annan (no.1), who in 1890 first printed photogravures from Hill and Adamson negatives held at his family's Glasgow printing firm, T. & R. Annan. As a child, Annan had met D.O. Hill when his father Thomas Annan was producing photographic reproductions of Hill's famous 'Disruption' painting (no.2).

James Craig Annan showed the prints at a number of venues, notably the final Linked Ring exhibition in 1909.[14] In the exhibition catalogue he made a clear case for the value of Hill's work, writing that 'at the very threshold of the new art of photography, there was a worker who realised its possibilities, – restricted though they were technically, – for pictorial and individual expression and for the production of results that have yet to be equalled'.[15] Annan's 1909 retrospect shows a medium with seventy years under its belt and its own old masters shaking out its wings as a fully fledged art.

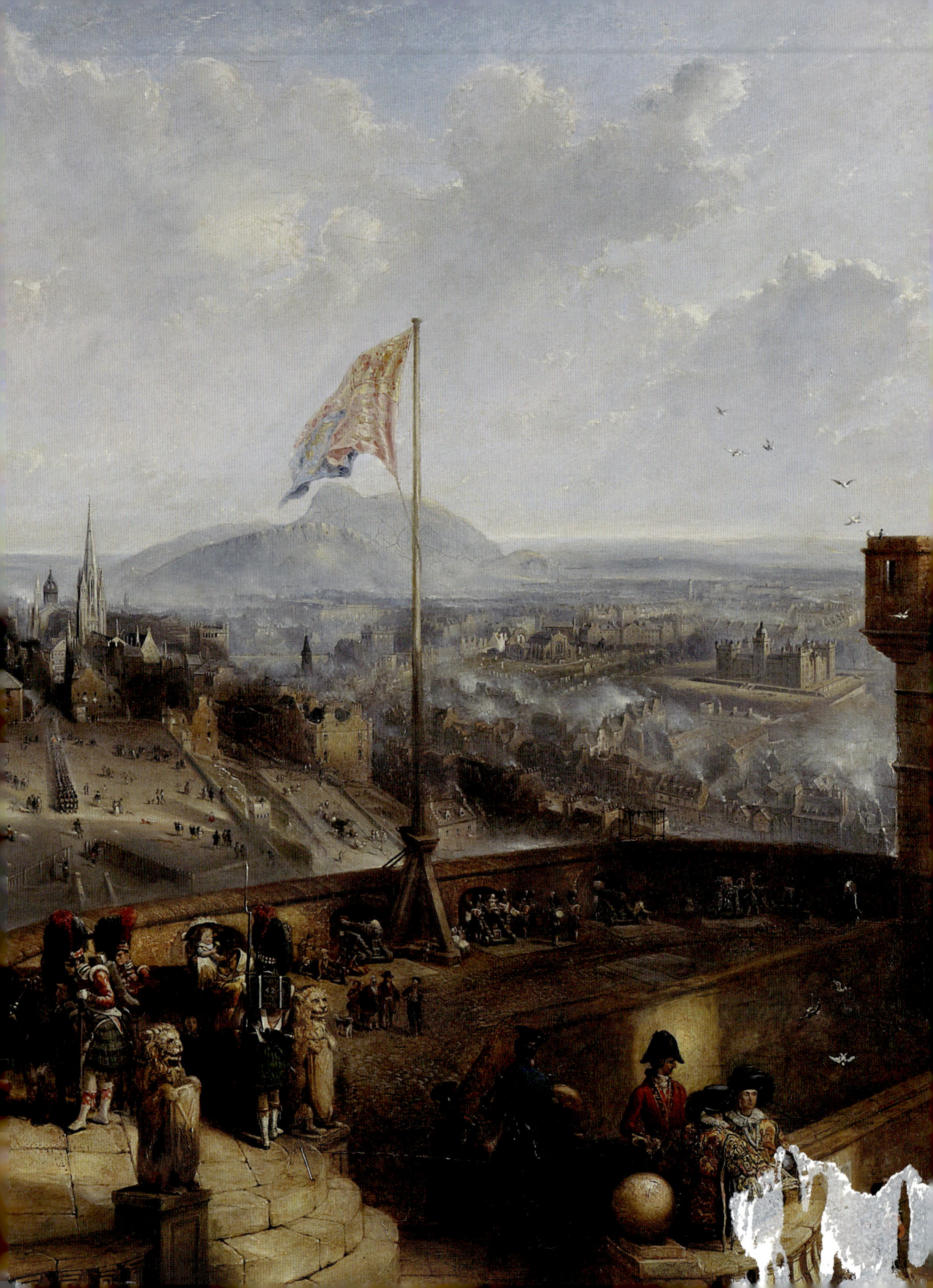

1 Painting with Light

Carol Jacobi

Nineteenth-century art was alert to its times and technology. One of the consequences of the Enlightenment and the Industrial Revolution was the spread of printing and literacy, making a new generation of artists aware of events of science, philosophy and history, and their breathless rate of change. Early photographers were frequently artists or closely associated with artistic and literary circles, and early discussion of photography was couched in artistic terms, such as the 'pencil of nature' (see p.9). The liaison between art and photography was, from the start, transformative to both media: the traditions and aesthetics of fine art informed photography, while photographs inspired art towards a more naturalistic and more democratic way of seeing and representing the world.

Edinburgh was an intellectual centre with a progressive community of scientists and artists. The Scottish painter David Octavius Hill (nos.9, 11) was typical: the son of a publishing family, he helped found and became Secretary of the Royal Scottish Academy. His circle included the scientist David Brewster (no.3), a close friend of Fox Talbot. Brewster and John Adamson pioneered photographic experiments at St Andrews University. In 1843 the reforming spirit led ministers of the Church of Scotland to walk out of the annual assembly to found the Free Church of Scotland, and Hill and Brewster were present. When Hill decided to commemorate the event, Brewster suggested he work with John Adamson's brother, Robert, and use photography to capture the likeness of the hundreds of participants.

Adamson had set up a studio at Rock House, Calton Hill Stairs, in Edinburgh, where Hill joined him, and, aided by Jessie Mann, they created more than 2,000 photographs over five years in Edinburgh and beyond. Members of their circle, the radical journalist Hugh Miller and art historian Elizabeth Rigby (later Lady Eastlake), started to write about art and photography.[16] Adamson's tragic death at only twenty-seven ended the photographic revolution, but the photographs remained to become world renowned as some of the earliest and most beautiful experiments in the medium.

Tate Britain's exhibition and accompanying book bring together Hill and Adamson's portraits (nos.3, 4, 5) with the 'Disruption Portrait' (see no.2) that engendered them. With William Etty's *Self-Portrait, after a Photograph by David Octavius Hill and Robert Adamson* 1844 (no.6), they reveal that painters explored the potential of photography as a new kind of preparatory study or source. Hill and Adamson's studio was highly successful and they are better remembered for perfecting the photographic portrait itself. Their synthesis of the lessons of the old masters and innovative aesthetics suited the chiaroscuro properties of their materials – paper negatives and salted paper prints. The seventeenth-century court portraits of Velázquez, with their strong arrangements of light and dark and attention to psychology, were one sympathetic precedent, and Hill and Adamson made photographic illustrations for Sir William Stirling Maxwell's *Annals of the Artists of Spain* (1848).

Hill and Adamson also addressed genre and landscape traditions in art, making 300 pictures of the fishing community in Newhaven, for example. Inspired by J.M.W. Turner, they pioneered the photographic panorama in two series, one taken from Calton Hill and the other from Edinburgh Castle (nos.8, 10). These have only survived as negatives but are shown here in the form of modern prints, alongside Hill's oil views.

David Octavius Hill
***Edinburgh Old and New* 1846–7**
(detail, no.9)

2 Amelia Robertson Hill, after David Octavius Hill
***Disruption Portrait, The First General Assembly of the Free Church of Scotland signing the Act of Separation and Deed of Demission on 23rd May 1843* c.1866**
Oil paint over three joined photographs, 61.3 x 137.5
The Hunterian, University of Glasgow

David Octavius Hill's original *Disruption Picture* is in the collection of the Free Church of Scotland, Edinburgh

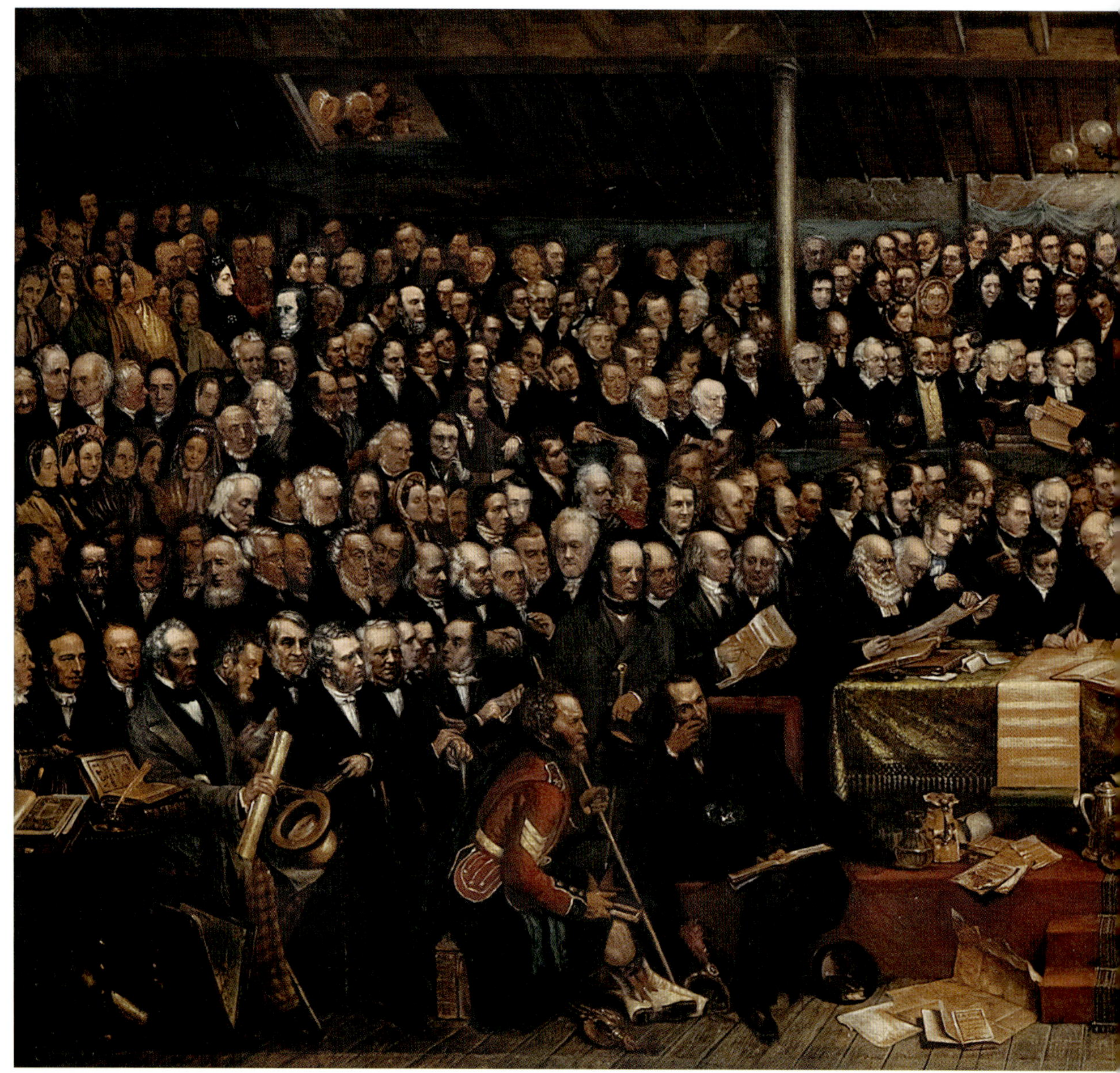

David Octavius Hill's *Disruption Picture* played an originating role in photography in several ways. It represented the dramatic secession of the Free Church of Scotland in an abandoned Edinburgh gasworks (Tanfield Hall) in 1843. The revolutionary use of photographic portrait studies, made with Robert Adamson, allowed Hill to depart from the traditional hierarchical composition of such assembly scenes and present a four-metre panorama of 457 individuals with equal attention to their roles and likenesses. This pictorial democracy was criticised in its own time, and is still strange to look at today, but was in keeping with the spirit of the event.

Hill worked on after Adamson's death in 1848. With the help of his second wife, the painter and sculptor Amelia Hill, he completed the picture in 1866. It was bought by the Free Church and reproductions hung in homes and institutions throughout Scotland. Rather than commission engravings, Hill engaged another photographer, Thomas Annan, who pioneered the use of a new stable form of photography for this purpose, the carbon print, invented by Joseph Swan. The largest of these reproductions was two metres across, made up of three mammoth prints. The version reproduced here was painted over by Amelia Hill to create a half-sized oil replica. CJ

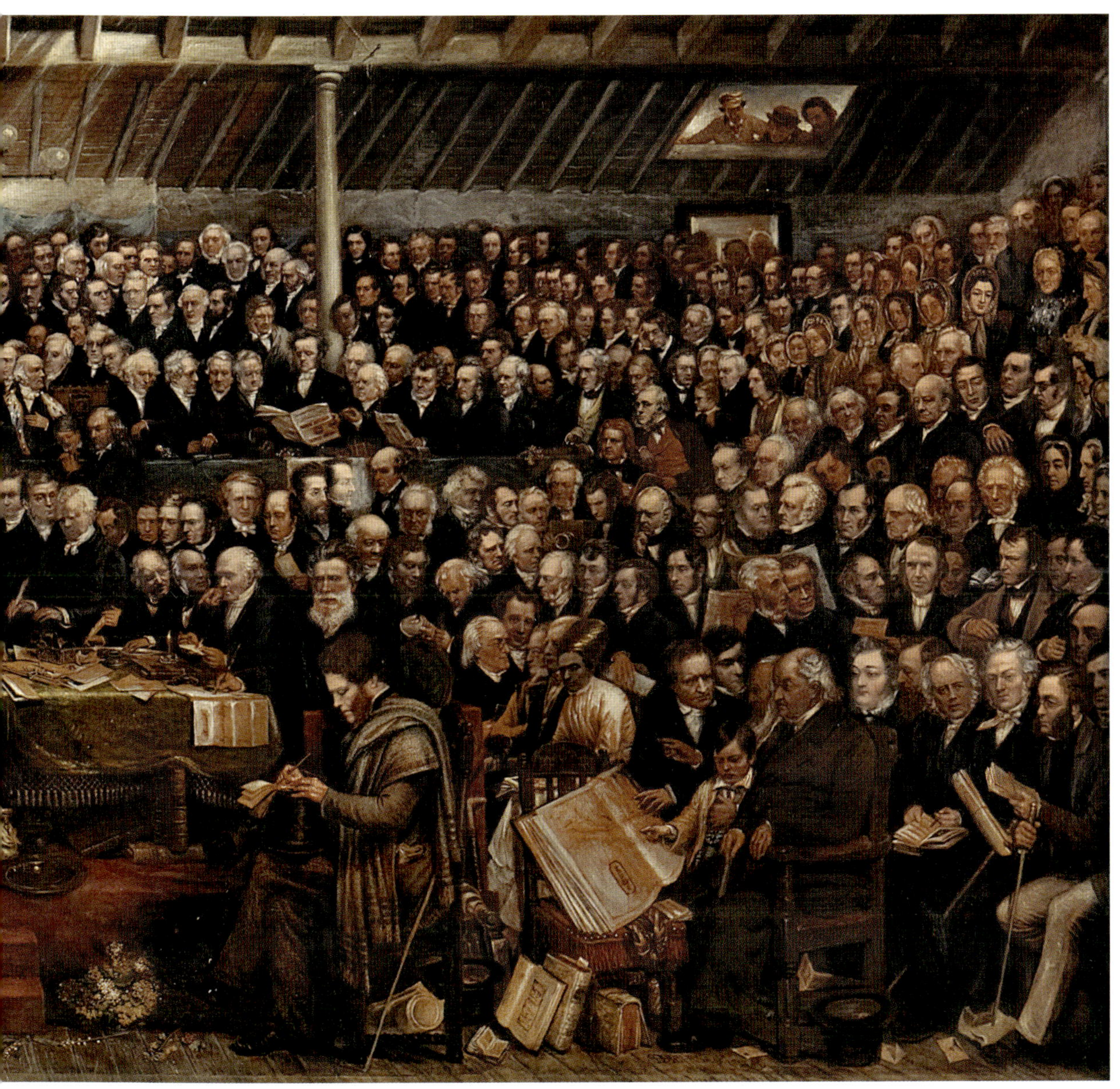

Sir David Brewster was one of Hill and Adamson's first portrait studies for the Disruption painting (no.2, left of centre). It is typical in the way it exploits the exaggerated chiaroscuro of the exposure to achieve a tonal beauty likened to Rembrandt. At the same time, the portrait includes elements that are distinctively modern. Photography emphasises the singular features of the sitter, registering – in a few moments – the creases and indentations of the face, and the configuration of tensed and relaxed skin and muscle that make up Brewster's individual presence. Hill and Adamson have also exploited the duration of the photographic exposure to find a new way of suggesting movement, the blur of the turned page.

The photograph *John Robertson and Hugh Miller* provided the details and pose for their appearance as two of those signing the Disruption agreement (foreground). The painting of the event records the folds and textures of Miller's Highland national dress differently from the rhythmic drapery inspired by classical sculpture that was traditional in academic painting. Miller was an illustrious journalist in Hill and Adamson's circle, a self-taught geologist and poet.

In the painting Hill included himself and other pioneers of photography who were not present, such as Robert Adamson with his camera (top right centre) and their studio assistant Jessie Mann (in a bonnet, far-right edge). Three of the Newhaven fishing community that they photographed so often look through the skylight. CJ

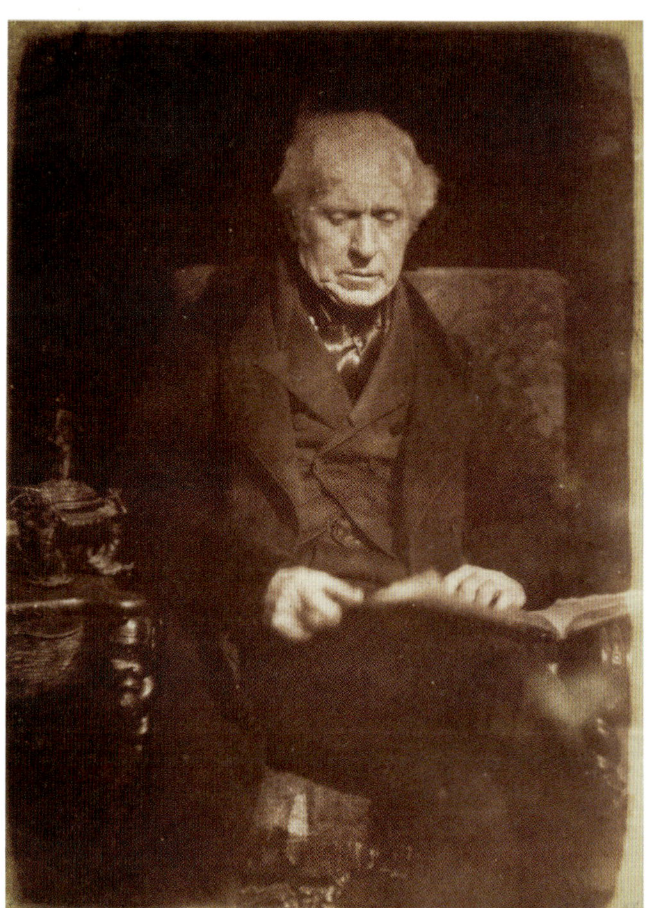

3 David Octavius Hill and Robert Adamson
***Sir David Brewster* c.1843**
Photograph, salted paper print 19.5 x 14.2
National Galleries of Scotland

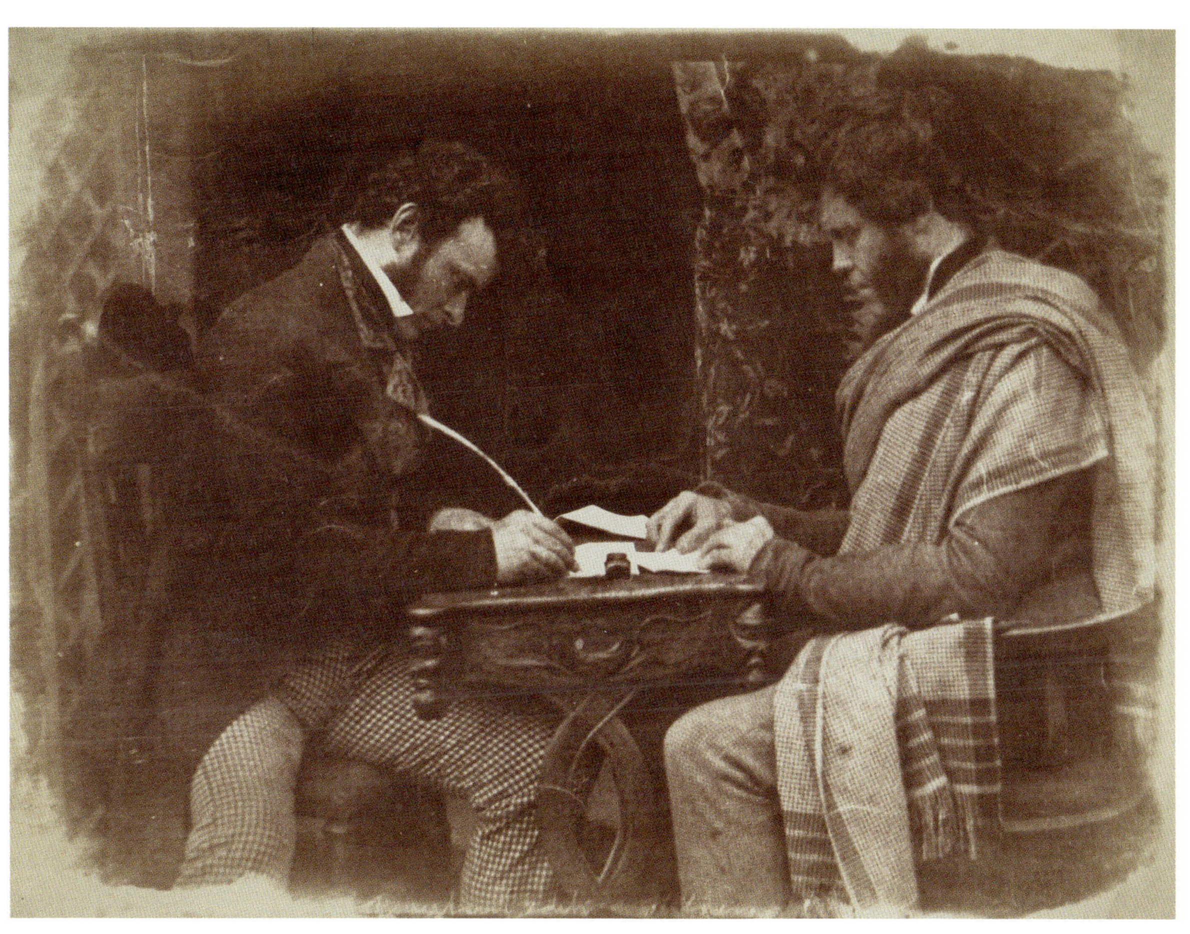

4 David Octavius Hill and Robert Adamson
John Robertson and Hugh Miller c.1843
Photograph, salted paper print 17.5 x 20.4
National Galleries of Scotland

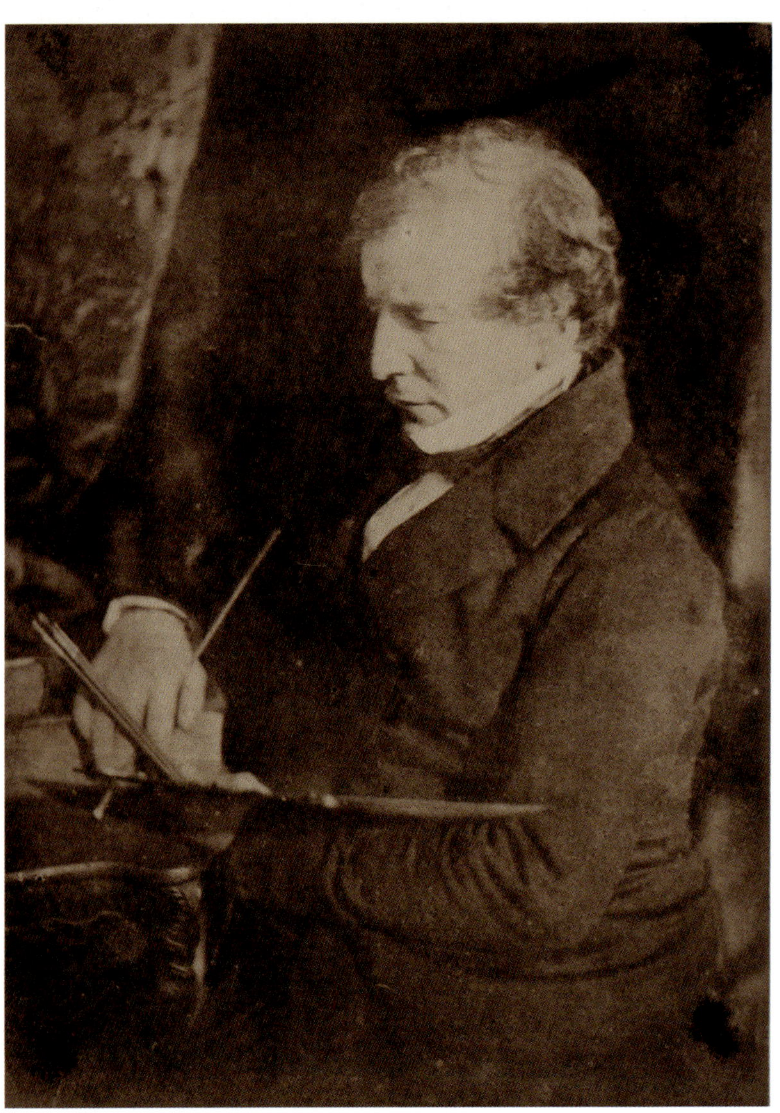

5 David Octavius Hill and Robert Adamson
***William Etty* 1844**
Photograph, salted paper print 19.7 x 14.4
University of Glasgow Library, Special Collections

Hill and Adamson took this photographic portrait when Etty was in Edinburgh for a Royal Scottish Academy dinner to celebrate the Academy's purchase of three of his paintings. Etty's visit was for only two days, but Hill persuaded him to come up to Rock House. They had met a month earlier at the British Association meeting in York, where Etty praised the artistry of Hill and Adamson's photographs, as Hill recorded in an 1845 letter to the painter David Roberts: '*Etty* saw in them revivals of Rembrandt, Titian and Spagnoletto.'[17]

Etty based his self-portrait on the photograph, reproducing Hill and Adamson's use of light and shadow to emphasise his face and hands. In 1898 the photograph was among the historical masterworks shown at the Royal Photographic Society's annual exhibition. HK

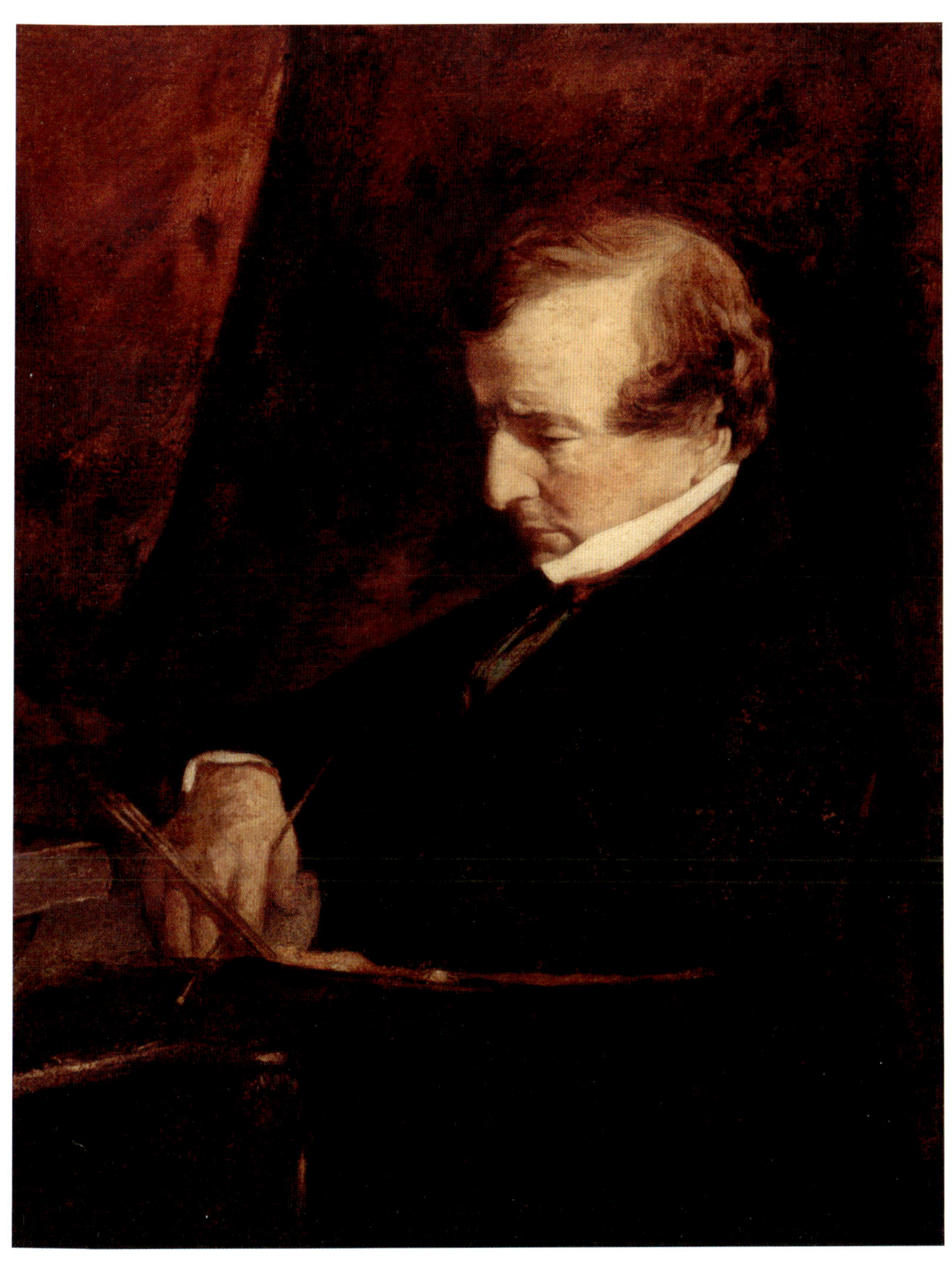

6 William Etty
***Self-Portrait, after a Photograph by David Octavius Hill and Robert Adamson* 1846**
Oil paint on millboard 41.3 x 31.8
National Portrait Gallery, London

Hill and Adamson's Rock House studio was on the slopes of Calton Hill, which had long served as a panoramic platform. Forty years earlier, Turner had made it a vantage point for *Edinburgh, from Caulton-hill*, and it was the location of the Calton Hill Observatory, whose large camera obscura was used by artists such as Alexander Nasmyth, with whom Hill studied.

Hill's painting *Edinburgh Old and New* updates these precedents with observations from photographic panoramas he made with Adamson between 1844 and 1846 (nos.8, 10). Those views provided perspectival references, along with contingent details such as window blinds on the city buildings below the castle. They were probably taken with the large camera made for Hill and Adamson by Thomas Davidson in 1844. The camera was intended for making life-sized portraits, but the format corresponds to the dimensions of Hill and Adamson's remarkable panoramas, the first of their kind in Britain. HK & CJ

7 J.M.W. Turner
***Edinburgh, from Caulton-hill* exh. 1804**
Pencil, watercolour and gouache on two overlapping sheets of white wove paper, together 66 x 100
Tate. Accepted by the nation as part of the Turner Bequest 1856

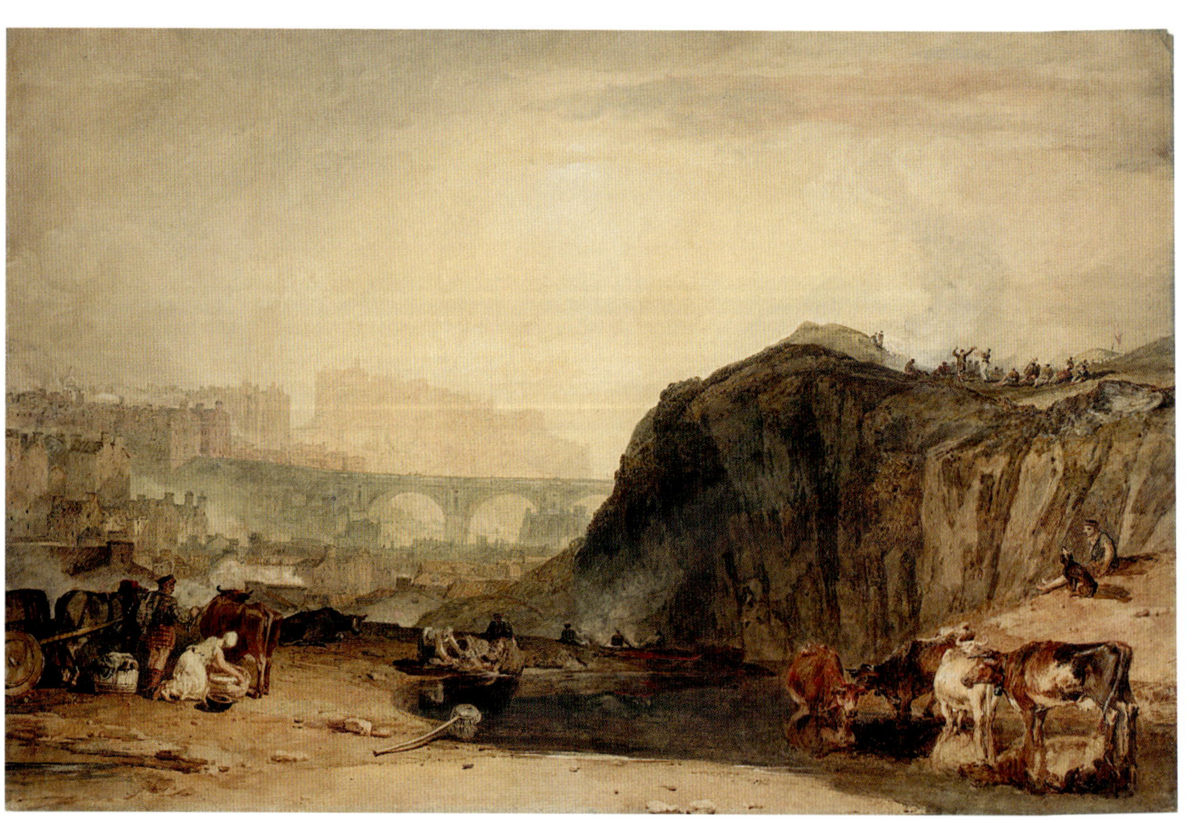

8 David Octavius Hill and Robert Adamson
Edinburgh from the Castle, looking south with castle wall and battlement in the foreground, part of a panorama
c.1844–6, printed 2016
Photograph, inkjet print on paper 32.1 x 40.6
University of Glasgow Library, Special Collections,

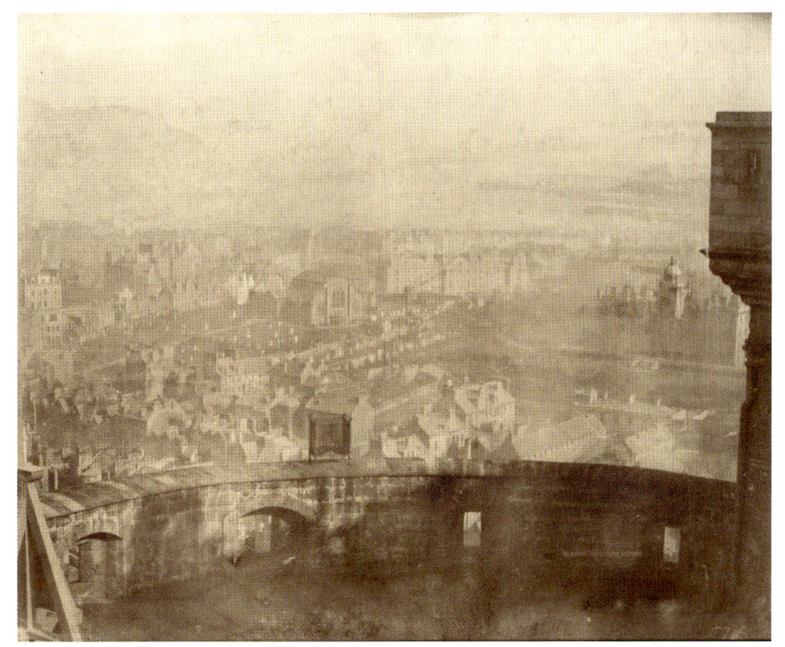

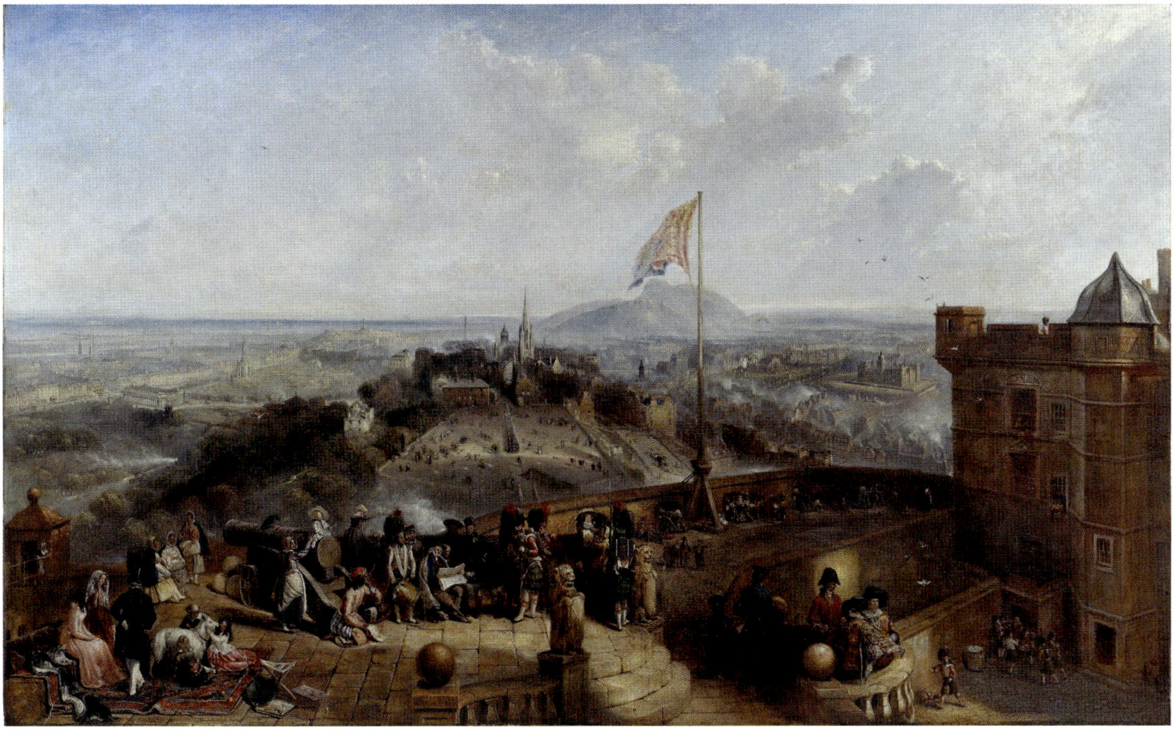

9 David Octavius Hill
***Edinburgh Old and New* 1846–7**
Oil paint on panel 117 x 193
National Galleries of Scotland

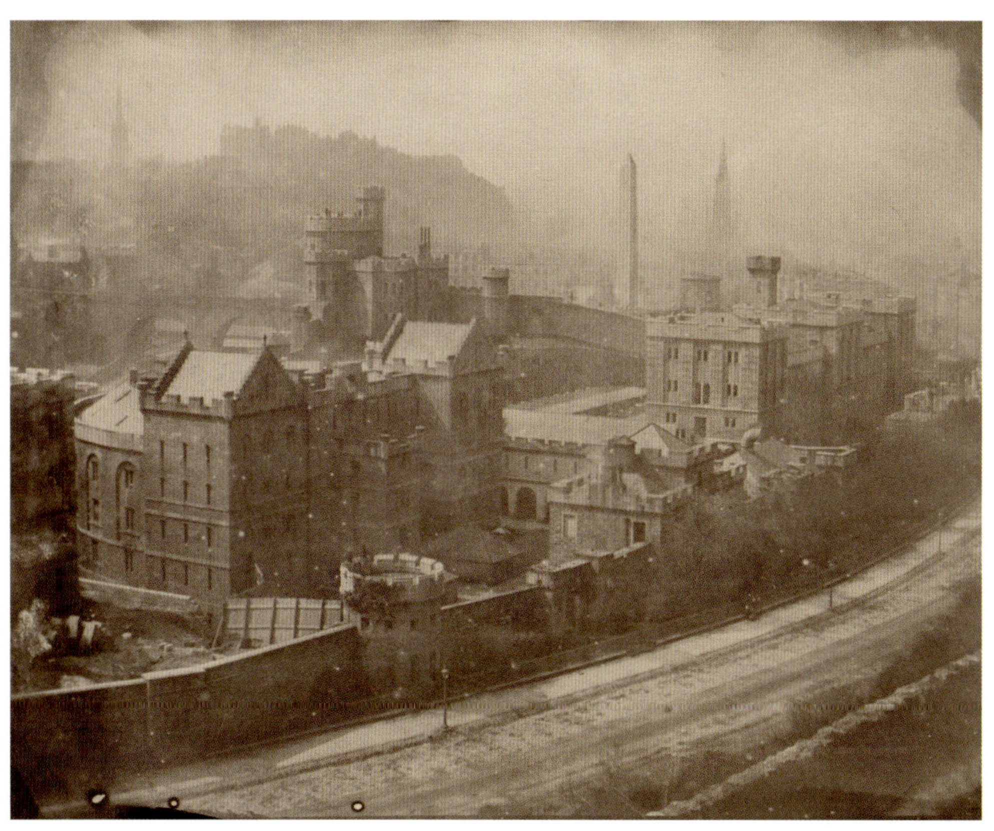

10 David Octavius Hill and Robert Adamson
***View from Calton Hill, looking South-West, with the Jail, the Castle, the Political Martyr's Monument and the Scott Monument* 1845 *or* 46, printed 2016**
Photograph, inkjet on paper 328 x 409
University of Glasgow Library, Special Collections

Hill painted *In Memoriam* on the death of his only daughter, Charlotte, in 1862. The scene is threaded with memories of the 1840s; Rock House holds the right foreground where Hill's easel stands at the far right in the garden, a painting in progress. On the opposite bank, Adamson's camera is draped in its dark-cloth, ready to take a photograph. Beyond, Edinburgh shimmers in a smoky haze, leading one reviewer to describe the painting as a gem 'of the opal kind with the colour and the fire, as it were, not laid upon the surface but all coming out from within'.[18] This careful account of specific qualities of light is reminiscent of Turner, whom Hill admired, describing him in a letter to David Roberts as a 'most glorious artist'.[19] HK

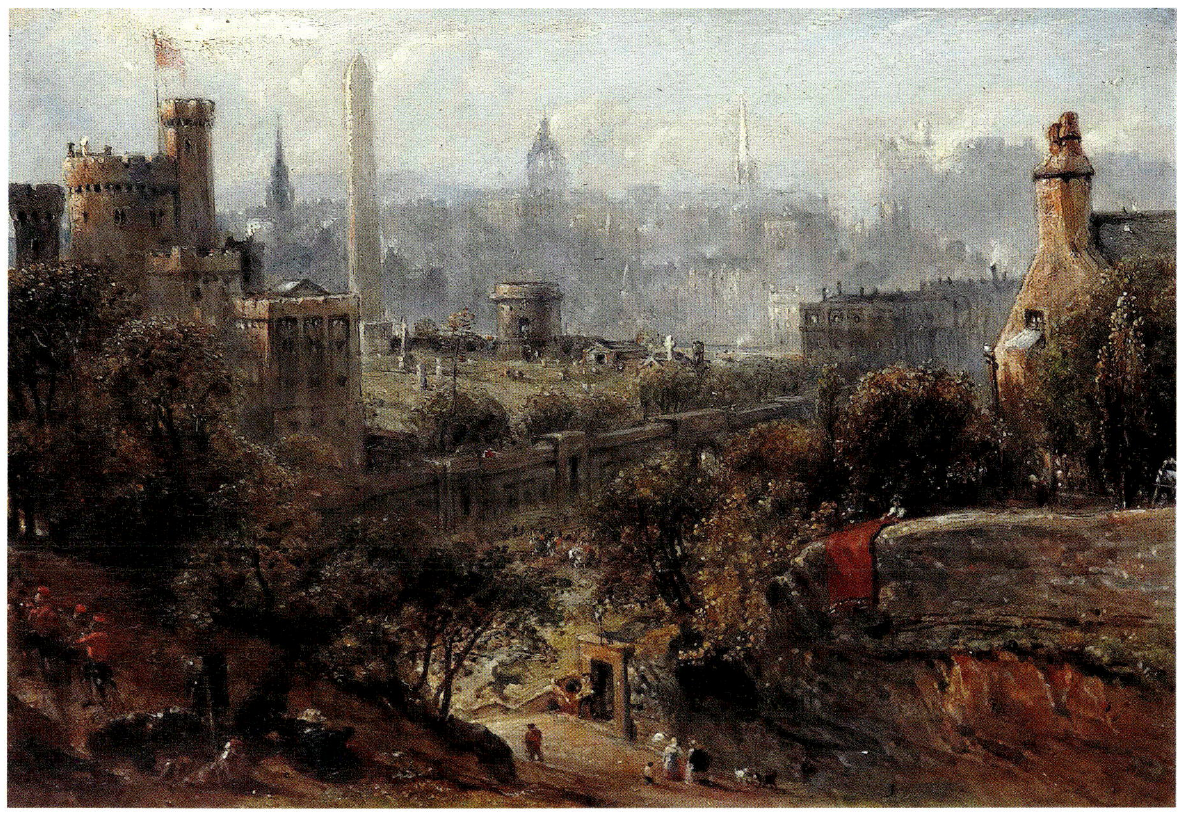

11 David Octavius Hill
***In Memoriam: The Calton* 1862**
Oil paint on panel 14.9 x 20
City Art Centre, Edinburgh Museums and Galleries

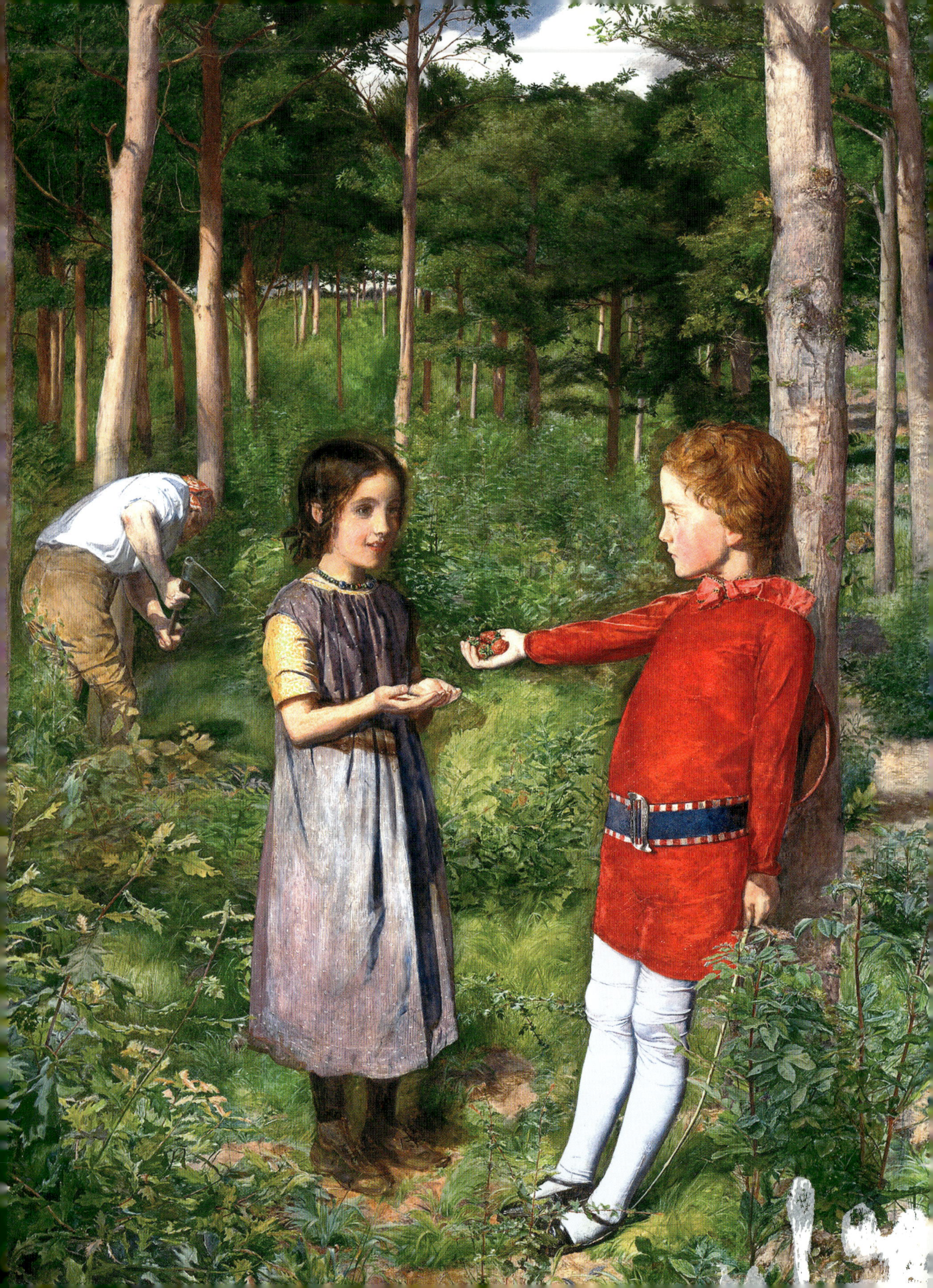

2 New Truths

Carol Jacobi

Innovations in the sciences and culture were distilled in the visual arts in intense debates about 'truth'. Writers as diverse as David Brewster and the art critic and social reformer John Ruskin promoted a natural philosophy that emphasised observation – a kind of seeing and representing that could escape habit and convention and directly penetrate the mysteries of nature. Influenced by their reading, the Pre-Raphaelite artists and their circle rejected the authority of the Royal Academy, which they felt was based on elitist habit, and claimed a new authority in the artist's vision. As they wrote in their journal *The Germ*: 'If this adherence to fact, to experiment not theory ... has added so much to the knowledge of man in science; why may it not greatly assist the moral purposes of the arts?'[20] Scientists and artists extended and questioned the bounds of perception and representation. Central to this was natural theology, a belief, expressed in the writings of Ruskin's and others, that the natural world was 'already a work of art', manifesting material and spiritual truth.

These ambitions informed simultaneous developments in photography, and the two main mentors of the Pre-Raphaelite artists, Ruskin and Ford Madox Brown, were early adopters. Ruskin incorporated photography into his art-making and writing in 1840 and Brown in 1847.[21] The *Art Journal* commented in 1849 that the study of photographs was already an established practice among some landscape painters.[22] Photographs were viewed at the Royal Society, at ad hoc photographic groups and, alongside conventional prints, drawings and paintings, at the progressive Graphic Society, attended by photographers and artists. The Pre-Raphaelite Brotherhood was founded in 1848. In 1850 Brown, Roger Fenton (who had studied painting in Paris during the same period as Brown), Thomas Seddon and Dante Gabriel Rossetti established the North London School of Drawing and Modelling for working men, an alternative to the Academy Schools. They rejected drawing from old masters and classical casts in favour of an appreciation of the complex variety of nature and real things.[23] Fenton took up photography the following year and became its leading exponent.

'We never see anything clearly,' Ruskin wrote, adding that even 'photographs never look entirely clear or sharp'. He praised photography that did not seek sharpness at all costs, but revealed to the eye 'the absolute infinity of things', be it dissolving distances or confusion of foreground detail;[24] for Ruskin it was here that the mysteries of nature began. Painters and photographers explored the implications of focus and indistinctness, atmospheric effects, the appearance of movement, form dissolved by darkness or by glare, and the discrete shapes of highlights and shadows. William Holman Hunt led the Pre-Raphaelite revolution in depicting effects of light in nature, and in 1850 introduced the practice of painting in the open from the motif like a camera, 'direct on the canvas itself, with every detail I can see, and with the sunlight brightness of the day itself'.[25] They observed that shadows were coloured and explored the challenges of finding an equivalent for the wide spectrums of light and dark within the narrower tonal range of pigment on a surface. These investigations were surveyed by a critic associated with the circle, Philip Hamerton, in an essay on 'The Relationship between Photography and Art'. For him painting, the result of long looking and many adjustments, was 'as true, and truer than the photograph'.[26]

John Everett Millais
The Woodman's Daughter
1859–61 (detail, no.18)

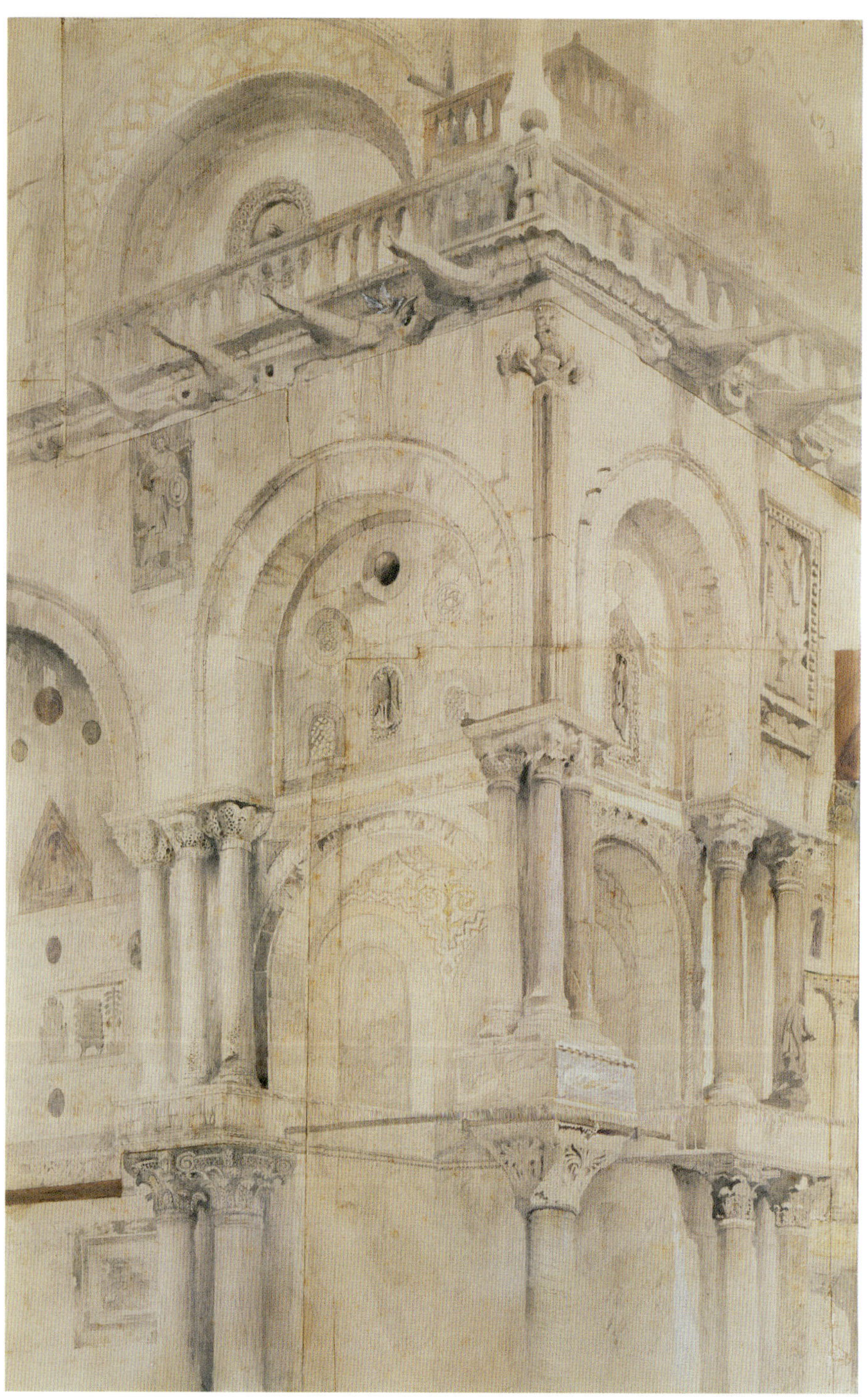

12 John Ruskin
The North-West Angle of the Facade of St Mark's, Venice
date unknown
Watercolour and graphite on paper 94 x 61
Tate. Presented by the Art Fund 1914

Daguerreotypes, small but extremely precise images on polished silver plates, were available to view, commission and buy from 1840. Ruskin had examples sent from France that year and had his valet, John Hobbs, experiment with them soon after. In 1845 he wrote to his father from Venice, where he had been drawing and photographing the architecture: 'It is a noble invention – say what they will of it – and anyone who has worked and blundered and stammered [at drawing] as I have done for four days, and then sees the thing he has been trying to do so long in vain done perfectly and faultlessly in half a minute won't abuse it.'[27] CJ

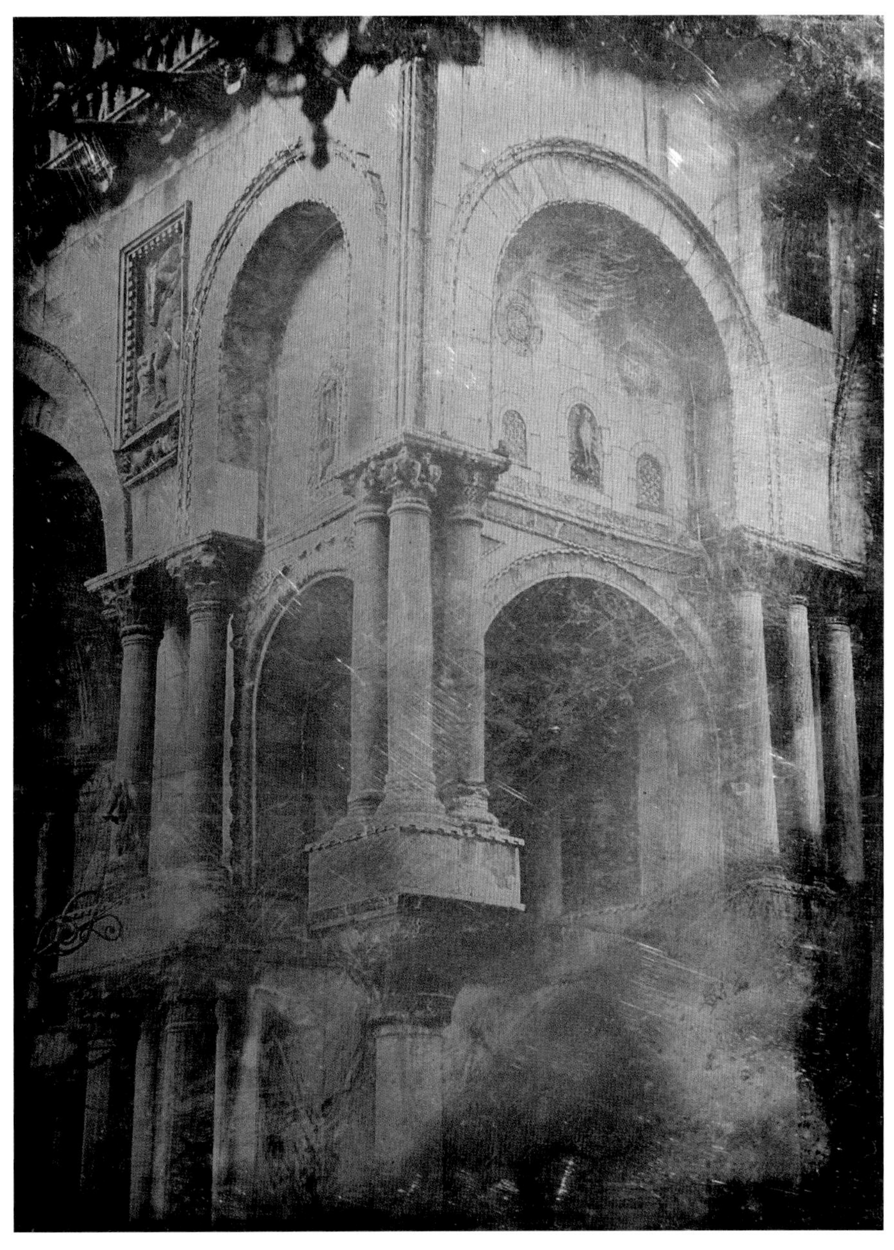

13 John Ruskin and John Hobbs
***North-West Angle of St Mark's, Venice* c.1850**
Daguerreotype plate 16.3 x 12.2
Ruskin Foundation (Ruskin Library, Lancaster University)

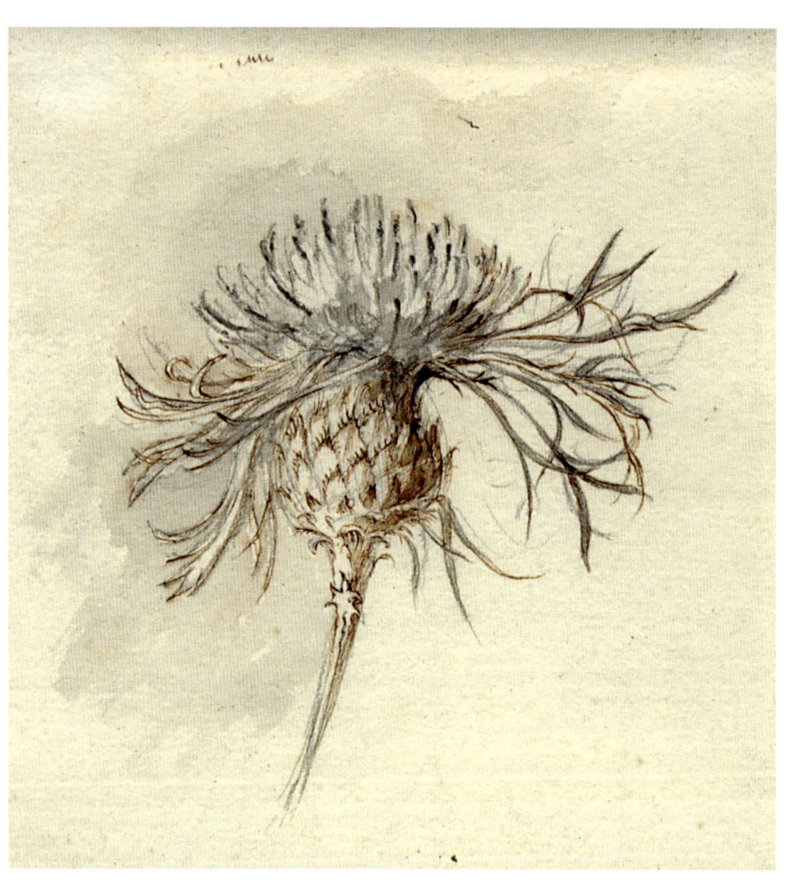

The botanical exactitude of many of Ruskin's drawings dramatises his ideals of observation: 'The greatest thing a human soul ever does in this world is to see something and tell what it saw in a plain way … To see clearly is poetry, prophecy and religion, all in one.'[28] Painters and photographers explored the close views like contemporary poets and novelists, complemented their scientific method by finding significance in marginal objects and minutiae. At the North London School, for example, Ruskin set students to draw a lichen-encrusted stick.

Talbot is renowned for inventing photography on paper, but he spent many more years researching photomechanical printing. His photoglyphic engravings were made on metal plates coated with photosensitive gelatin. The coating was exposed to light beneath an object (such as these dandelion seeds), after which the unexposed areas were washed off to leave a resist. The plate was etched with ferric chloride (also Talbot's discovery), then inked and printed like an ordinary engraving. CJ & HK

14 John Ruskin
Perennial Cornflower
Pencil and ink on paper 11 x 10
Ruskin Foundation (Ruskin Library, Lancaster University)

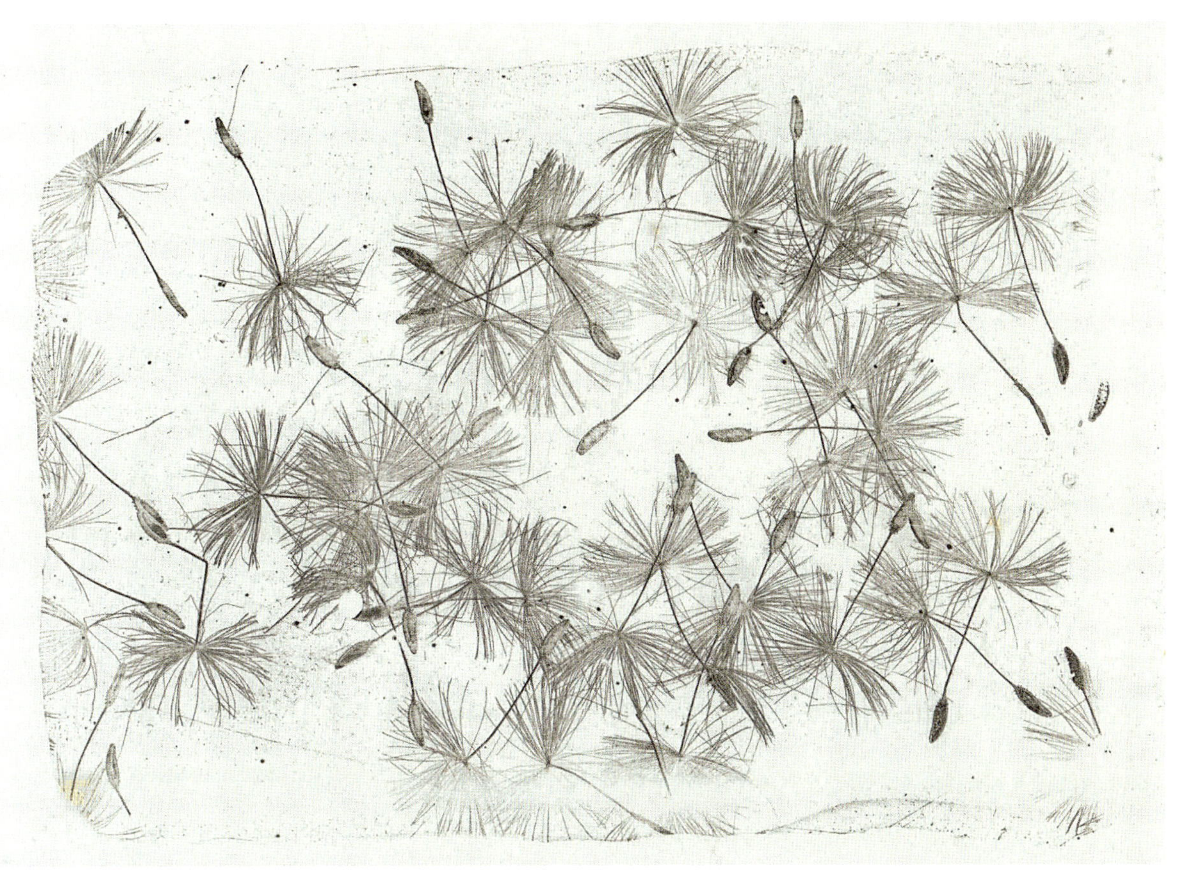

15 William Henry Fox Talbot
***Dandelion Seeds* c.1858 or later**
Photoglyphic engraving on paper 7.1 x 10.2
The National Media Museum, Bradford

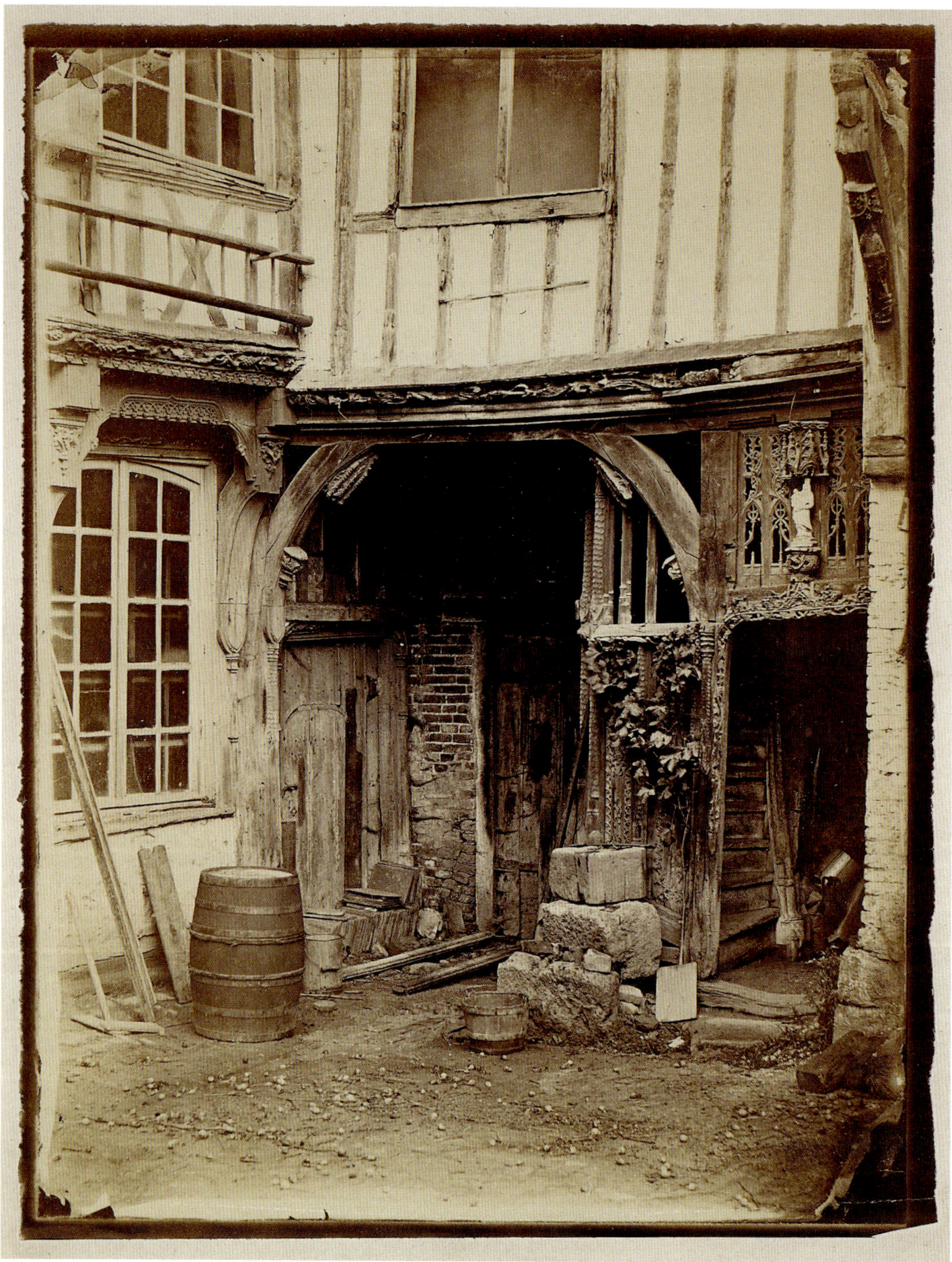

16 John Ruskin
***The Courtyard of a Late Gothic Wooden House at Abbeville* 1868**
Photograph, albumen print on paper 22.3 x 17.3
The Ashmolean Museum, Oxford.
Presented by John Ruskin to the Ruskin Drawing School (University of Oxford), 1875

Ruskin employed photographs as preparatory studies for paintings and drawings, and collected photographs of old masters and other subjects. They informed his writings on art and architecture, and were included in his lectures and a library of teaching materials created for the Ruskin School of Art, which he founded in 1871. This image of the courtyard of a fifteenth-century royal house was used in a lecture on Pre-Raphaelite painting. It was made during a stay in Abbeville in northern France and emulated French photographic surveys of national historic sites. Ruskin chose a closer point of view, however; for him the photograph helped the viewer to look, 'rejecting nothing, selecting nothing', and find poetry in the incidental details: battered medieval carving, abandoned tools, vines, 'the little angle of the courtyard ... tenderly *painted* in the depression of its fate [Ruskin's emphasis]'.[29]

In contrast with his admiration of daguerreotype detail, Ruskin appreciated the qualities of mystery in the more tonal characteristics of the albumen print. His notes for the School of Art collection advised students to observe and copy the exaggerated shadows of the vine, and included two examples in sepia. For Ruskin this inconsequential shadow exemplifies the purpose and poetry to be found in art and nature, expressing a 'mingling' of the 'declining shadows of the past and the hardships of the present day' that he saw in the photograph as a whole:

> *Now begin the study of Effects of Foliage diminished in distance ... I take, therefore, an actual group of leaves, vine, seen in this Photograph at a distance of about twenty-five feet ... Though the Photograph exaggerates the shadows, it gives us in other respects accurately the conditions of Mystery required at such distance. I take the group here shown in association with French Sculpture that the student may learn the qualities of good Painting and Sculpture at once. When he has learned to draw these leaves as the Photograph represents them, he will know how to admire the imaged leaves carved at the side of them.*[30]

CJ

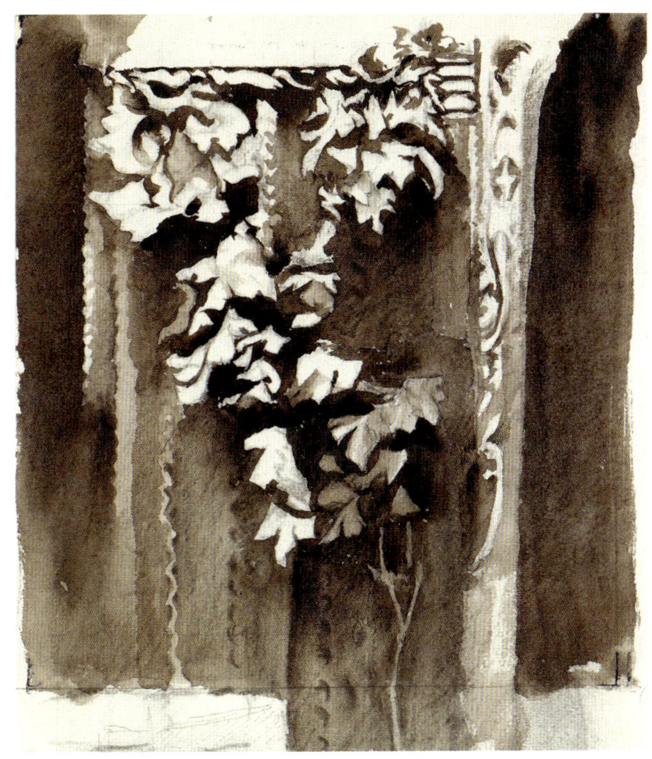

17 After John Ruskin
***First Process of Sepia Sketch of Leafage: Study from Ruskin's Photograph of the Courtyard of a Late Gothic Wooden House at Abbeville* 1868**
Watercolour over graphite on wove paper 27.3 x 24.2
The Ashmolean Museum, Oxford.
Presented by John Ruskin to the Ruskin Drawing School (University of Oxford), 1875

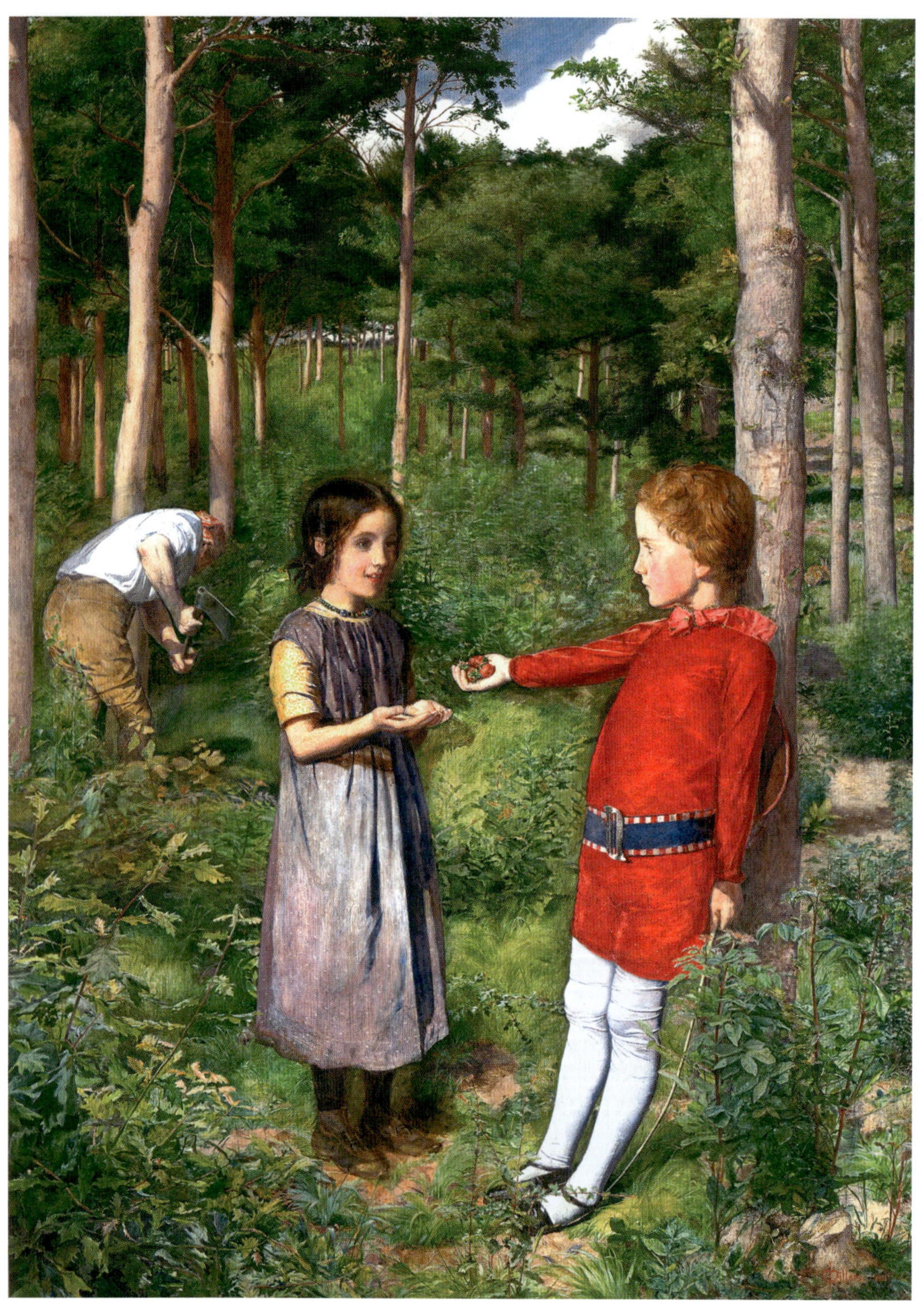

18 John Everett Millais
***The Woodman's Daughter* 1850–51**
Oil paint on canvas 88.9 x 64.8
Guildhall Art Gallery, Corporation of London

The Woodman's Daughter, based on a poem by Coventry Patmore (1844), was painted in a secluded part of Marley Wood near Oxford. Millais's shift to intensely realised detail attracted extreme criticism and this painting was the first to be defended by Ruskin. It echoed the Pre-Raphaelite aim, published in *The Germ*, to see nature 'in the actual place, let the water damp your feet, stand in the chill of the shadow itself'.[31] In his later account of *The Woodman's Daughter* Millais's son, the naturalist John Guille Millais, observed how his father had recorded 'every blade of grass, every leaf and bough and every shadow they cast'.[32] The horizon is almost excluded, and the viewer, like the artist, is immersed within the wood, where 'the eye cannot follow the mysterious interlacing of all the wonderful green things that spring up all about'. The parallels between art and photography were obvious to contemporaries. A friend, William Bell Scott, remarked: 'The seed of the flower of Pre-Raphaelitism was photography ... History, genre, medievalism, or any poetry or literality, were allowable as subject, but the execution was to be like the binocular representations of leaves that the stereoscope was then beginning to show.'[33]

Some criticised Millais's precision as 'mechanical' and lacking poetry. *The Germ*, however, explained the poetic associations of the detail: 'Objects they [artists] depict excite the beholder, just as those objects in nature would excite his [the artist's] interest, if by any associations of idea in the one case, by the same in the other.'[34] This Pre-Raphaelite idea of excitation and association echoed Fox Talbot's claim: 'A painter's eye will often be arrested where ordinary people see nothing remarkable. A casual gleam of sunshine, a time withered Oak, or a moss covered stone, may awaken a train of thoughts and feeling.'[35]

For Millais's son the 'tender greys' of the oak saplings, vulnerable to the axe's swing, and the fallen feather in the foreground suggested the natural innocence of Maud and her world, endangered by the intrusion of the aristocratic boy. The ambivalence of his pose and artifice of his clothing hint at his cruelty to Maud much later in their lives. The poem goes on to describe her seduction by him, followed by abandonment and the madness that drives her to drown her own child in a woodland pool. The poet made a similar use of telling natural imagery to hint at the death below the water: 'Is it the twisting water-eft / That dimples the green slime?'

By the 1850s many British photographers were making experiments with woodland scenes. The immersive composition was helpful in excluding skies that were incompatible with the long exposures needed to capture the monochrome complexities of green foliage and filtered light. Stereoscopic photographs, which appeared three-dimensional when looked at through a viewer, enhanced the effect. At the first independent photography exhibition, held at the Society of Arts in 1852, Roger Fenton's opening address on the 'Art of Photography' defended photographic ideals as well as the medium's continuity with longer landscape traditions shared with Ruskin and the Pre-Raphaelites. He contrasted the grand historic sites that were a favourite of French photography with a British perception of meaning in modest, everyday motifs like 'the guarded oak, standing alone in the forest; intricate mazes of tangled wood, reflected in some dark pool'.[36] CJ

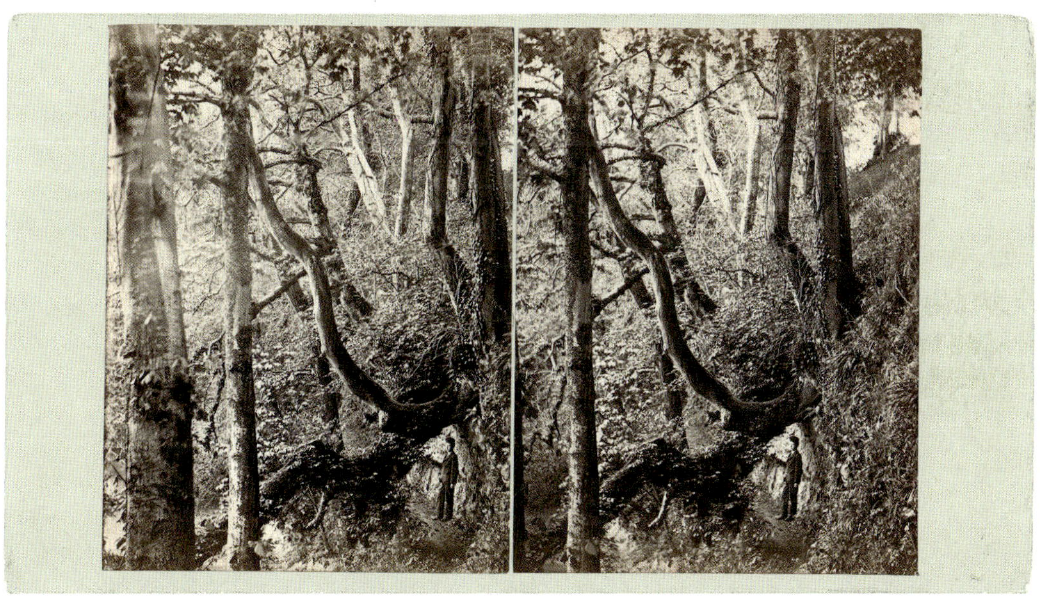

19 Photographer Unknown
***Figure in a Wood* 1850s**
2 photographs, albumen print on stereo card
Collection of Dr Brian May

Railways expanded tourism in the nineteenth century, and painters and photographers were drawn to similar tourist destinations. Albums, guidebooks and souvenirs began to illustrate sites of special beauty with photographs instead of engravings, and painters naturally used them as studies. Leeds artist John Atkinson Grimshaw gave up his post as a railway clerk in 1861 to become a painter. He was influenced by the Pre-Raphaelites and from his earliest years he employed photographs as preparatory studies for his beautiful and meticulous landscapes. CJ

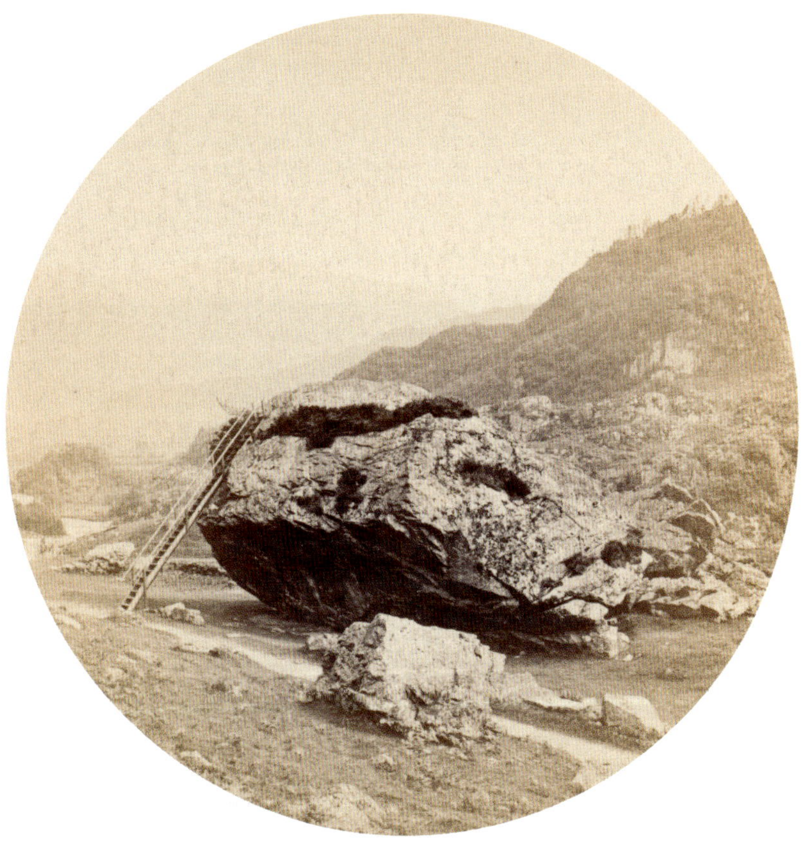

20 Thomas Ogle
***The Bowder Stone, Borrowdale* 1864**
Photograph, albumen print on paper 8.5 x 9
William Wordsworth, *Our English Lakes, Mountains and Waterfalls, as Seen by William Wordsworth*, London 1864
Tate

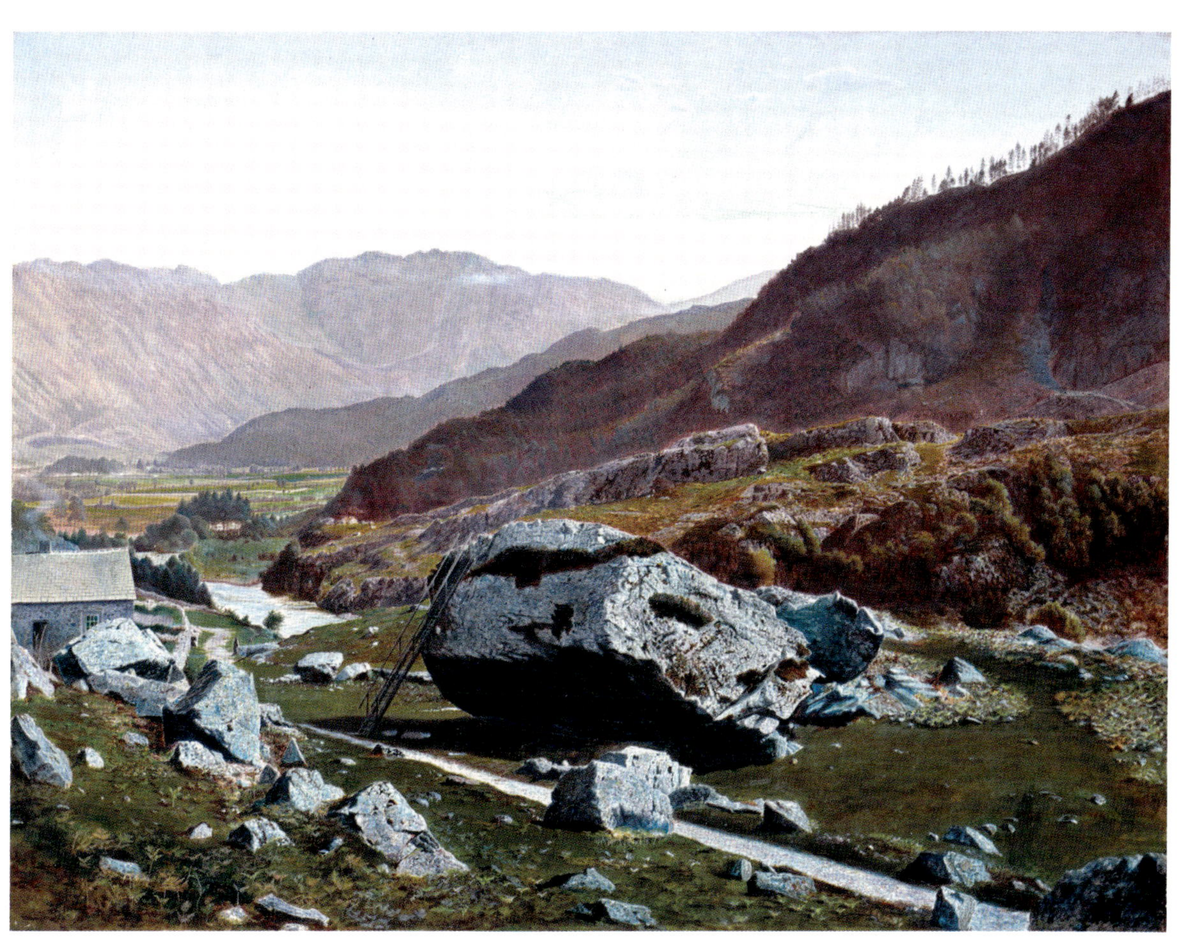

21 John Atkinson Grimshaw
***The Bowder Stone, Borrowdale* c.1863–8**
Oil paint on canvas 40 x 53.6
Tate. Purchased with assistance from the Friends of the Tate Gallery 1983

The Alps were celebrated subjects for artists, notably Turner. By the mid-nineteenth century new geological understandings of the vast forces of nature and expanses of time that had formed the Earth began to inform images of the mountains. John Ruskin and Friedrich von Martens were among the first photographers to capture them. Martens was well known at the Graphic Society and in 1851 he included an alpine panorama in his display at the Great Exhibition at Crystal Palace. The jury awarded him a medal and praised photography generally: 'We may safely predict; that from the date of the general application of Photography to the illustration of scenes daily passing around us, will commence a new era in pictorial representation.'[37]

Ruskin mentored John Brett, a younger associate of the Pre-Raphaelite circle, and encouraged him to paint in the Alps. Brett, too, drew on photographic sources, amassing a large collection by the end of his life. Hamerton described the difficulties thrown up by studying photographic 'memoranda' of Alpine subjects:

> *The whitest flake white is not so white as snow …*
>
> *When not illuminated by direct sunshine the snow is in many instances darker than the sky; darker even than grey clouds.*
>
> *And yet I know that the flake white I have to imitate* snow *in sunshine with is, in reality, darker than the snow in shadow.*
>
> *Our whitest white is darker than many of Nature's ordinary blues and greens and reds.*
>
> *And our blackest black is lighter than many of Nature's greys.*[38]

CJ

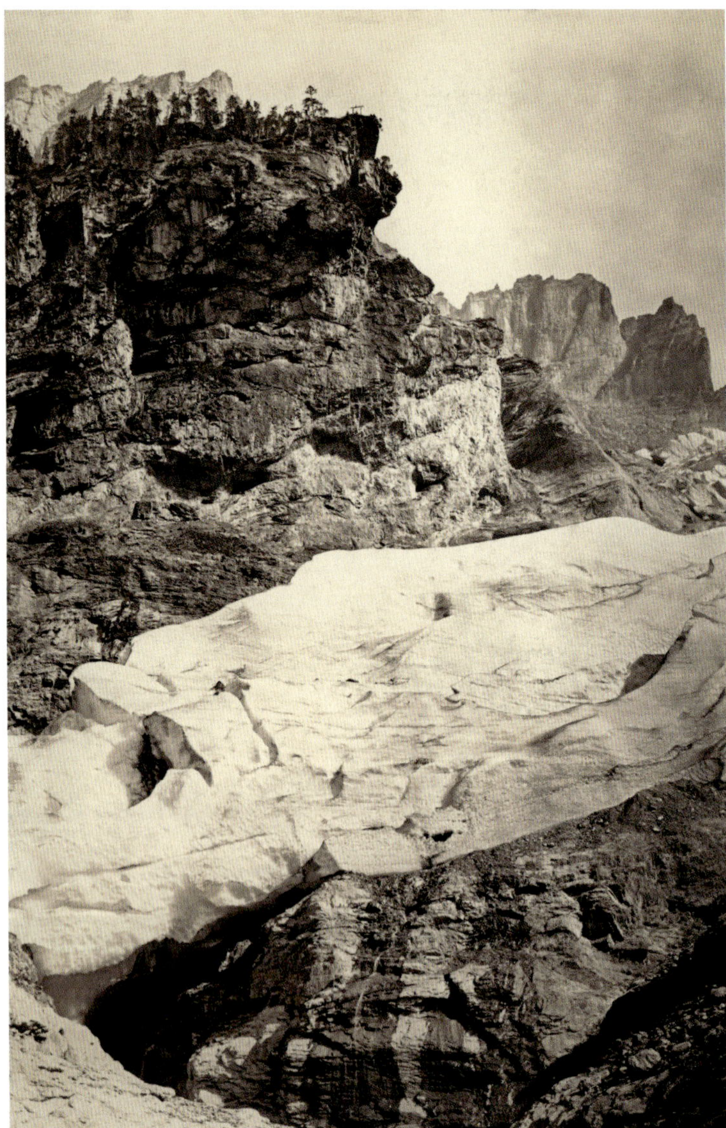

22 Friedrich von Martens
***The Glacier of Rosenlaui* 1850s**
Photograph, albumen print on paper 32 x 26
Alpine Club Photo Library, London

23 John Brett
***Glacier of Rosenlaui* 1856**
Oil paint on canvas 44.5 x 41.9
Tate. Purchased 1946

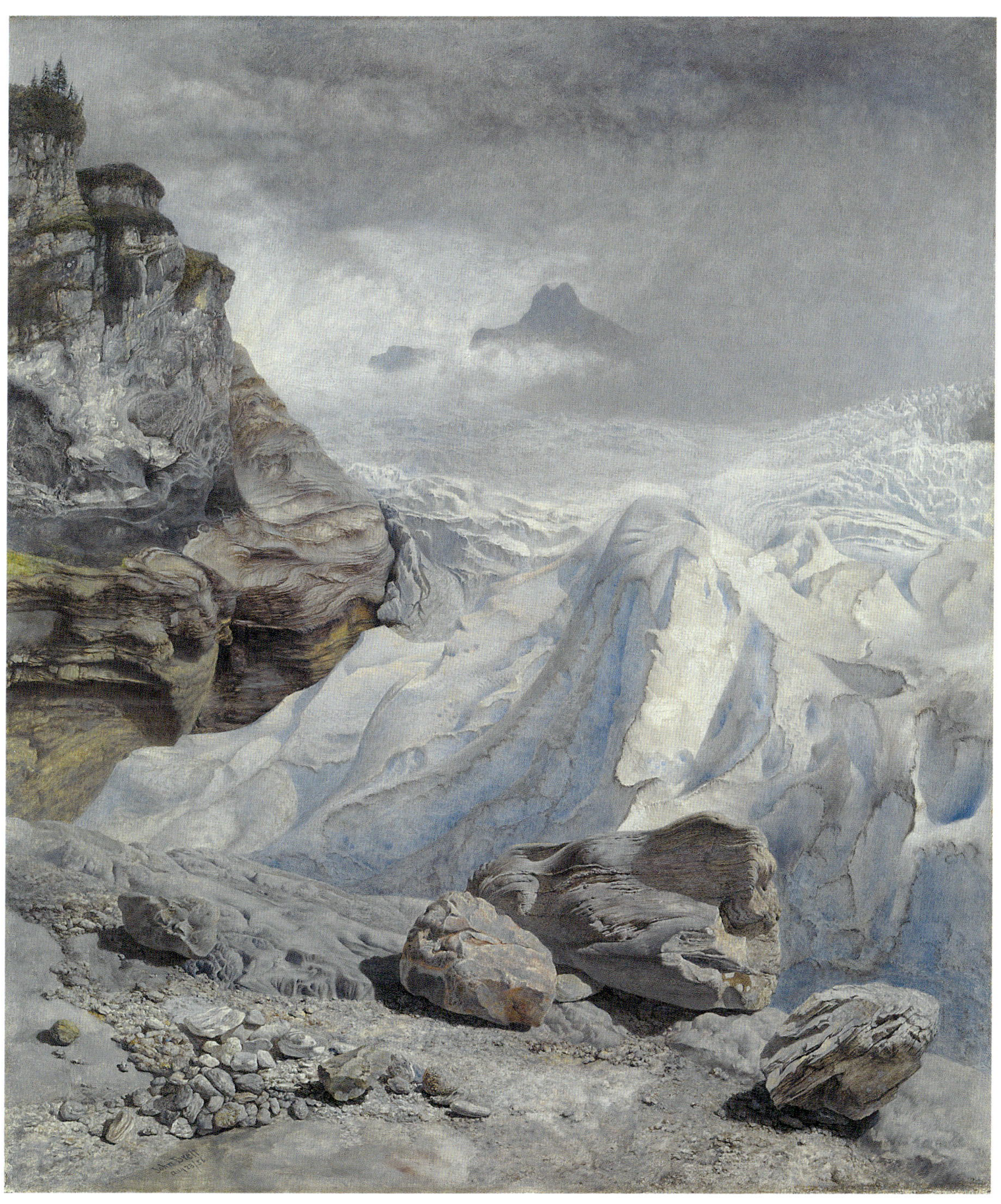

24 James Graham
***Nazareth from the North* 1855**
Photograph, albumen print on paper 21.1 x 25.8
Palestine Exploration Fund

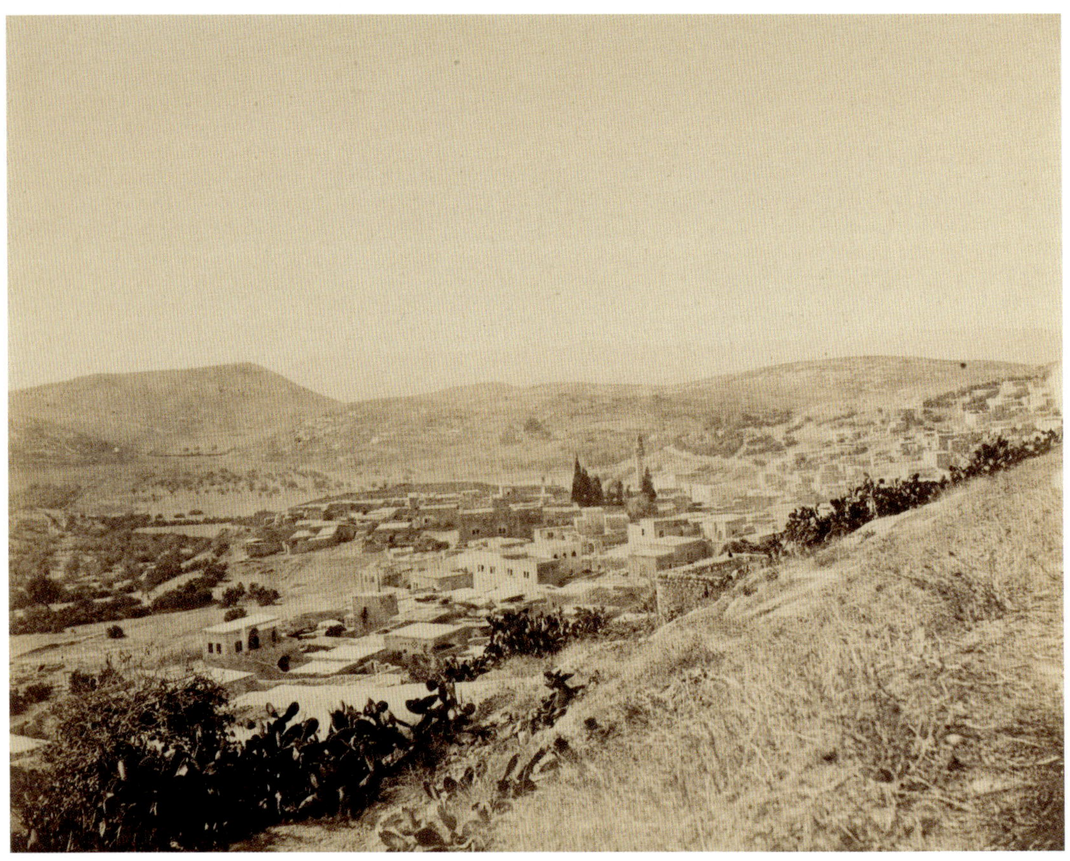

In 1854 Hunt and Seddon travelled to the Middle East and transcribed several views side by side with the photographer James Graham. Hunt's view of the town of Nazareth was painted over three days, 24–27 October, and Graham's photograph *Nazareth from the North* was taken on 27 October. Hunt did not quite complete the watercolour and used the photograph as an aide-memoire. It recorded light and shade as a mosaic of angular facets, which, when rendered in Hunt's *Nazareth* in prismatic colour, presented a new vision of light. *Nazareth* is also typical of the Pre-Raphaelite technique of creating expansive views with the continuity of detail from foreground to background exhibited in topographical photography. The rhythmic layers and hazy distance of traditional, picturesque landscape painting were abandoned for the striking exaggerated perspective and tonal geometries brought out by the camera. CJ

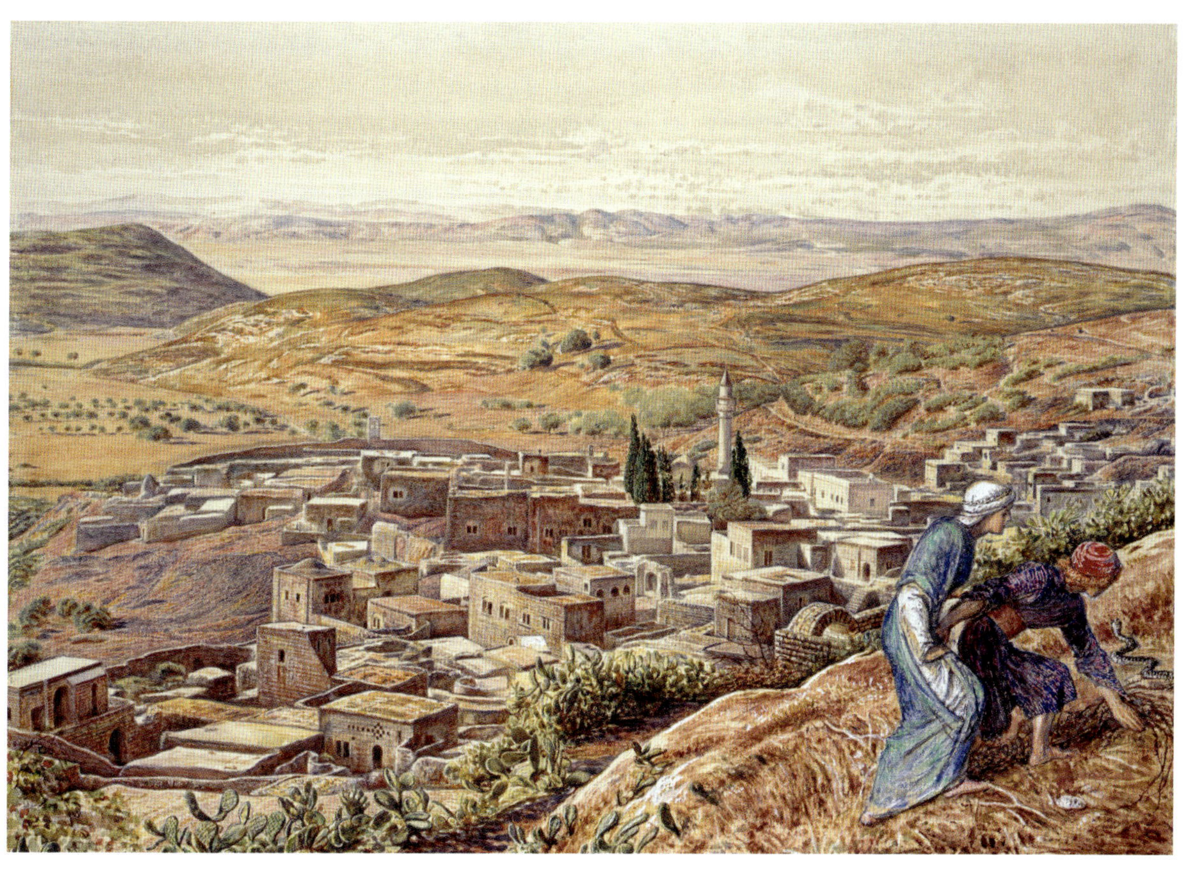

25 William Holman Hunt
***View of Nazareth* 1855, 1860–61**
Watercolour on paper 35.3 x 49.8
The Whitworth, The University of Manchester

Brown's *Carrying Corn*, painted near London, was inspired by noticing 'corn shocks in long perspective' and, despite its small size, required seventy hours of on-the-spot labour to accumulate the all-over detail.[39] In 1855 White purchased *Carrying Corn*, but his own images of cornfields (no.27) aspire to more traditionally picturesque arrangements and softer backgrounds. The poetry of these photographs was admired in London and Paris and pronounced 'more artistic and more like pictures, than anything else'.[40] CJ

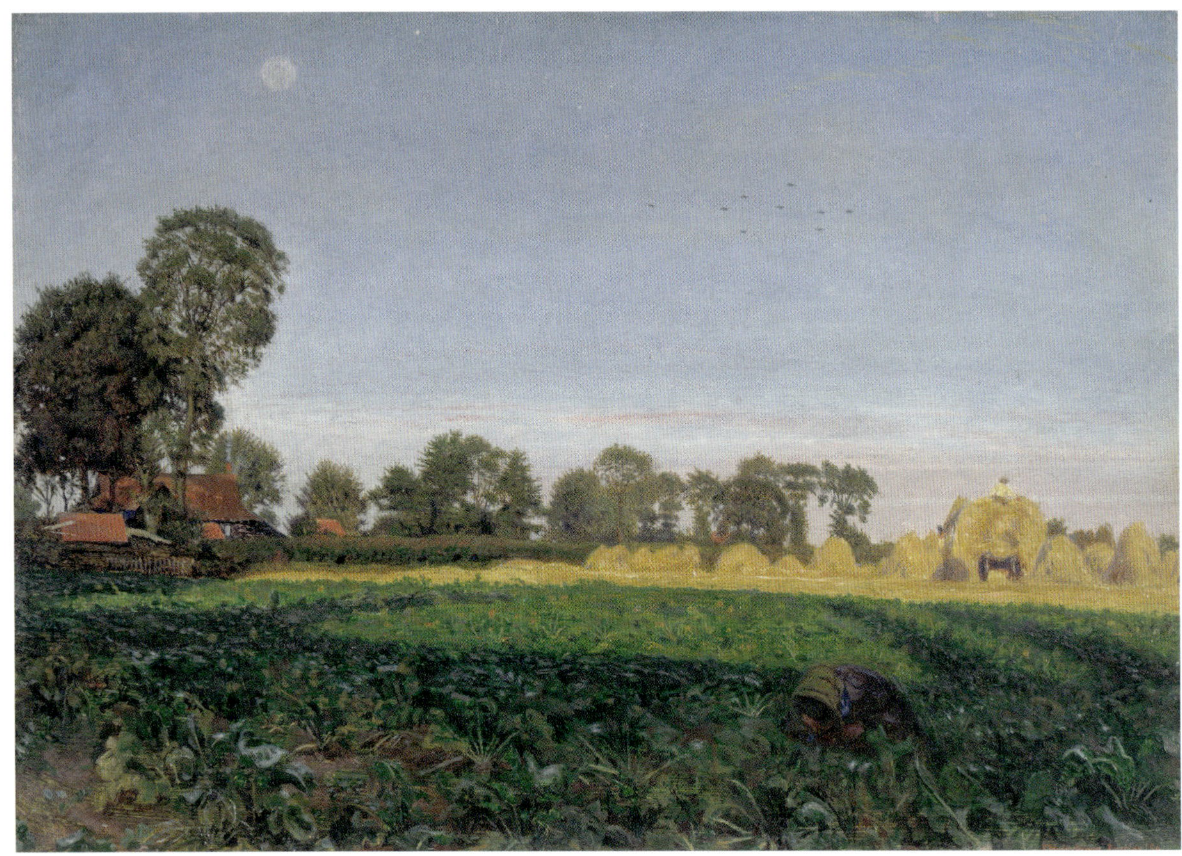

26 Ford Madox Brown
***Carrying Corn* 1854–5**
Oil paint on mahogany 19.7 x 27.6
Tate. Purchased 1934

27 Henry White
***Sheaves of Wheat* c.1856**
Photograph, albumen print on paper 18.5 x 24.5
Wilson Centre for Photography

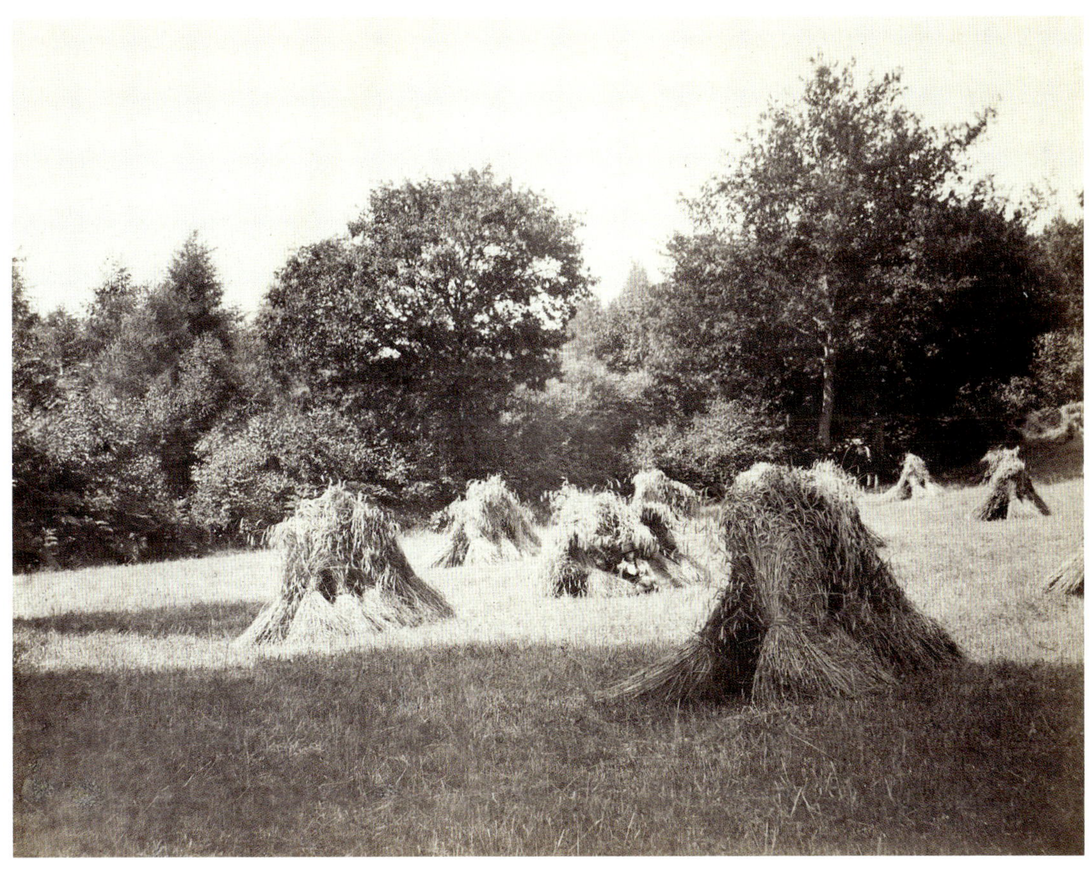

28 Gustave Le Gray
Ciel chargé – Mer Mediteranée
***(Cloudy Sky – Mediterranean Sea)* 1857**
Photograph, albumen print on paper 30 x 41
Victoria and Albert Museum

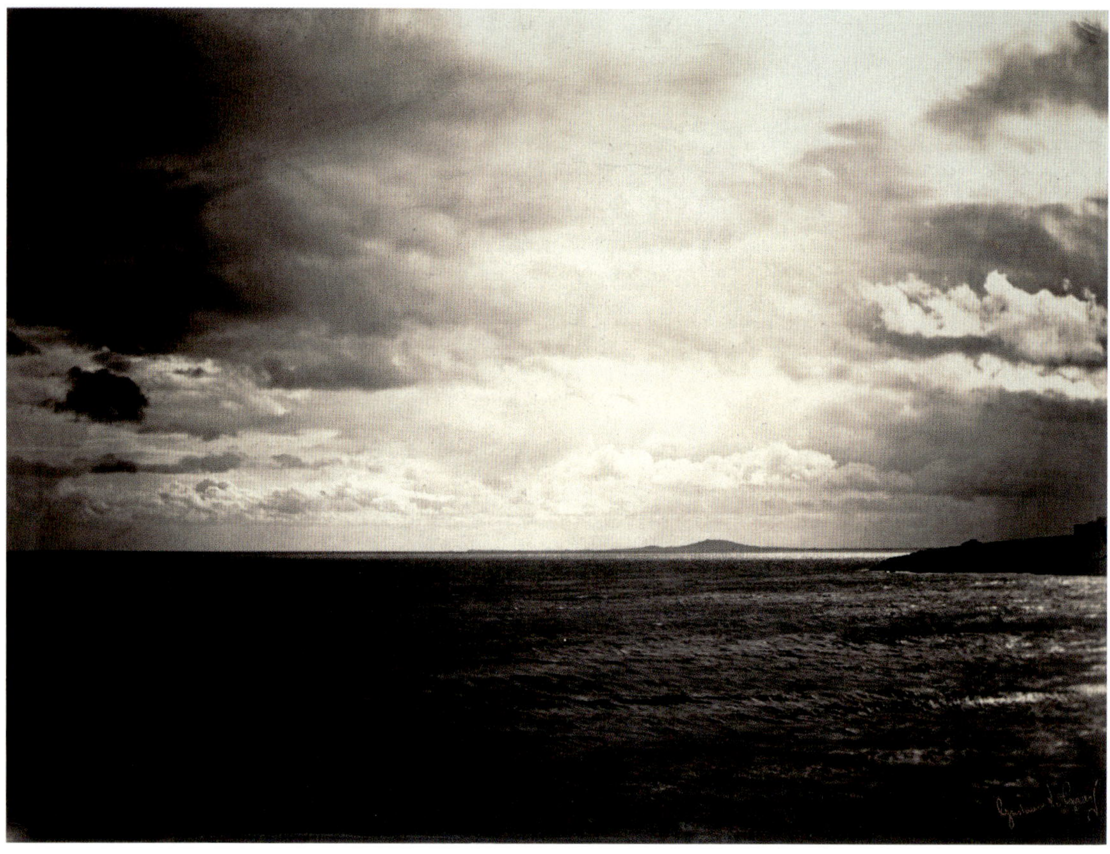

The critic Philip Hamerton compared Hunt's seascape effects to the celebrated photographs of Gustave Le Gray.
Le Gray's seascapes had been read as moonlight views and were considered the most painterly landscape photographs of the time. Hamerton admired them but believed Hunt was able to get more into his picture 'because painting is … an art of compromise … capable of moderation'. He analysed the limitations of the photograph:

In the photograph the blaze of light upon the sea is given with perfect fidelity; but in order to get this, and the light on the edges of the clouds, all else has been sacrificed: the shaded sides of the clouds, in nature of a dazzling grey, brighter than any white paper, are positively black in the photograph, and the pale splendour of the sunlit sea – except where it flashes light – is heavy and impenetrable darkness.[41]

CJ

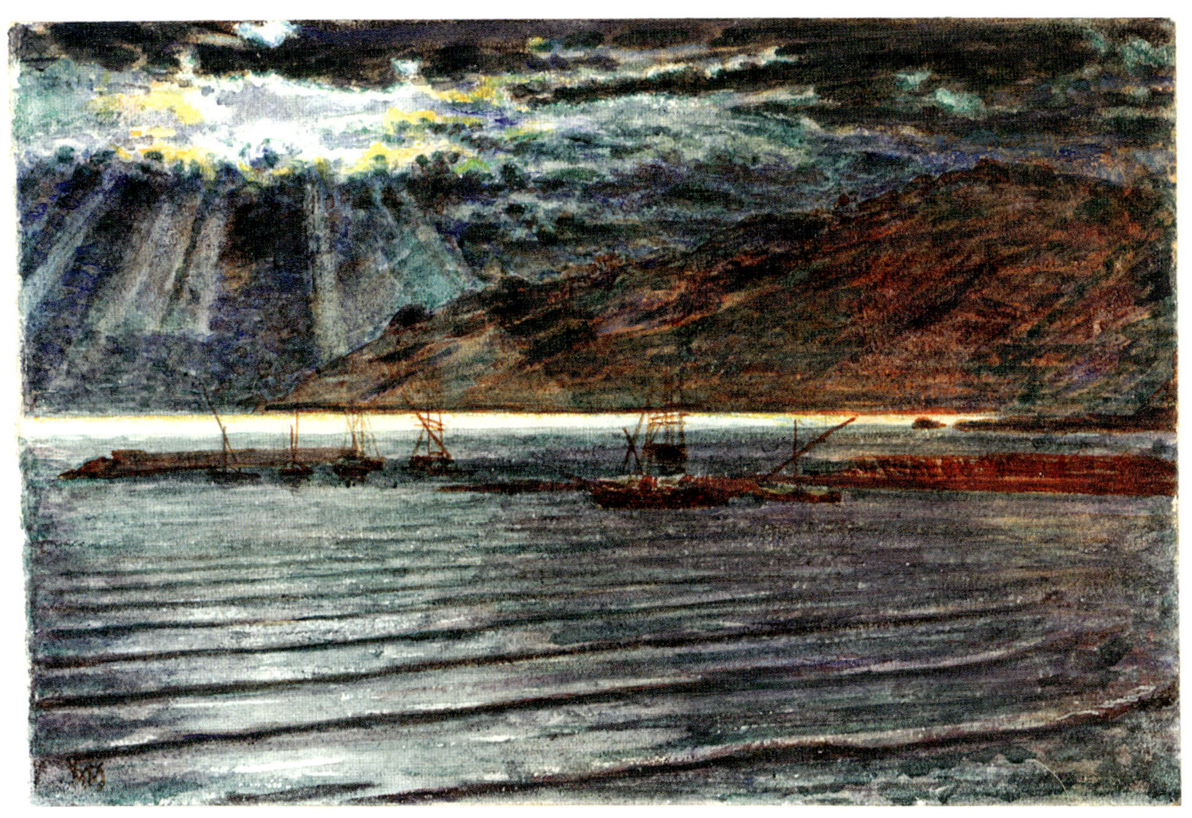

29 William Holman Hunt
***Fishing Boats by Moonlight* c.1869**
Watercolour, heightened with white
and traces of pencil on paper 40.4 x 55.6
Trustees of the Cecil Higgins Art Gallery, Bedford

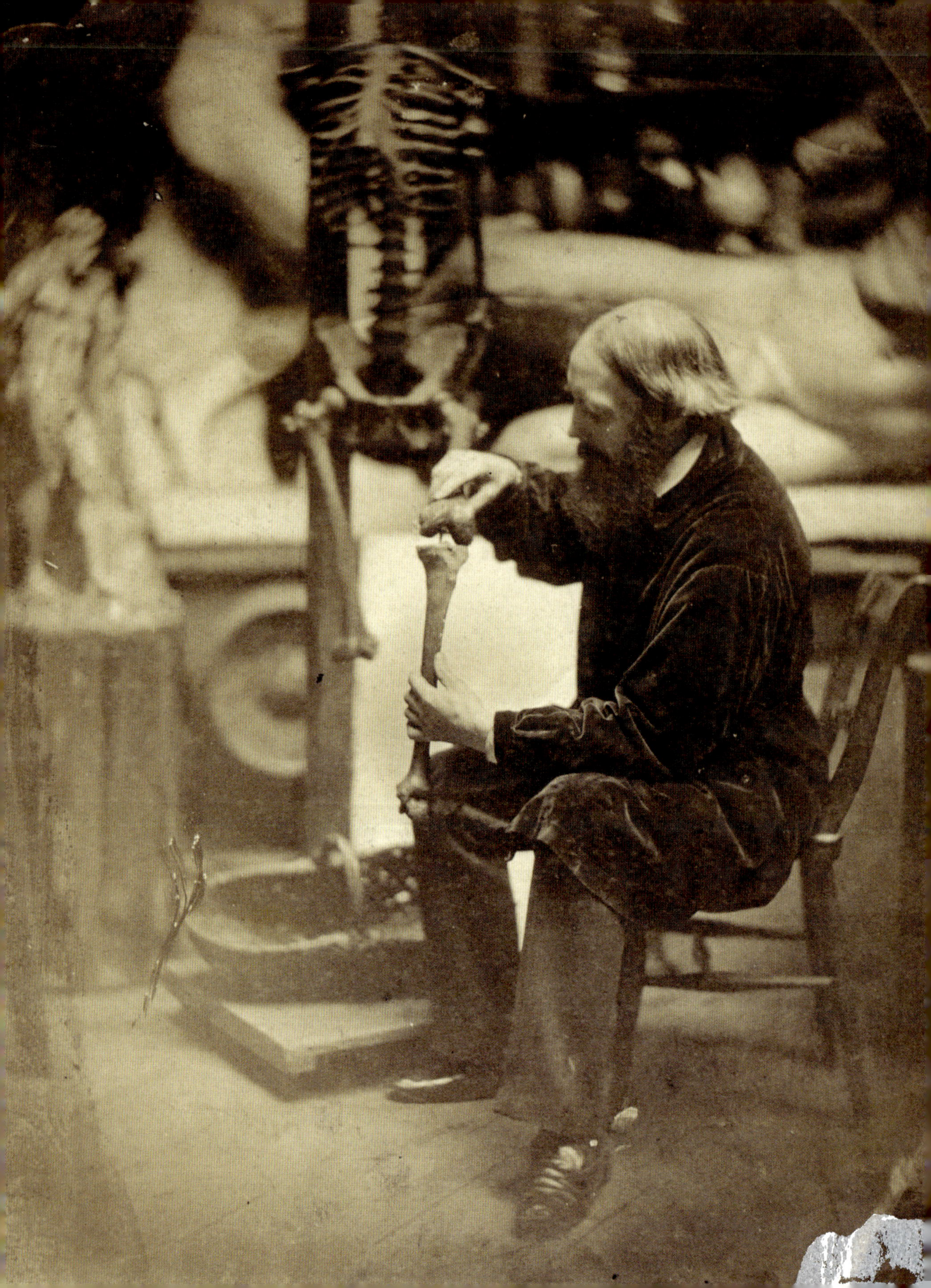

3 In the Studio

Carol Jacobi

Exchanges between photographers and painters took place in the studio as well as in the field. The selecting and arranging of models, costumes and settings provided common ground across the two media, and there were close associations between photographic and painting practice. Some photographers trained as artists, and photographic and painting materials were often purchased from the same suppliers. In 1851 the Wolverhampton painter Oscar Rejlander abandoned his painting profession for photography. 'What really hurried me forward', he later recalled in an essay, 'Apology for Art-Photography', 'was my having seen the photograph of a gentleman, and the fold in his coat sleeve was just the very thing I required for a portrait I was then painting at home.'[42] Painter-turned-photographer Roger Fenton collaborated with painter associates and in 1853 became the first Secretary of the Photographic Society (later the Royal Photographic Society).

Daguerreotypes of 'figures of the living model' were advertised for artists from the early 1840s.[43] As the training and practice of artists diversified, photographs were used as preparatory studies or substitutes for props, lay figures or models in the studio. Some photographers created images specifically for artists (no.40), but more often, painters purchased pictures imported from the continent, where so-called *études* or *académies* were well established. It has been argued that Fenton intended his oriental scenes for this purpose, as well as standing as self-sufficient works. Dickenson's Drawing Gallery, an art school set up as an alternative to the Royal Academy and latterly known as Heatherley's after its proprietor Thomas Heatherley (no.35), created an archive of images for students, many of whom were from Pre-Raphaelite circles. John Everett Millais attended the school and became known for his habit of making records of models, many commissioned from his friend, the amateur photographer Rupert Potter.

In 1853 Fenton was commissioned to survey the collections of the British Museum, traditionally the subject of artists' study (no.38). Photography, particularly stereoscopic photography that could be viewed in three dimensions, became an accepted way of recording and viewing sculpture. Photographers were, in turn, alert to the lessons of sculpture, its exploitation of light fall and its grace of physique and pose, as Julia Margaret Cameron advertises in her reinterpretation of Phidias' antique *Sister Fates* in *Teachings from the Elgin Marbles* (no.39).

Photographers recruited artists' models, as they were the only subjects who were able to hold a difficult pose for the time it took to expose the image. Their figures were also less distorted by corsets. The training and practice of artists diversified and photographic studies increasingly stood in for the casts and models in the studio and in art schools. As photography advanced and exposure time shortened, models were captured in a new range of spontaneous poses that could not be held long enough to paint. Rejlander became interested in facial countenance and in 1872 illustrated Darwin's *The Expression of the Emotions in Man and Animals*. However, fidelity to the appearance of the models used in paintings of historical and literary scenes, especially the friends and family portrayed by the Pre-Raphaelites, frequently gave rise to criticism for their absence of idealisation. Representations of modern individuals distilled issues of standards in art and photography in the nineteenth century, and raised questions about modern beauty and expression.

Samuel Butler
Mr Heatherley Himself **c.1870**
(no.35)

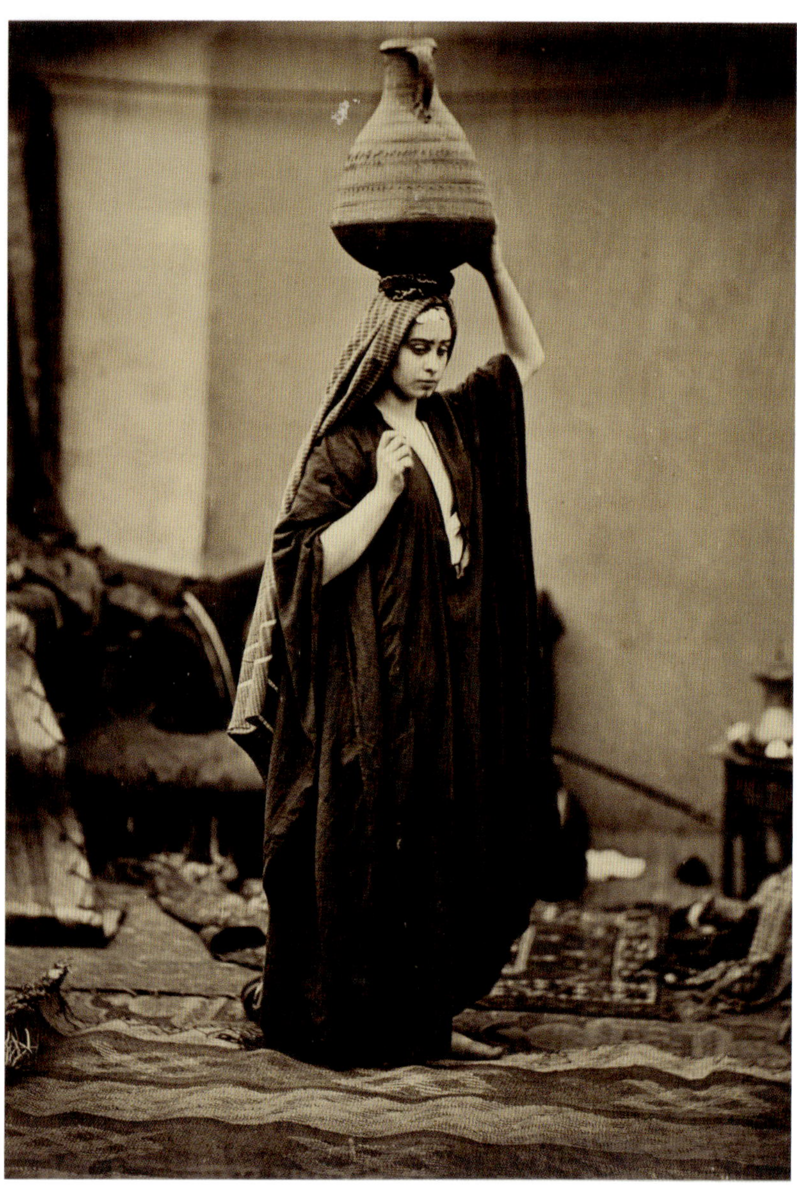

30 Roger Fenton
***Nubian Water-Carrier* 1858**
Photograph, albumen print on paper 36 x 25.7
Wilson Centre for Photography

In January 1859 Roger Fenton exhibited eight orientalist scenes at the Photographic Society of London. Titles like 'Pasha and Bayadère' and 'Nubian Water Carrier' signalled a popular motif in painting, seen in works by William Holman Hunt, Thomas Seddon and John Frederick Lewis. Lewis's Egyptian and Turkish subjects were especially acclaimed, and cited in a review describing one of Fenton's photographs as having 'more than all the detail of a water-colour drawing by John Lewis, and at the same time a low tone of singular breadth and sweetness'.[44]

The photographs were among fifty-one studies Fenton made at his north London studio the previous summer. They give a glimpse behind the scenes: in *Nubian Water-Carrier* wires were used to steady the heavy jug on the model's head. Another photograph (no.32) is a proof print that includes the studio skylight with its pleated velarium. These details would be effaced in the final prints – retouched out of the first image and cropped from the second.

The images show Fenton's artistic connections, not least in the remarkable similarity between *Nubian Water-Carrier* and an equivalent figure in Frederick Goodall's painting. Fenton had met Goodall's brother Edward in the Crimea, where in 1855 Fenton was photographing the British military and Edward was making studies for the *Illustrated London News*. Carl Haag may be a more direct link, for he and Goodall belonged to Clipstone Street Artists Society in London and Haag appears in some of Fenton's orientalist photographs. Shortly after those were made, he and Goodall embarked on a seven-month Egyptian sojourn that launched Goodall's successful career as a painter of Near Eastern subjects. HK

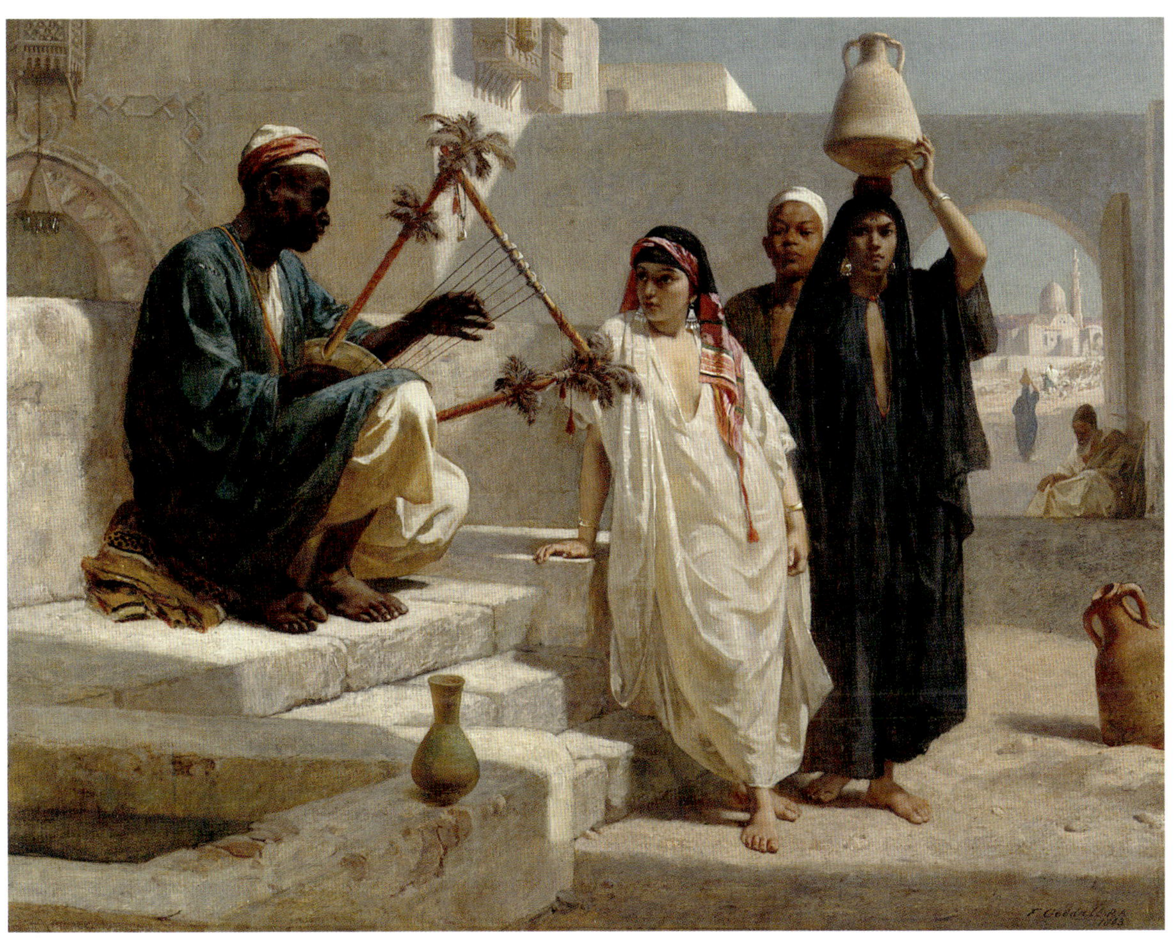

31 Frederick Goodall
***The Song of the Nubian Slave* 1863**
Oil paint on canvas 71.2 x 92
Royal Academy of Arts, London

Frank Dillon was very prominent among Fenton's sitters; he appears in most of the orientalist photographs (no.46) and is thought to have contributed many of the props. Dillon had travelled in Egypt in 1854, returning to exhibit Near Eastern subjects at the Royal Academy in 1856, 1857 and 1858. When his wife died in 1860, he returned to Egypt, where from the autumn of 1861 until the winter of 1862 he shared a house in Giza with fellow artists George Price Boyce and Egron Lundgren. Back in London, Dillon settled in Kensington, fitting out his 'Arab Studio' in the Mamluk style he so admired. Clarke photographed him there, leaning against a wall with recessed niches modelled on the Cairo house in his watercolour, and holding a long-stemmed Turkish pipe like that in Fenton's photographs. HK

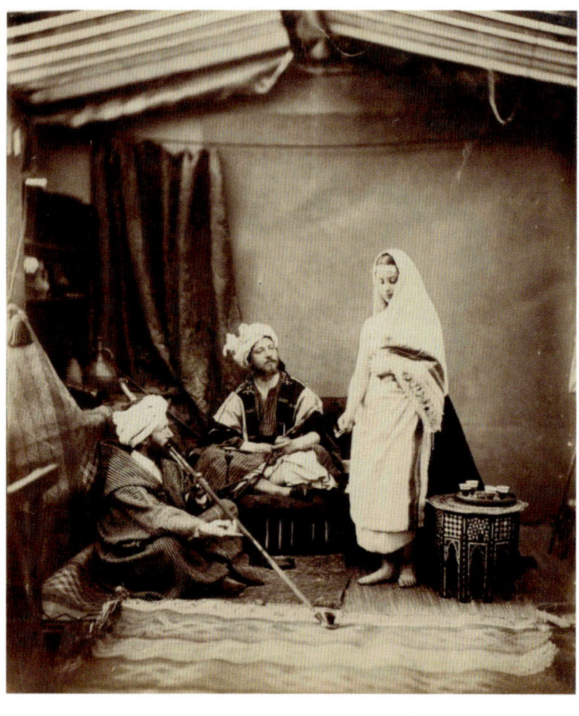

32 Roger Fenton
***Frank Dillon and another man in orientalist costume seated, one woman standing* 1858**
Photograph, albumen print on paper 31.3 x 27
Wilson Centre for Photography

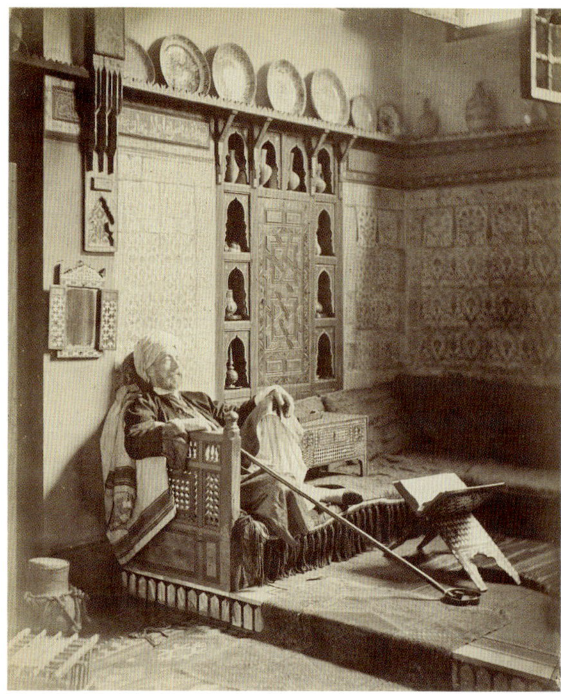

33 C.H. Clarke
***Frank Dillon* c.1870s**
Photograph, albumen print on paper 29.2 x 24.4
Wilson Centre for Photography

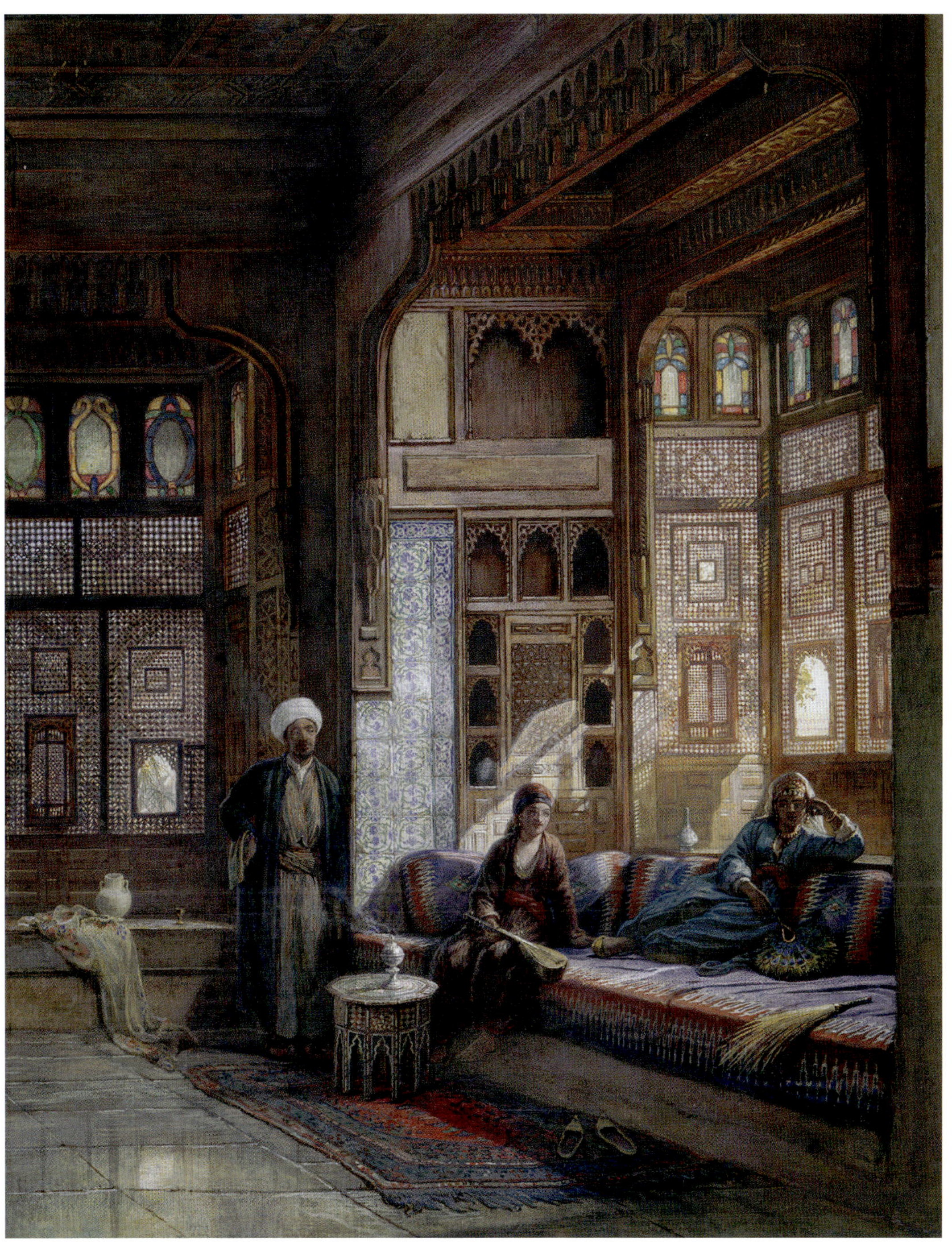

34 Frank Dillon
A Room in the House of Sheikh al-Sadat al-Wafa'iya, Cairo c.1875
Bodycolour on paper, stretched over panel 74.5 x 58.5
Victoria and Albert Museum
Purchased with the assistance of The Art Fund, the National Heritage Memorial Fund, Shell International and the Friends of the V&A

37 Samuel Butler
***Mr Heatherley's Holiday: An Incident in Studio Life* 1874**
Oil paint on canvas 92.1 x 70.8
Tate. Presented by representatives of Jason Smith 1911

The artist and writer Samuel Butler studied at Heatherley's Art School in the mid-1860s. He photographed Mr Heatherley and the models in preparation for his oil paintings. *Rose the Model* was one of the first he took, and he wrote in his notebook: 'All the markings which we see in the antique and accept, though we never see them in real life, were not only there but in as full development as I ever saw in the antique.'[45] CJ

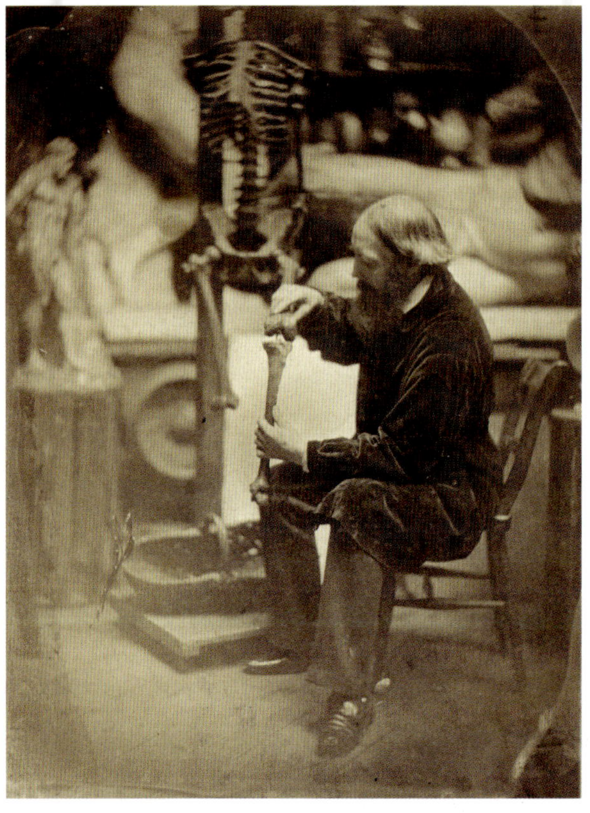

35 Samuel Butler
***Mr Heatherley Himself* c.1870**
Photograph, albumen print on paper 23.3 x 17.3
By permission of the Master and Fellows of St John's College, Cambridge

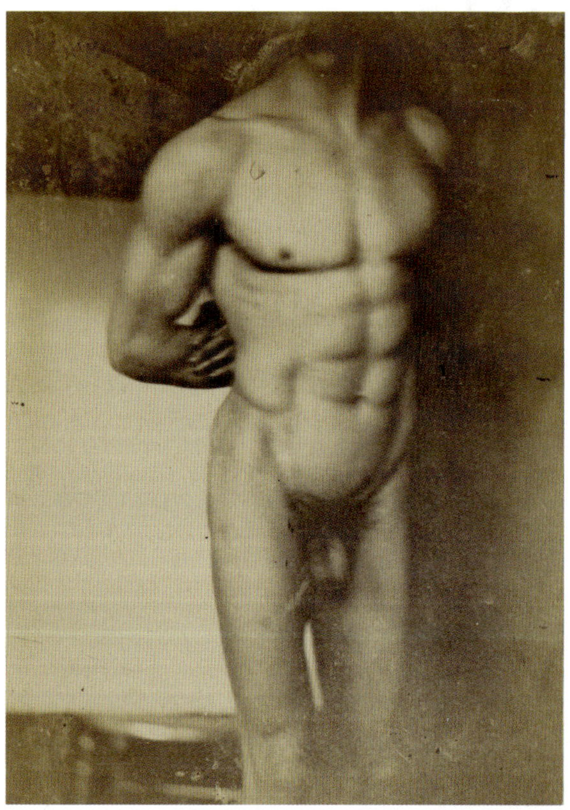

36 Samuel Butler
***Rose the Model* c.1865**
Photograph, albumen print on paper 21 x 15.2
By permission of the Master and Fellows of St John's College, Cambridge

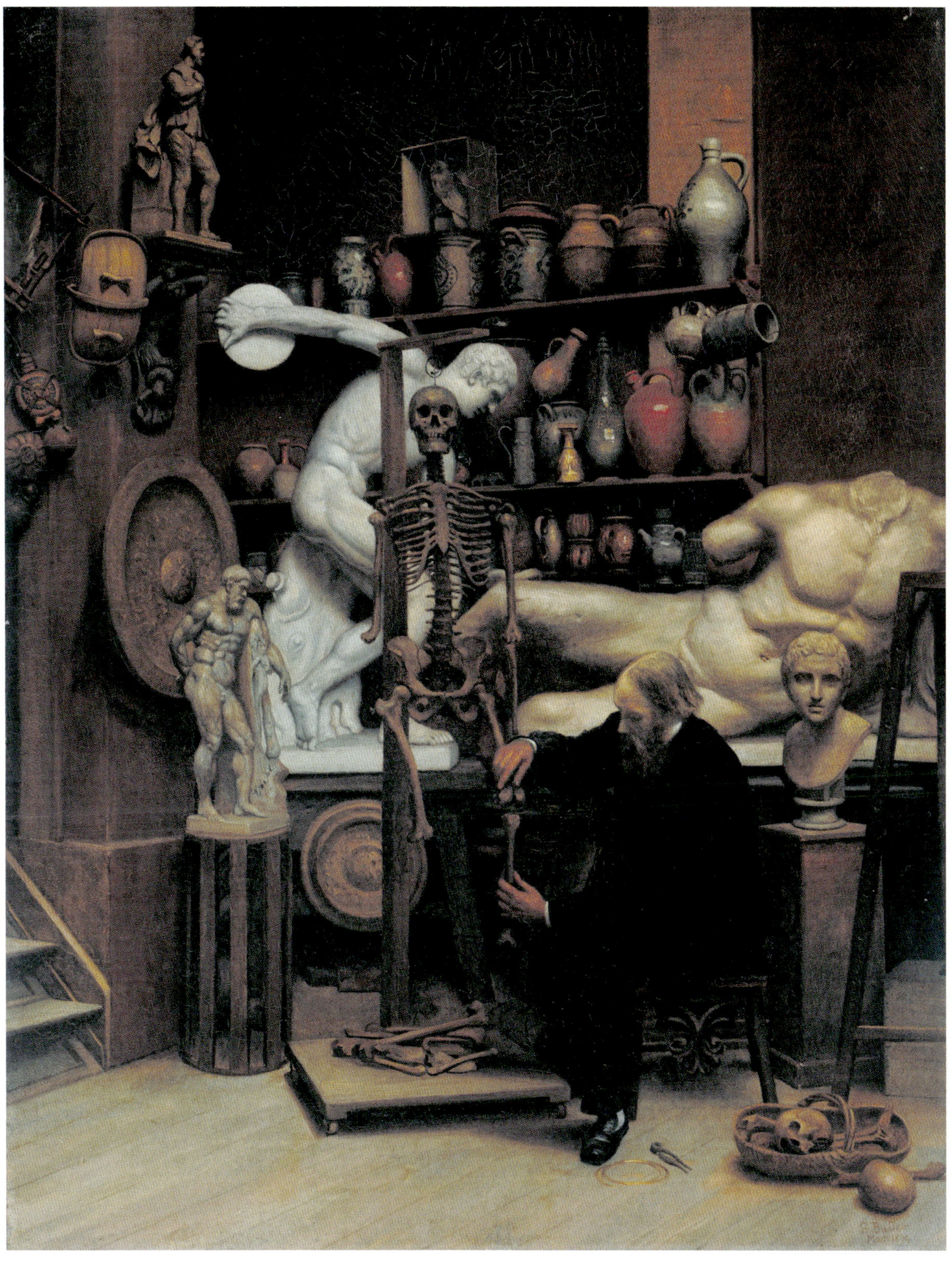

The Elgin Marbles, classical Greek carvings in the British Museum, were considered paradigms of art. The artist Benjamin Robert Haydon proclaimed the marbles as a distillation of human anatomy and in the year of his death, 1846, he even wrote to Hill and Adamson comparing Fenton's *Sister Fates* to their photographs of fisherwomen, a comparison published shortly after.[46]

Julia Margaret Cameron was a member of the Arundel Society, which published reproductions of works of art including the Elgin Marbles. In 1863 the *Athenaeum* discussed the want of 'nerve and vitality ... breathing and intelligent spirit' in these copies, however.[47] Cameron visited the British Museum with Tennyson, with whom she discussed the marbles at length, and made her own versions of the *Sister Fates*, represented by the draped figures of two models, Mary Hillier and Cylene Wilson, and inscribed 'From Life'. Her photographs varied the attitude of the heads of the figures, missing in the sculpture itself, to suggest a relationship between them. CJ

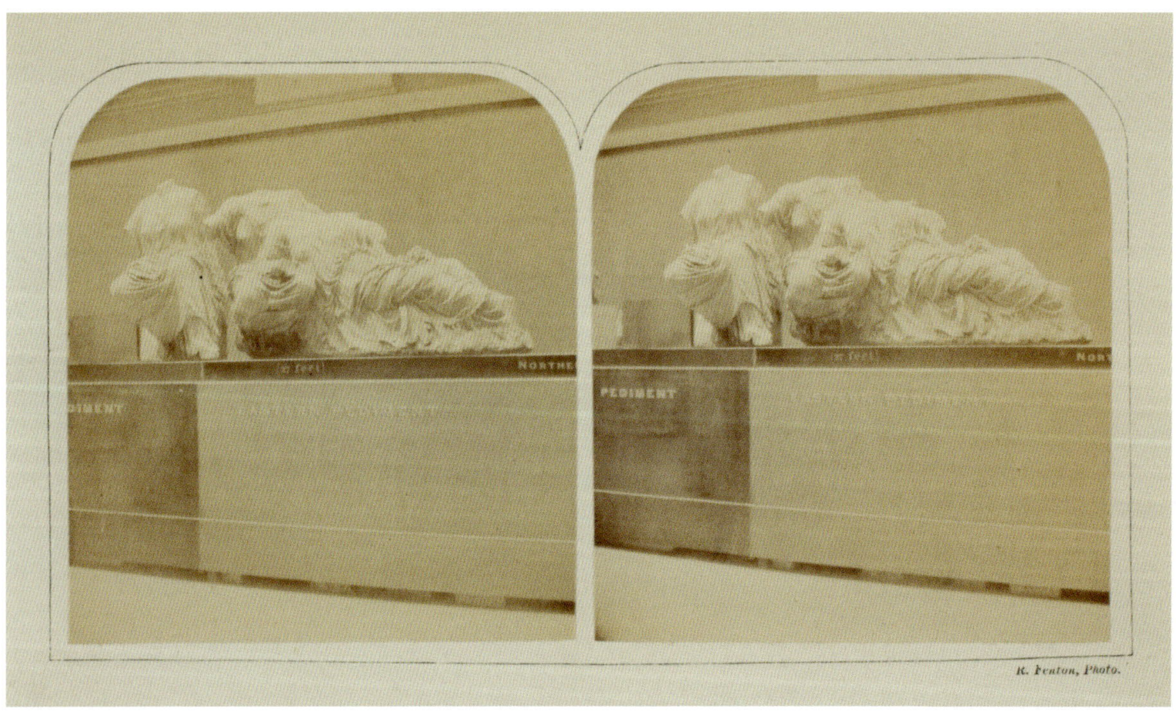

38 Roger Fenton
***The Elgin Marbles, British Museum II* 1859**
2 photographs, albumen prints on stereo card 7 x 7 each, on 8.5 x 17.3 mount
George Eastman House

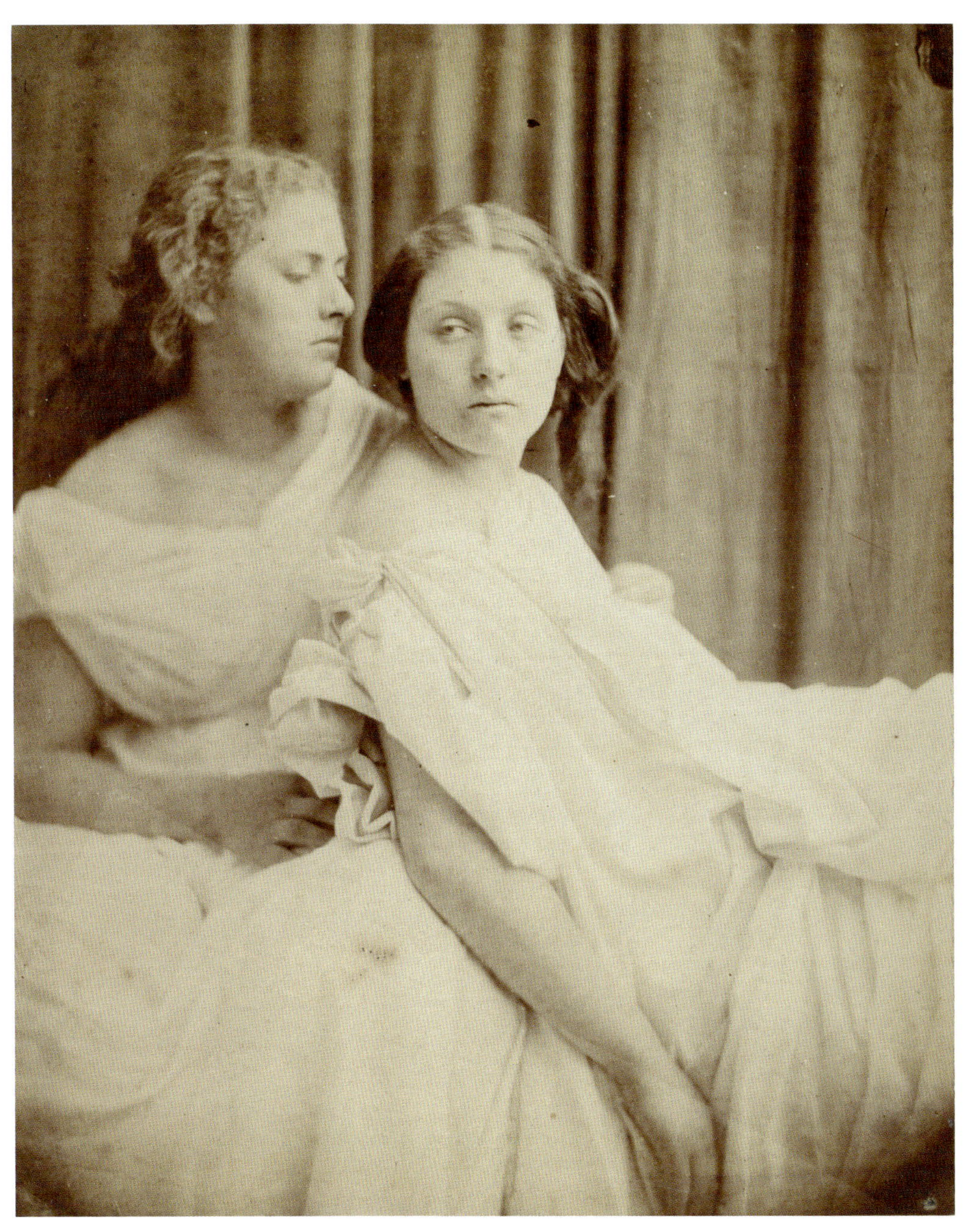

39 Julia Margaret Cameron
Teachings from the Elgin Marbles
***(Cyllena Wilson and Mary Hillier)* 1867**
Photograph, albumen print on paper 28.4 x 23.3
The Ashmolean Museum, Oxford.
Bequeathed by Humphrey Case, 2009

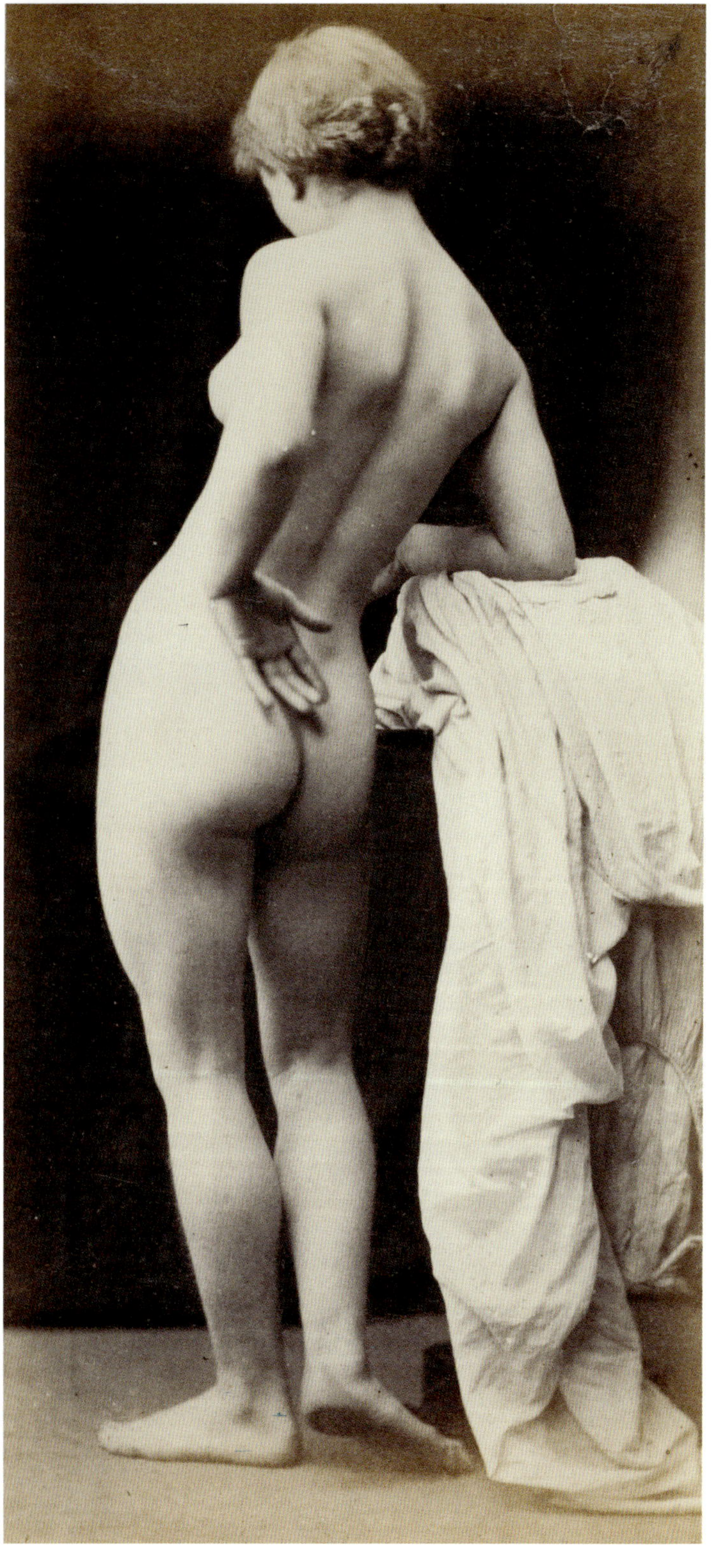

Most *études* or *académies* made for the use of artists were characterised by poses that recalled classical art. Rejlander's model bears no mark of modern garters or corsets. She stands in contrapposto, with one leg bent, and leans against a draped support, emulating marble figures in classical sculpture, as did John Gibson's *Venus* c.1850, of which Rejlander owned photographs. Rejlander also photographed models in the poses of figures in paintings by Titian, Rubens and others in the belief that they might help artists improve on them.

The graphic artist Edward Linley Sambourne was an illustrator for the weekly *Punch* and other journals. He worked at great speed and began collecting and making reference photographs in 1889, employing the leading artists' models of the time. He also borrowed classical poses and drapery, but became increasingly interested in catching the body in expressive movement. Sambourne made hundreds of images, many taken in a rooftop photographic studio that was provided for members of the Camera Club. CJ

40 Oscar Gustav Rejlander
***Untitled* c.1860**
Photograph, albumen print on paper 18.3 x 8.8
Wilson Centre for Photography

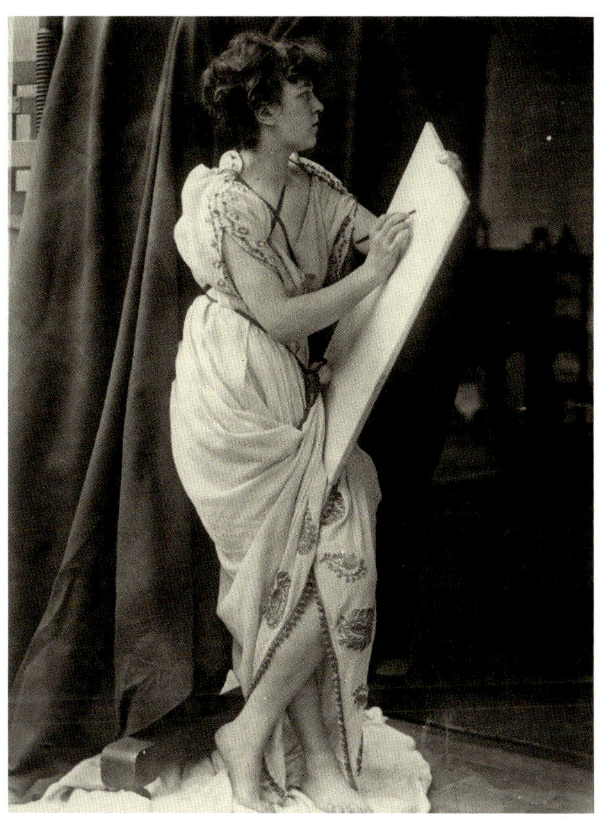

41 Edward Linley Sambourne
Ada Fletcher as an Allegory of Art **1890**
Photograph, platinum print on paper 21.1 x 16.3
18 Stafford Terrace, The Royal Borough of Kensington and Chelsea

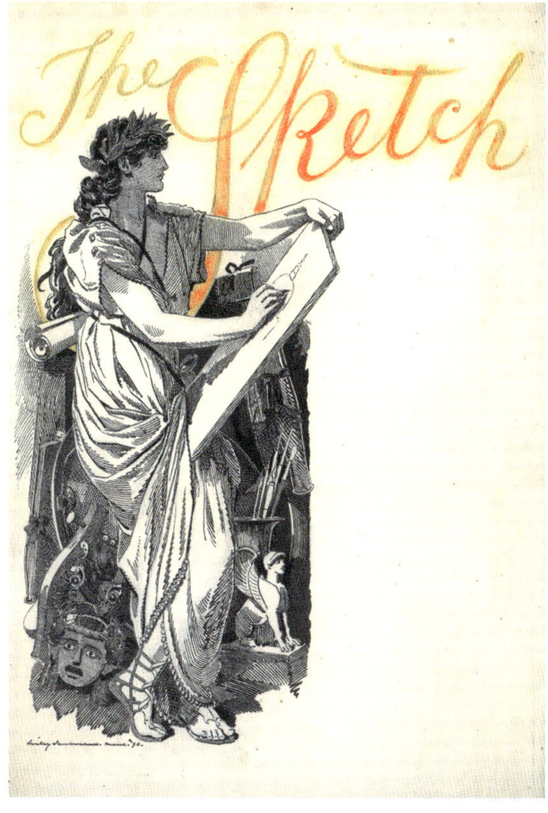

42 Edward Linley Sambourne
Design for 'The Sketch' **1893**
Pen and ink on paper 44.4 x 34
18 Stafford Terrace, The Royal Borough of Kensington and Chelsea

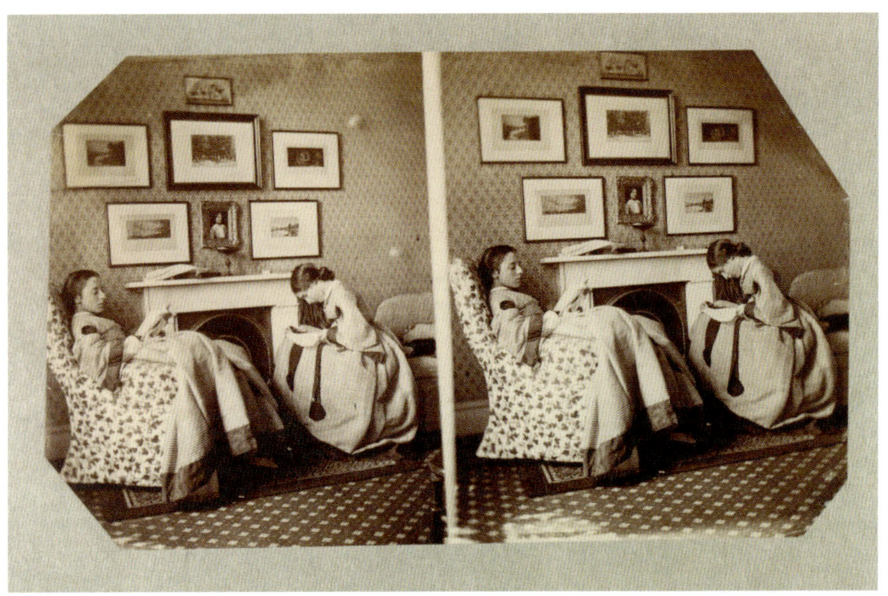

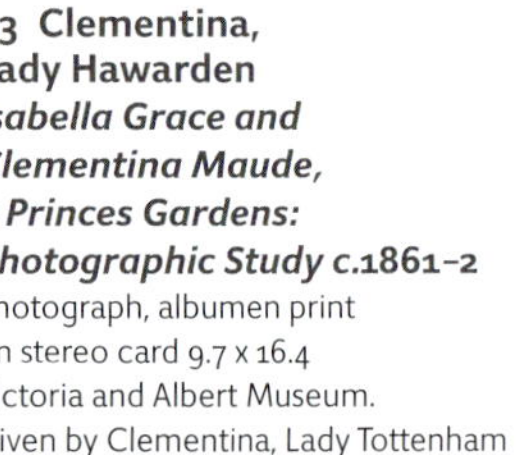

43 Clementina, Lady Hawarden
Isabella Grace and Clementina Maude, 5 Princes Gardens: Photographic Study c.1861–2
Photograph, albumen print on stereo card 9.7 x 16.4
Victoria and Albert Museum.
Given by Clementina, Lady Tottenham

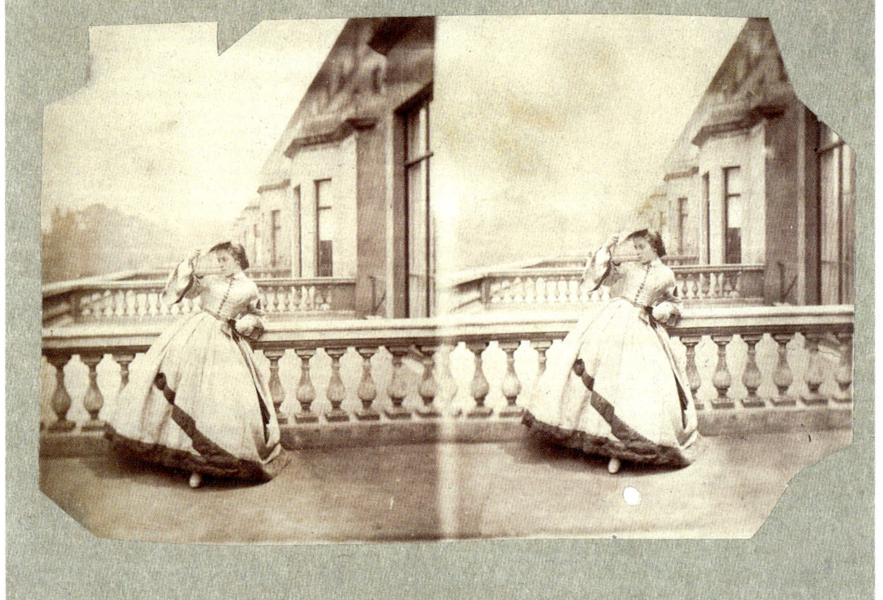

44 Clementina, Lady Hawarden
Isabella Grace on the terrace, 5 Princes Gardens: Photographic Study c.1861–2
Photograph, albumen print on stereo card 9.7 x 16.4
Victoria and Albert Museum.
Given by Clementina, Lady Tottenham

Etchings by the surgeon Francis Seymour Haden, including a view of the Hawarden family estate in Tipperary, are visible in the background of one of the stereoscopic photographs (no.43) by Clementina, Lady Hawarden, hinting at an artistic as well as a social connection. Comparison of Haden's print *The Assignation* with another of Hawarden's photographs (no.44) provides further evidence of artistic dialogue, as Virginia Dodier has noted.[48] The photograph features – as was Hawarden's practice – one of her daughters as her model, here wearing a distinctive dress and holding a fan to her head in a carefully arranged pose. In Haden's etching we see the same figure echoed: reversed by the printmaking process and leaning against a tree rather than a balustrade, she is nonetheless recognisably borrowed from Hawarden's photograph. Haden, whose brother-in-law was James McNeill Whistler, became a leading voice in the promotion of etching as a fine art and was rewarded by a knighthood in 1894. EJ

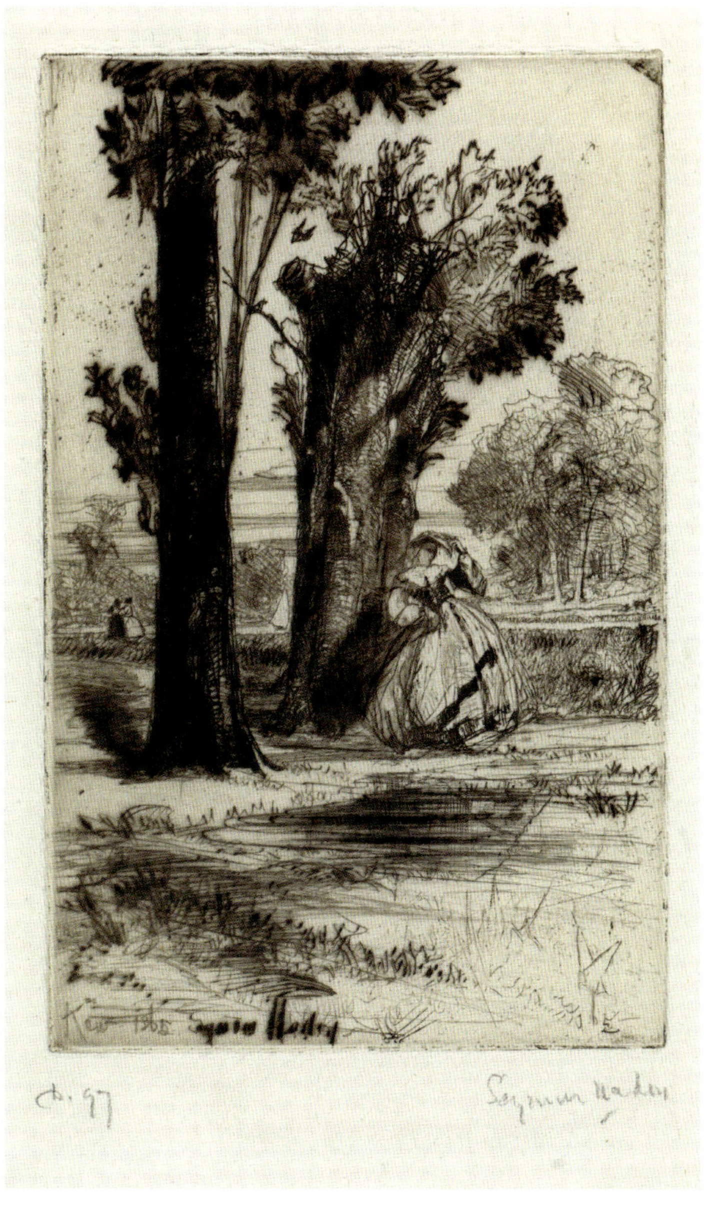

45 Francis Seymour Haden
***The Assignation* 1865**
Etching and drypoint on paper 21.3 x 13.6
The Hunterian, University of Glasgow

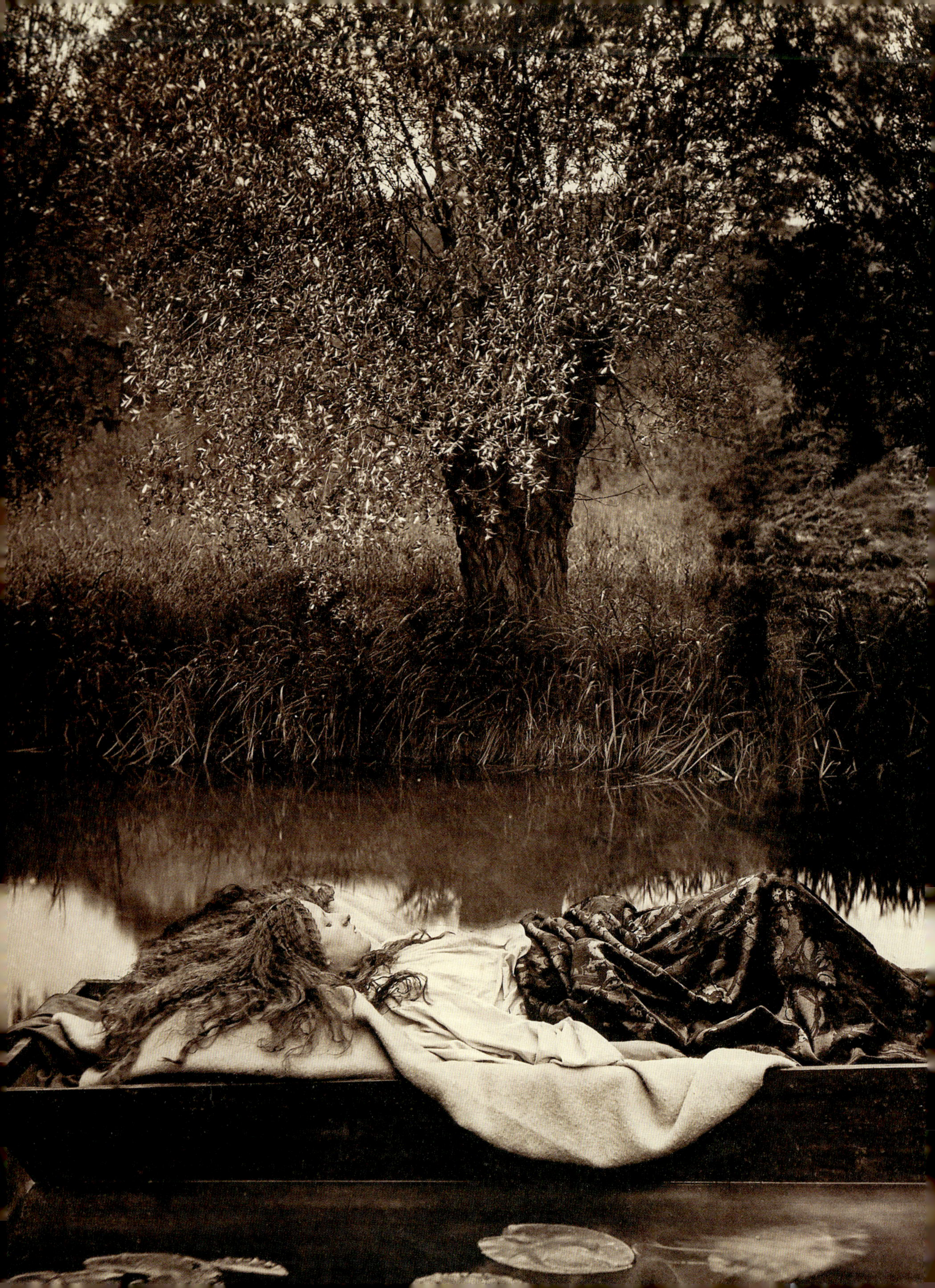

4 Tableaux

Carol Jacobi

The narrative tableau – the representation of models, props and sets arranged to tell a story – was a technique employed by painters and photographers. It appealed to the expanding middle-class and urban audiences who were enjoying the literature of popular writers like Charles Dickens. Photography formed part of a growing trade in prints, illustrated books and journals, reaching a broader public through new markets in Britain and abroad, especially in America and the British Empire. In 1855 the publication of engravings of Roger Fenton's ground-breaking photographs from the Crimean War in the *Illustrated London News* swelled its readership to 150,000, for example. Oscar Rejlander and Henry Peach Robinson created composite photographs that brought figures and settings together into narratives of new complexity. Stereographic photographs reached a wide international market. The small, portable cards, often hand-tinted in colour, could be collected and enjoyed using a three-dimensional viewer in the home. Photographers such as James Elliot brought together large casts of characters in his spacious studio, using props and sets from London theatres.

These new pictorial technologies, uses and audiences catalysed an age of innovation in the visual arts, but brought, at the same time, questions about standards and discriminating viewing that were reflected in contemporary writings on art and photography. Artists aimed to encourage the quality of art and design, many becoming involved in illustration and the applied arts, for example. Some photographers sought to distinguish their work from more commercial uses such as society portraits and the lucrative cartes-de-visite. Amateur photographers, often collaborating through exchange clubs and, from 1859, the Amateur Photographic Association, played a significant role. All kinds of photographers drew on works of art. Stereographic photographers re-staged celebrated paintings in three dimensions, sometimes expanding the action into several sequential scenes that unfolded over time. Amateur photographers would create and record private tableaux, using friends and family to evoke well-known characters from art and literature.

Britain's proud literary tradition, from Shakespeare to contemporary writers, played a distinctively progressive role in Victorian art and photography, and was especially central to Pre-Raphaelite painting. Tennyson was the leading figure in modern poetry and also personally known to a group of artists who frequently interpreted his visually evocative imagery. Book design gained new attention and Edward Moxon's 1857 edition of Tennyson's *Poems*, illustrated with woodblock prints by Millais, Hunt, Dante Gabriel Rossetti, Daniel Maclise and others, raised the standards. The original, condensed designs reverberated in subsequent illustrations, paintings and photographs within the circle, including new editions of the poems illustrated by Julia Margaret Cameron.

Henry Peach Robinson
***The Lady of Shalott* 1860–61**
(detail, no.56)

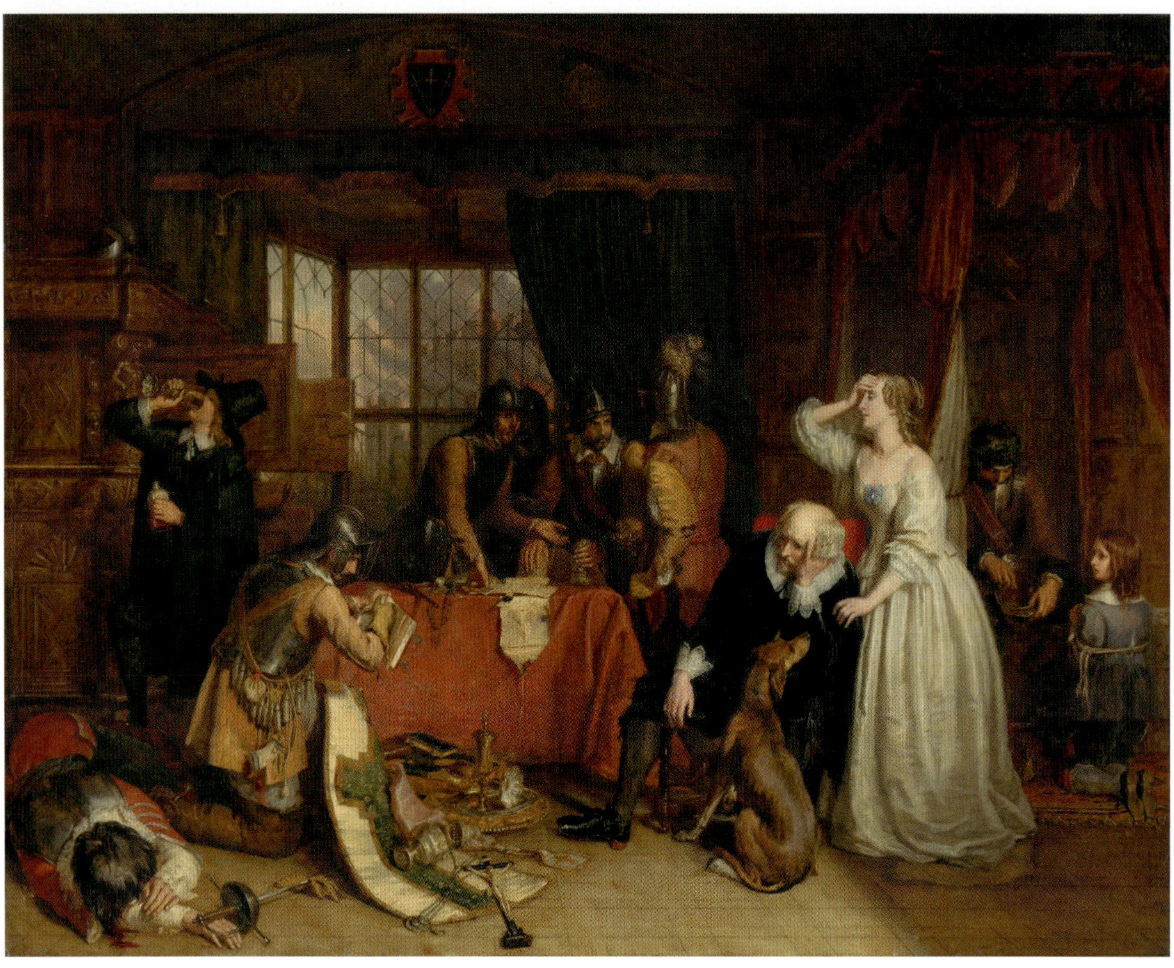

46 Charles Landseer
***The Plundering of Basing House* exh. 1836**
Oil paint on canvas 100.3 x 125.7
Tate. Bequeathed by Jacob Bell 1859

Charles Landseer made his name as a history painter and this, the first of his successful series depicting the Civil War, shows Oliver Cromwell's troops sacking Basing House, a stronghold loyal to Charles I, on 14 October 1645, while Marquess John Paulet looks on in despair. The plunder included the religious objects of the Catholic household, and the Puritan preacher Hugh Peters is shown drinking from a golden goblet. The Civil War gained a new relevance after the revolutions in France in 1789, 1830 and 1848, and Landseer's painting, which became well known as an engraving, entered the National Gallery in 1859.

In 1856 Sir David Brewster, the inventor of the lenticular stereoscope, suggested that 'the most interesting scenes in our best comedies and tragedies might be represented with the same distinctness and relief as if the actors were on the stage. Events and scenes in modern history might be similarly exhibited.'[49] The following year, James Elliot advertised in *The Times* 'a series of illustrations from English history from the Time of the Romans to the Present date'. His version of *The Plundering of the Basing House* expanded Landseer's narrative into sequential scenes, and in the first we see a soldier run his sword through the cavalier who lies at the left of the painting. CJ

47 James Elliot
***The Plundering of Basing House: Puritan Soldiers with Prisoners (Attacked)* 1858**
2 photographs, albumen prints on stereo card 8.8 x 17.8
Collection of Dr Brian May

48 James Elliot
***The Plundering of Basing House: Puritan Soldiers with Prisoners (Bound)* 1858**
2 photographs, hand-tinted albumen prints on stereo card 8.8 x 17.8
Collection of Dr Brian May

49 James Elliot
***The Plundering of Basing House: Puritan Soldiers with Prisoners (Given Water)* 1858**
2 photographs, hand-tinted albumen prints on stereo card 8.8 x 17.8
Collection of Dr Brian May

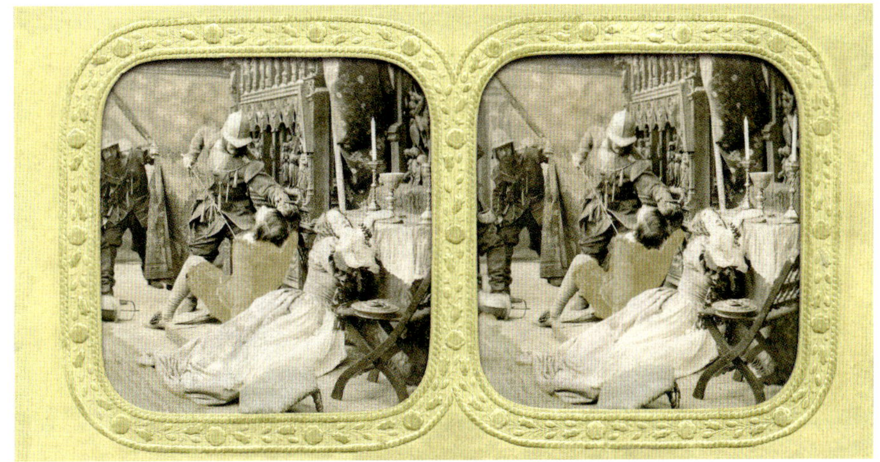

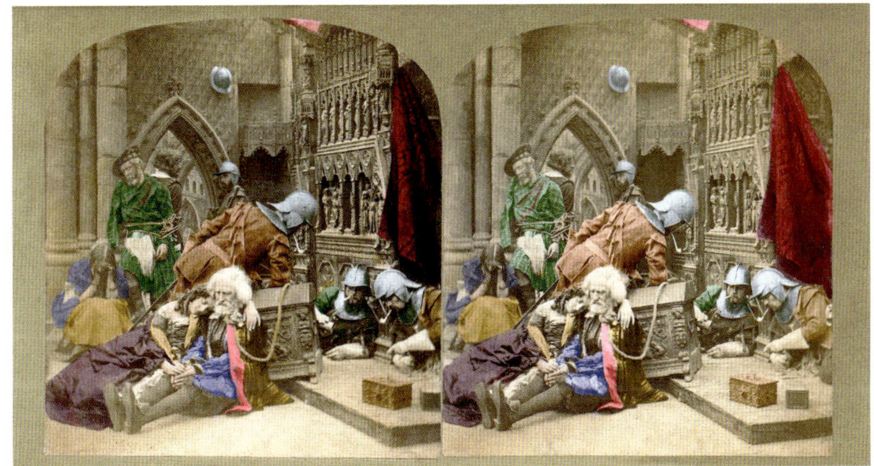

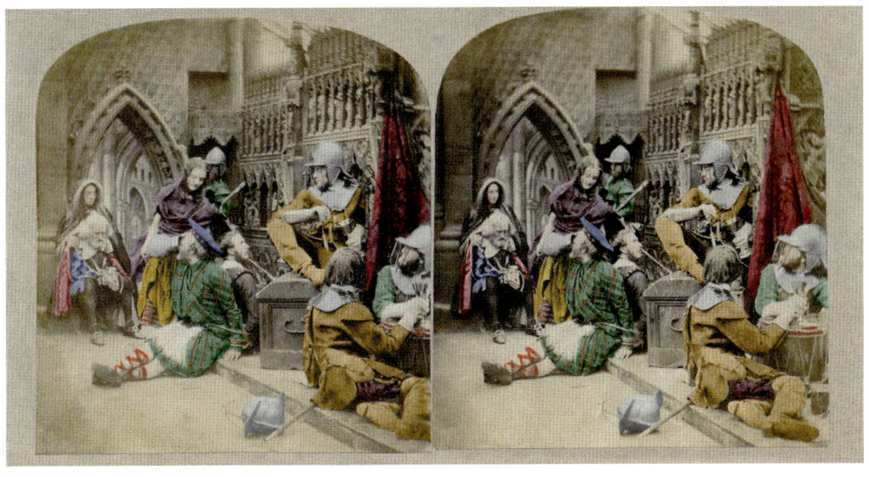

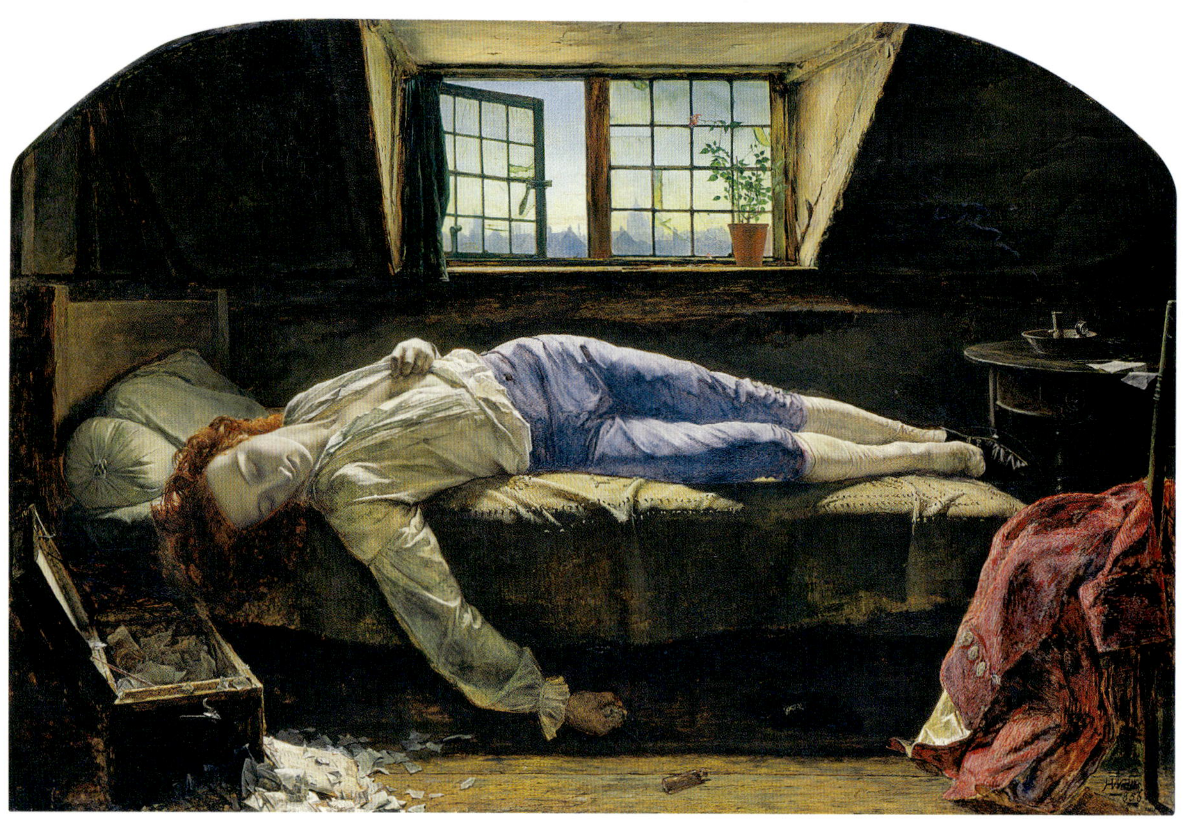

50 Henry Wallis
***Chatterton* 1856**
Oil paint on canvas 62.2 x 93.3
Tate. Bequeathed by Charles Gent Clement 1899

Henry Wallis's *Chatterton* represents the suicide of a poor eighteenth-century poet and was one of the most famous paintings of its time. Wallis set the death in a bare attic overlooking the City of London, which evoked the urban poverty of his own age. The figure was based on the likenesses of Pre-Raphaelite poets Algernon Swinburne and George Meredith. The picture toured the British Isles and hundreds of thousands flocked to pay a shilling to view it. James Robinson saw the painting in Dublin and conceived a stereographic series of Chatterton's life, beginning with *The Death of Chatterton* 1859. Legal procedures were brought against him to protect the income of the printmaker who had the lucrative copyright to publish engravings. The ensuing court battles were the first art copyright cases.

In the same year Oliver Wendell Holmes argued that stereography had its own artistic possibilities: 'The first effect of looking at a good photograph through the stereoscope is a surprise such as no painting ever produced,'

51 James Robinson
***The Death of Chatterton* 1859**
2 photographs, hand-tinted albumen prints on stereo card 8 x 18
Collection of Dr Brian May

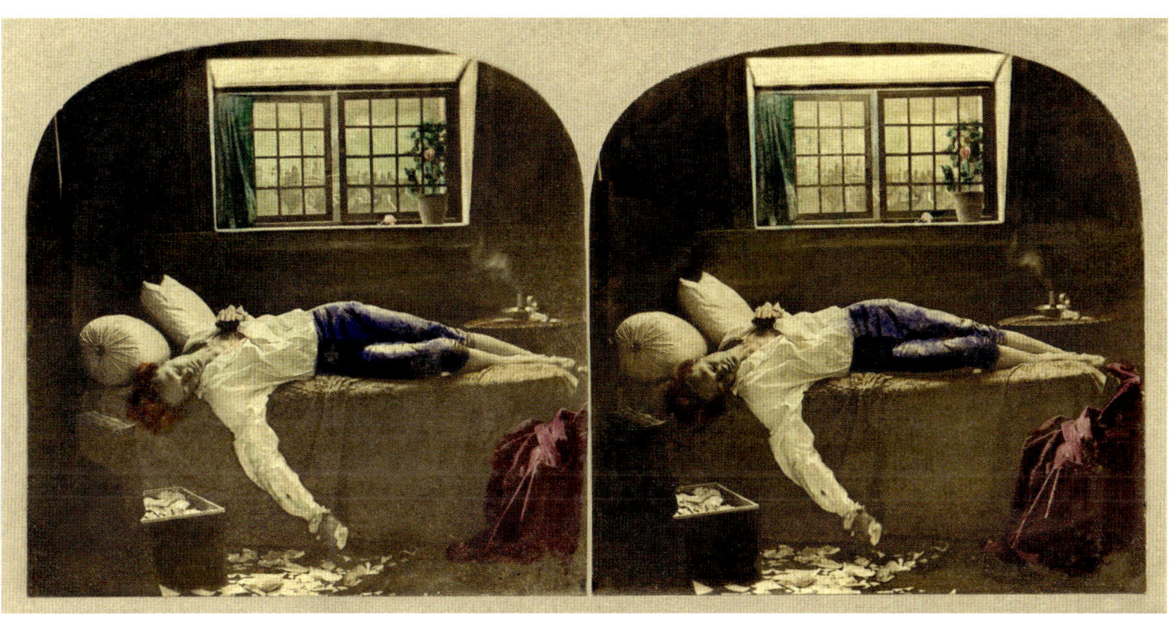

he declared. 'The mind feels its way into the very depths of the picture … The very things which an artist would leave out, or render imperfectly, the photograph takes infinite care with'; there will be 'incidental truths which interest us more than the central object of the picture'.[50] The individuality of the boy in eighteenth-century costume adds potency to his death. The haphazard creases of the bed sheet are more suggestive of restless movement, now stilled, than Wallis's elegant drapery. The backdrop was painted, but the chest, discarded coat and candle were real. The torn paper pieces, animated by their three-dimensionality, trace the poet's recent agitation, while the candle smoke, representing his extinguished life, is different in each photograph due to their being taken at separate moments. The tinting is crude in comparison with the painting but the stereoscope summons in three dimensions 'every stick, straw, scratch' in a manner that even Pre-Raphaelite-style painting could not.[51] CJ

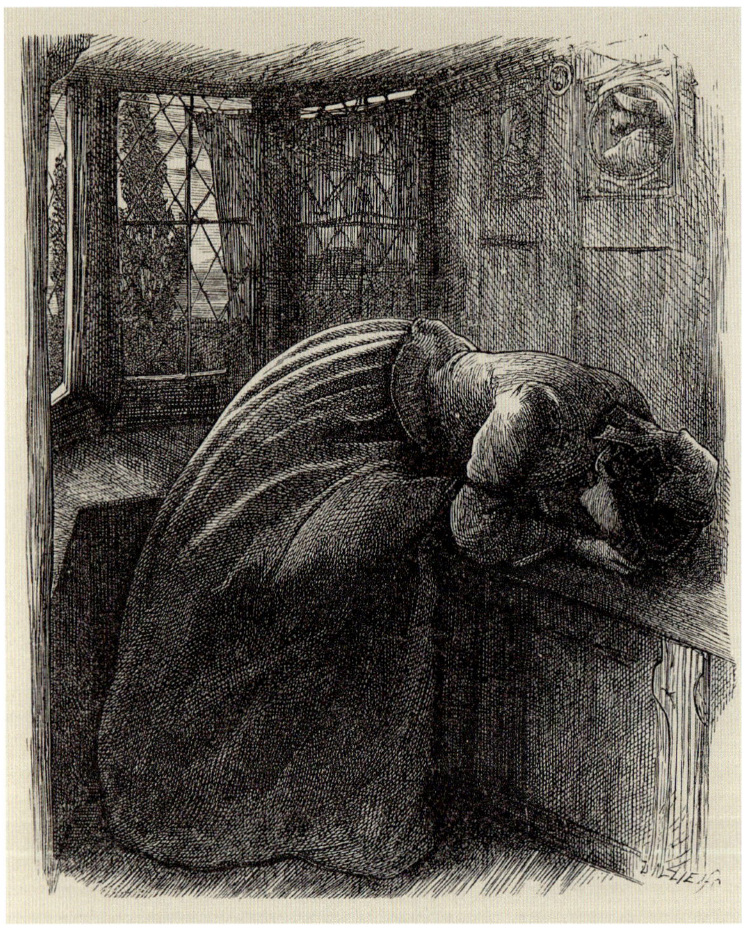

52 John Everett Millais
***Mariana,* illustration from *Poems* by Alfred, Lord Tennyson, published by Edward Moxon, London, 1857**
Wood engraving on paper by the Brothers Dalziel 9.4 x 7.9
Tate

The prolific photographer Clementina, Lady Hawarden won success after taking up the camera in 1857. She exhibited her work with the Photographic Society of London in 1863 and 1864 and was awarded the society's silver medal in both years, but died shortly afterwards at only forty-two. Hawarden called her poetic photographs of her daughters 'studies'. Some of these echo Pre-Raphaelite illustrations of Tennyson's *Poems*, reprinted in 1862, and reflect the affinities between photography and print illustration. She adapted the drama of light and dark and the compressed, shallow spaces that were fundamental to the woodblock medium. Tennyson's Mariana was a young woman abandoned by her betrothed, and such allusions provided literary content for Hawarden's images. CJ

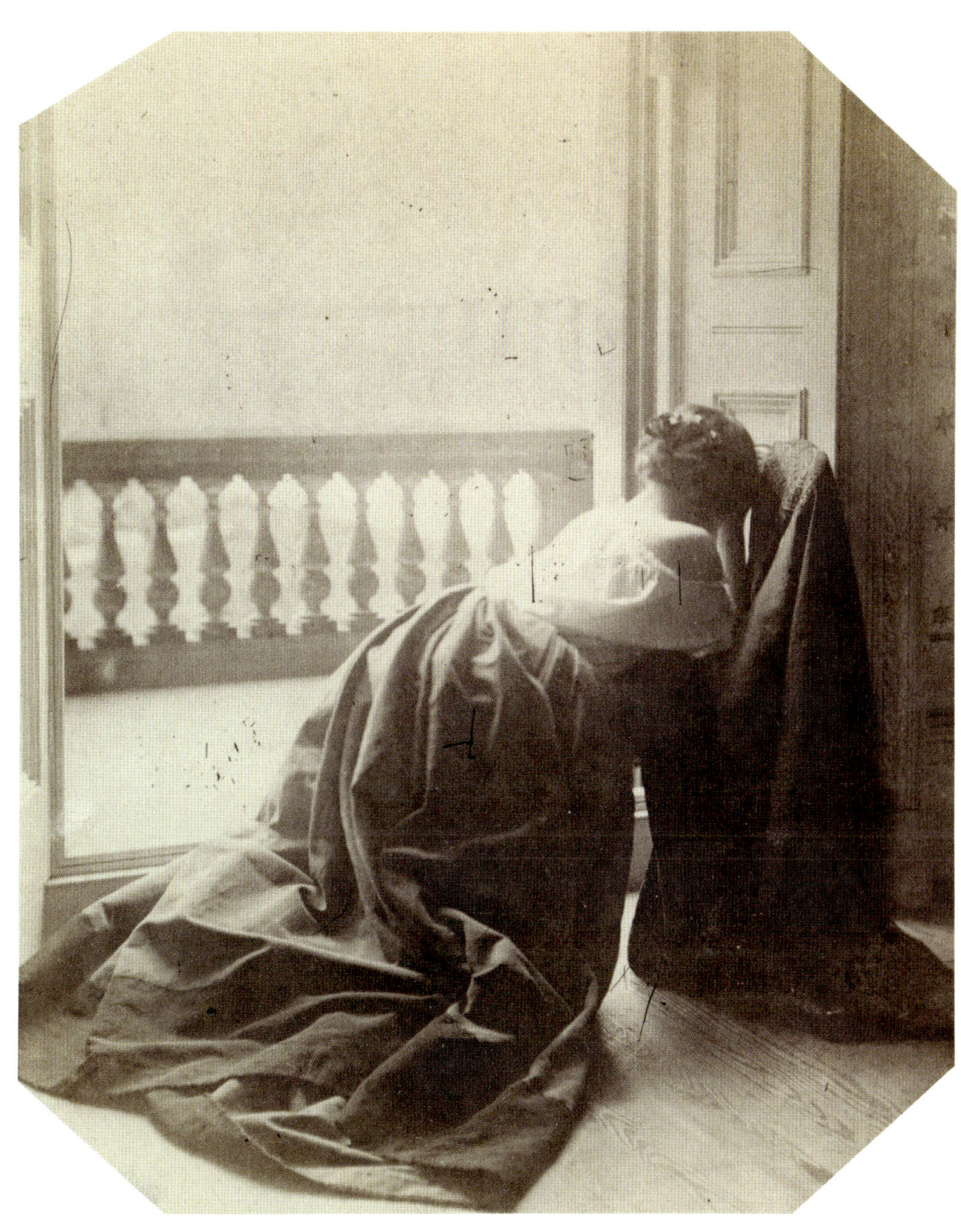

53 Clementina, Lady Hawarden
Clementina Maude, 5 Princes Gardens c.1862
Photograph, albumen print on paper 10.8 x 8.9
Victoria and Albert Museum
Given by Clementina, Lady Tottenham

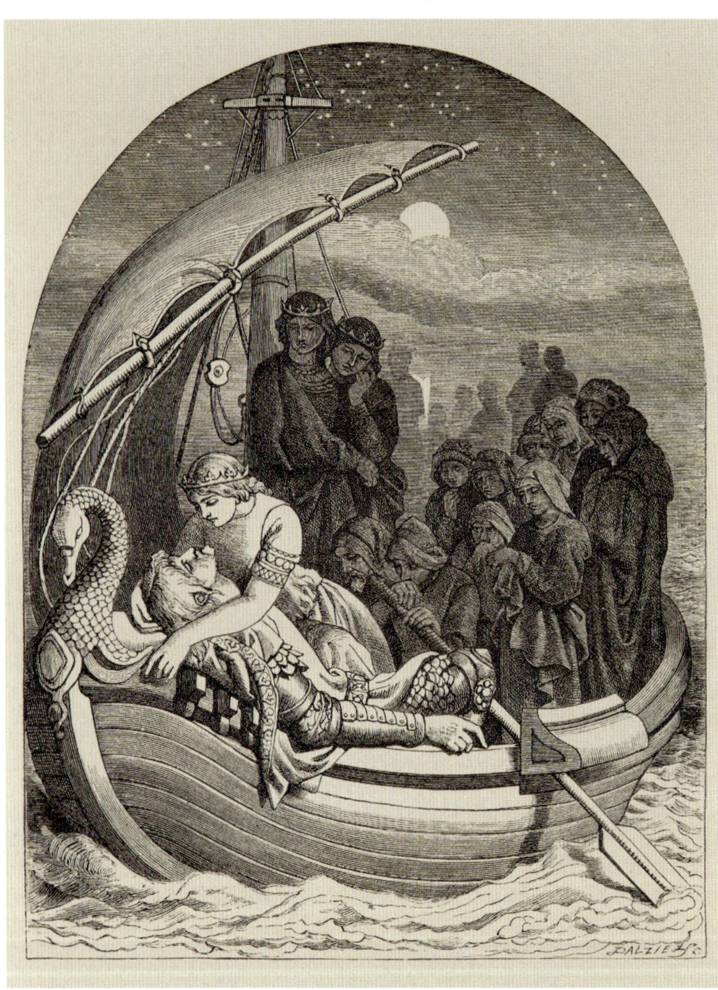

54 Daniel Maclise
***Morte d'Arthur,* illustration from *Poems* by Alfred, Lord Tennyson, published by Edward Moxon, London, 1857**
Wood engraving on paper by J Thompson 12 x 9.2
Tate

Cameron knew Maclise's work through his illustrations for her 1847 translation of the poetic ballad *Leonora* by Gottfried August Bürger. Cameron's description of her translation presages the ethos that would characterise her photographs more than twenty-five years later. In her Preface she argued that other versions – including that by Sir Walter Scott in 1796 – effaced Bürger beneath the translator's 'own genius'.[52] By contrast, her intention was to defer to the creator, and simply 'catch the likeness of a beautiful picture, and to copy faithfully each feature and expression of the original'.[53] This is reminiscent of her later insistence on inscribing her photographs 'From Life' to signal a faithful photographic representation without enlargement or retouching. Cameron wrote 'From Life' on the mount for *King Arthur*, yet diverged from that ideal and retouched the negative plate, adding a moon, partially camouflaging the ceiling beams and giving a smoke-like effect to the waves beneath the boat. HK

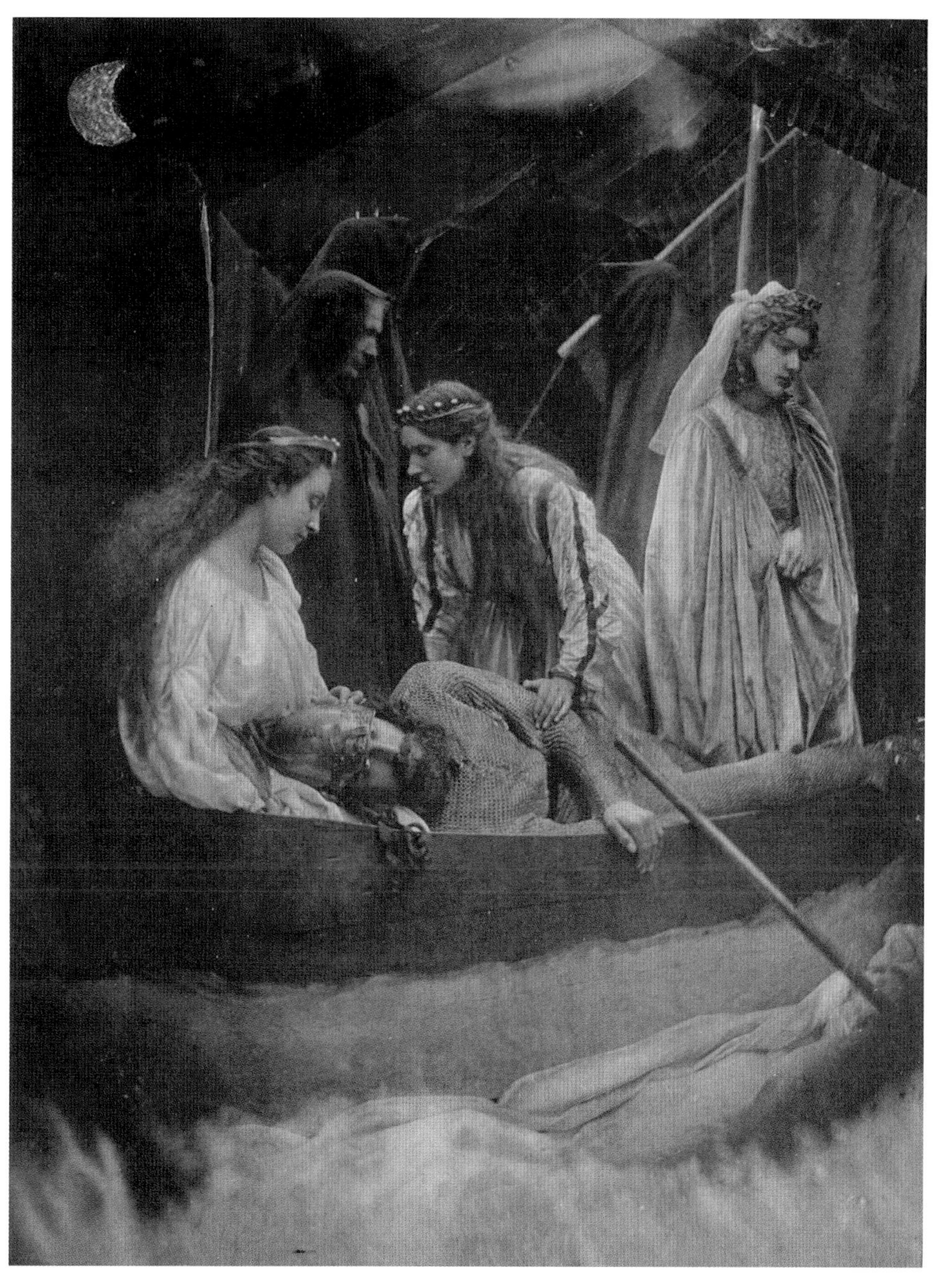

55 **Julia Margaret Cameron**
The Passing of Arthur (So like a Shatter'd Column Lay the King)
(Mary Hiller, William Warder, Mrs Hardinge, unknown woman, unknown hooded figures), illustration to Tennysons's *Idylls of the King and Other Poems* (May 1875), vol.2, pl.10
Photograph, carbon print on paper 35 x 27.5
The Royal Photographic Society Collection at the National Media Museum, Bradford

56 Henry Peach Robinson
***The Lady of Shalott* 1861**
Photograph, albumen print on paper from two negatives 30.7 x 51
Tunbridge Wells Museums and Art Gallery

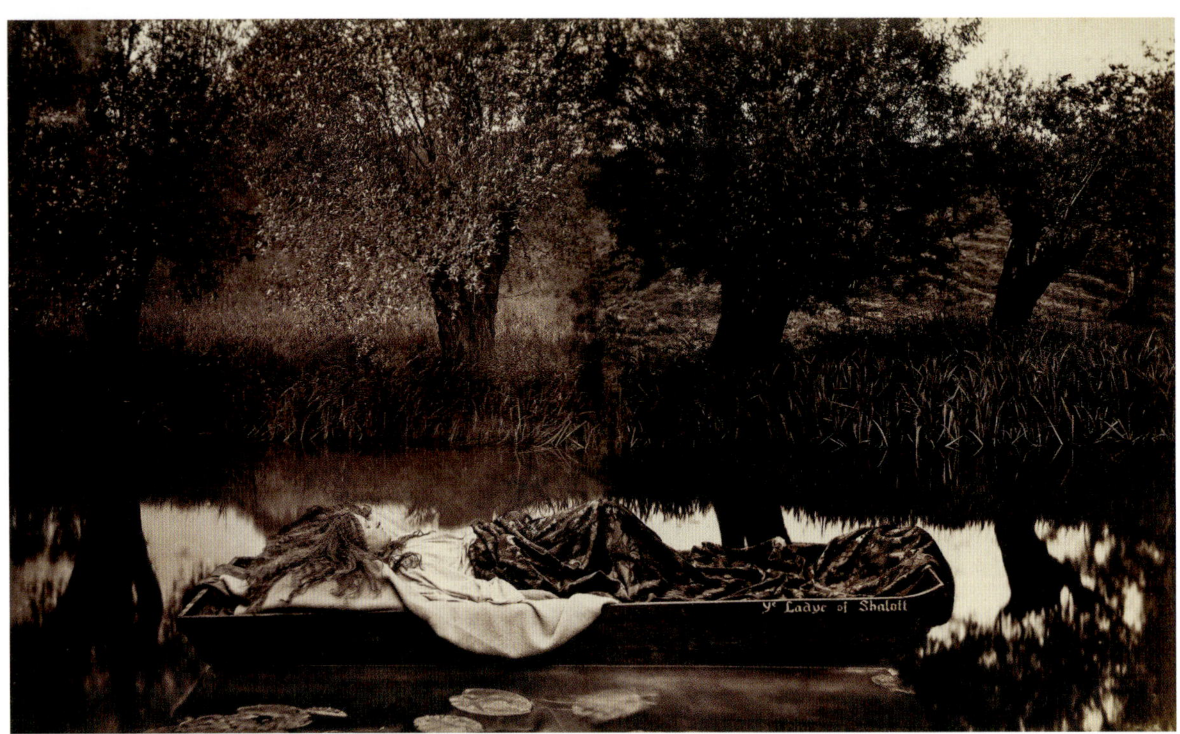

In 1862 Henry Peach Robinson exhibited *The Lady of Shalott*, a large photograph based on Alfred Tennyson's 1832 poem. The photograph was widely praised; the critic A.J. Wall described 'this beautiful picture' as having 'poetry and sentiment … in perfect accordance with those of the poem'.[54]

Robinson's choice of subject was astute. Tennyson's Arthurian tale of unrequited love and death was tremendously popular; in the 1850s alone, Rossetti, Holman Hunt, Millais and Burne-Jones all treated the subject, and Walter Crane made eighteen watercolour illustrations between 1858 and 1859. In the summer of 1862 Crane showed this oil at the Royal Academy, as Wall noted:

> *No. 359, a small oil painting … is either a very palpable copy from Mr. Robinson's* Lady of Shalott, *with a few alterations (which are not improvements), of the most trivial description, or a most unusually remarkable and astonishing coincidence of idea and execution. The painting is as inferior to the photograph in all the higher, as well as in all the less important, qualities of such a picture as it well could be.*

Wall described Robinson as a 'successful artist-photographer',[55] but his method of combination printing was often criticised. Robinson later agreed that such manipulations 'overstepped the limits by which the practice of our art ought to be bound'. But regarding *The Lady of Shalott*, he demurred: 'My excuse is that both the art and the artist were young.
And anyhow the picture had the desired effect and attracted still more attention to pictorial photography.'[56] HK

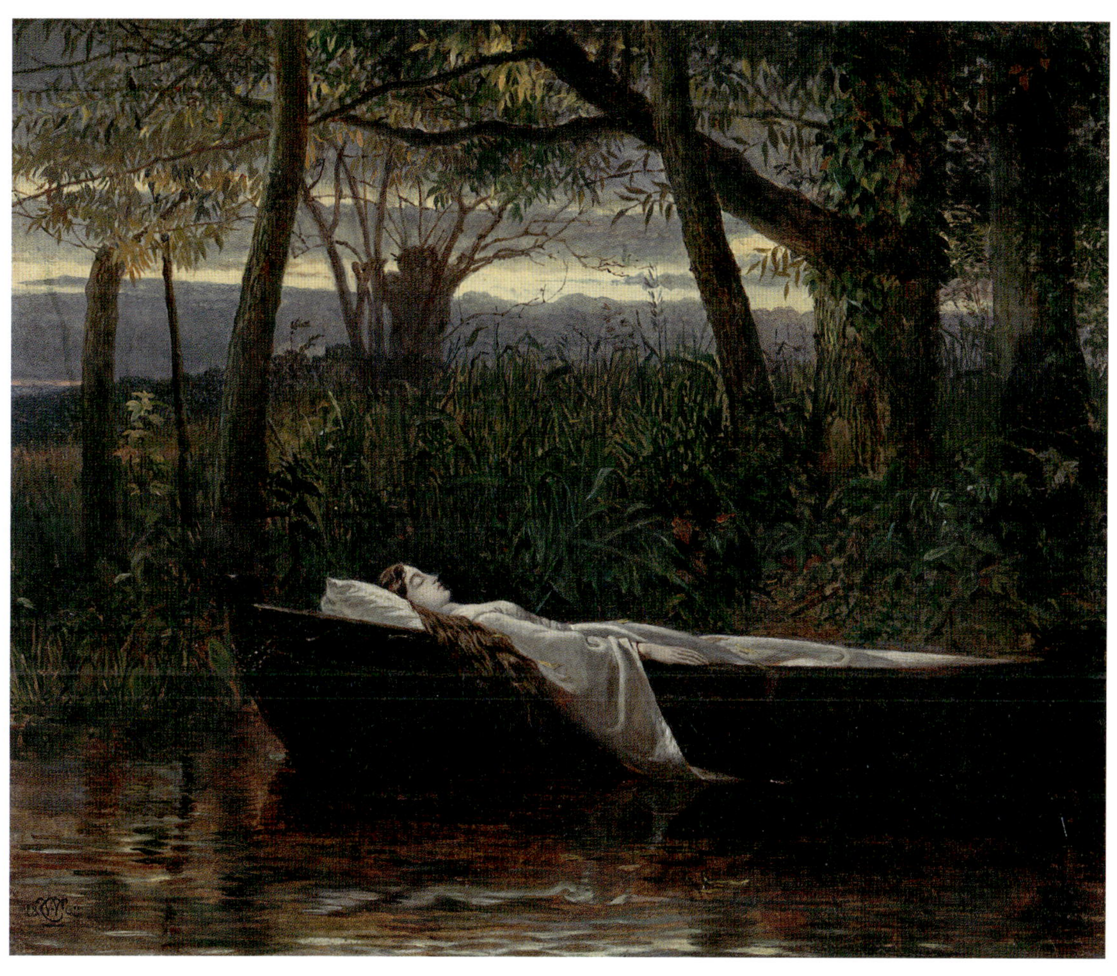

57 Walter Crane
***The Lady of Shalott* 1862**
Oil paint on canvas 24.1 x 29.2
Yale Center for British Art, Paul Mellon Fund

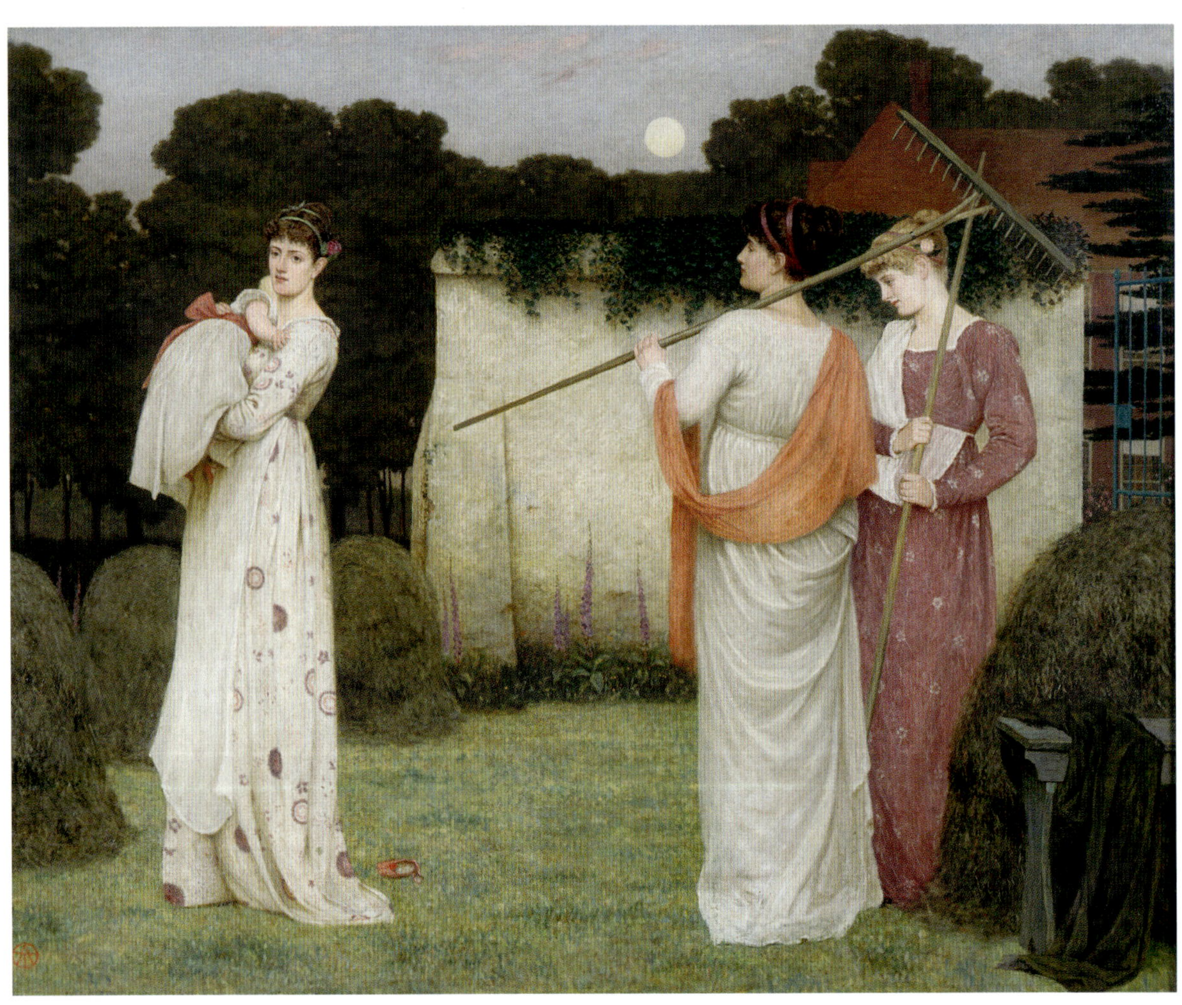

58 Thomas Armstrong
***The Hay Field* 1869**
Oil paint on canvas 113.7 x 157.2
Victoria and Albert Museum.
Bequeathed by Mrs Ellen Coltart, 1917

From the 1860s the aesthetic circle and the arts and crafts movement, led by William Morris, brought writers, artists and designers of all kinds together. The painter Thomas Armstrong was part of the milieu and became a leading educationalist. *The Hay Field* imagines an ideal pastoral scene synthesising classical and modern Pre-Raphaelite beauty. The ribbons and loose, flowing costumes worn by the four figures represent modern aesthetic dress, and the pinks and whites and natural motifs harmonise with the four foxgloves against the white wall behind.

Walter Crane was an aesthetic painter and designer and a close associate of Morris. He was in the forefront of dress reform movements and, with other artists, a member of the Healthy and Artistic Dress Union. The Union promoted 'greater beauty in ordinary life' and the idea that freedom of dress expressed personal freedom of other kinds, especially for women.[57] Aesthetic designs were circulated by Arthur Lasenby Liberty, a member of the Union, through his London shop. In May 1896 Liberty, Crane and others collaborated in arranging a series of 'Living Pictures' for a Liverpool event promoting aesthetic dress. The Union drew on the un-corseted, aesthetic dress and variations of classical, Renaissance and oriental styles represented in the paintings of the aesthetic movement. The tableaux were based on individual works and staged over three days. Most were photographed, possibly by Edgar Scamell, whose credit stamp appears on every photographic mount.

CJ & HK

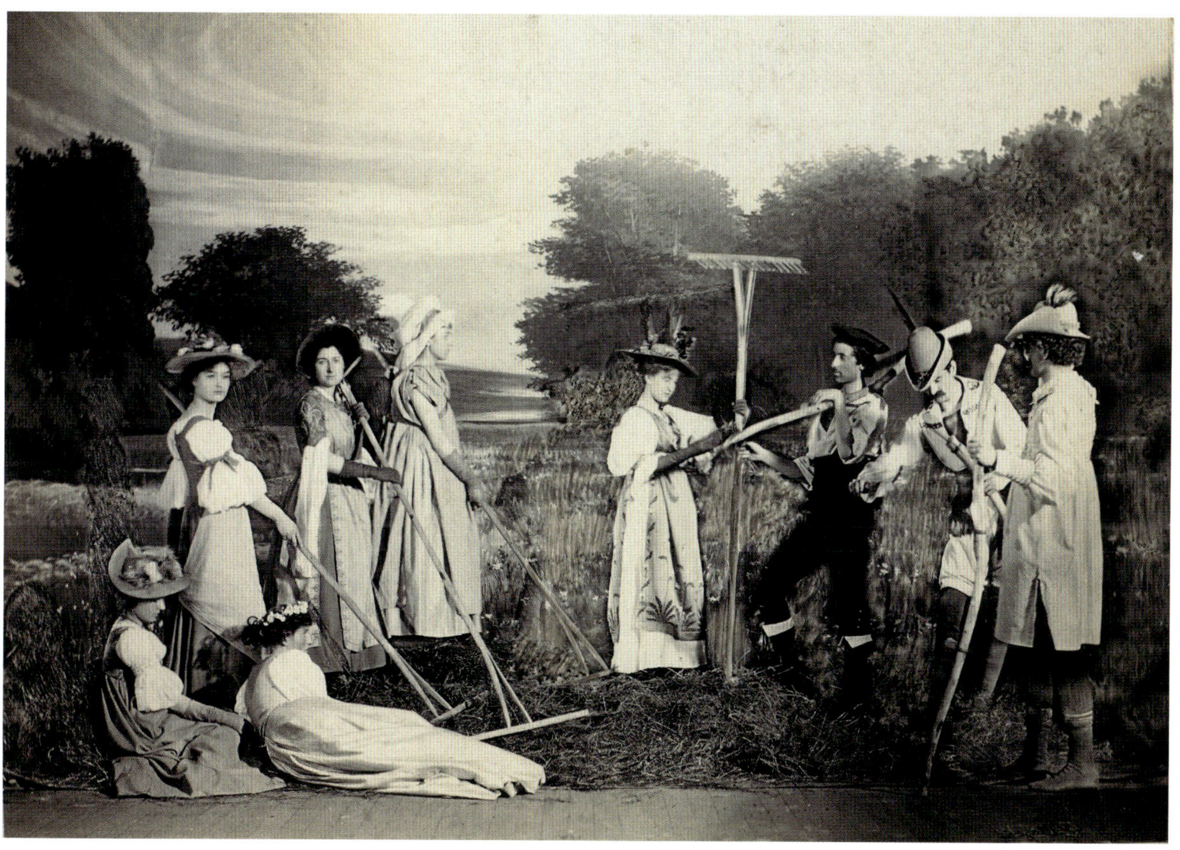

59 Photographer Unknown, arranged by Walter Crane
***Living Picture: Pastoral Scene* 1896**
Photograph, gelatin silver print on paper 19.4 x 28
The Whitworth, The University of Manchester

The photograph at right comes from an album of *tableaux vivants* made between 1890–93, when Prince Alfred, the Duke of Edinburgh, commanded the Royal Navy's base at Devonport. His older daughters, Victoria, Alexandra and Marie, enjoyed the social world of a service town, including Government House, the home of the general-in-command, Sir Richard Harrison. His three daughters were close friends with the princesses and feature in most of the tableaux. Another haunt was Mount Edgcumbe, whose grand orangery was probably the backdrop for the larger scenes; the young Earl of Mount Edgcumbe appears in 'The Sleeping Beauty'.

The album records nineteen performances, from Shakespeare plays to five tableaux that match paintings by Marcus Stone, a Royal Academician whose sentimental scenes were tremendously popular. They show the Victorian love of amateur theatricals and have the same generous field of view and depth of field as Gustav Mullins's photographs of tableaux performed by the royal family at Balmoral and Osborne between 1890 and 1893. Such scenes could also be captured by any professional photographer with a camera large enough to take group portraits, such as those for official occasions at the naval base.

These charming pantomimes mark a joyous interlude that ended in 1893, when the duke succeeded to the Duchy of Saxe-Coburg and the family left for Germany. Over the next three years each girl was married off to European aristocracy and three versions of unhappy matrimony very different to the romantic tableaux enacted at Devonport. HK

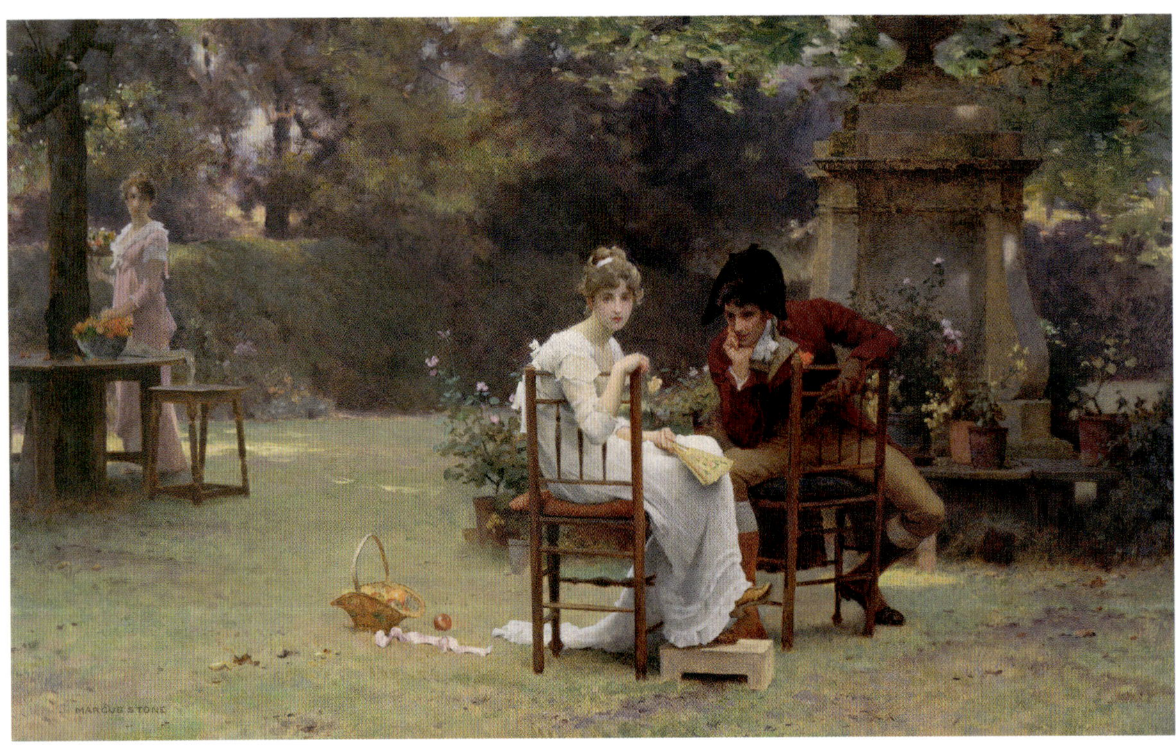

60 Marcus Stone
***Two's Company, Three's None* 1892**
Oil paint on panel 31.1 x 51.6
Manchester City Galleries

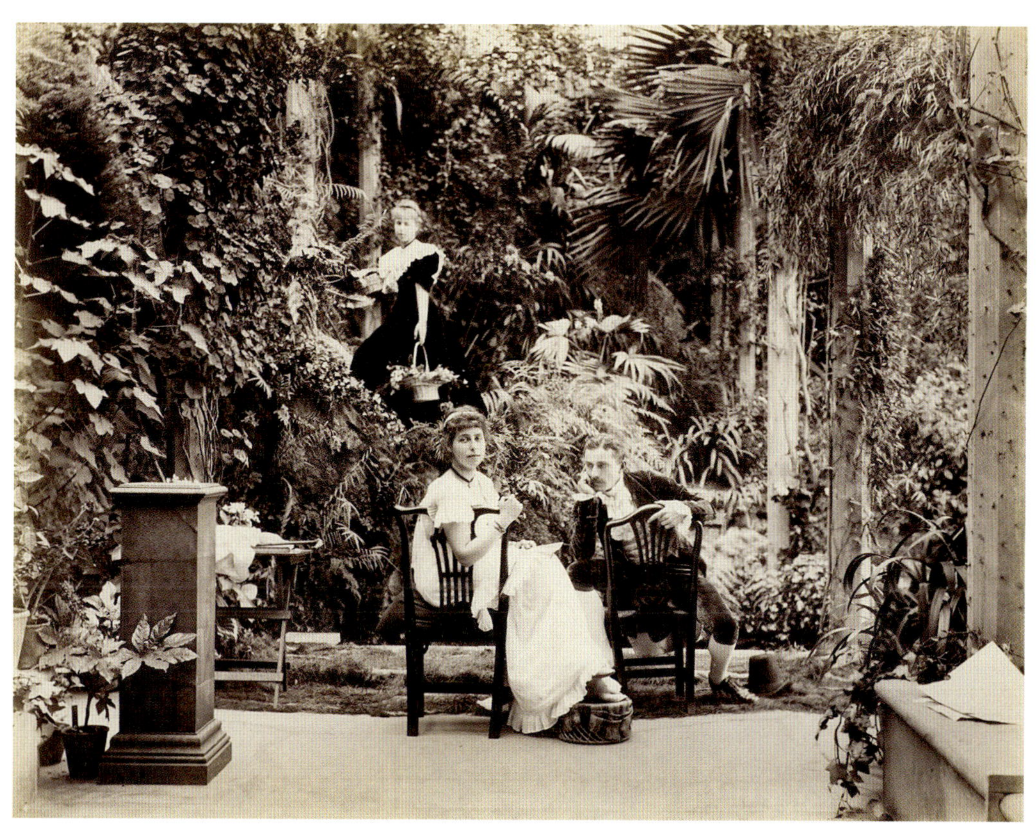

61 Photographer Unknown
H.R.H. Princess Alexandra,
H.R.H. Princess Victoria & Mr Savile
"Two's Company, Three's None" (Marcus Stone)
in 'Tableaux Vivants Devonport' *c.*1892-3
Photograph, albumen print on paper 27 x 34.5
Wilson Centre for Photography

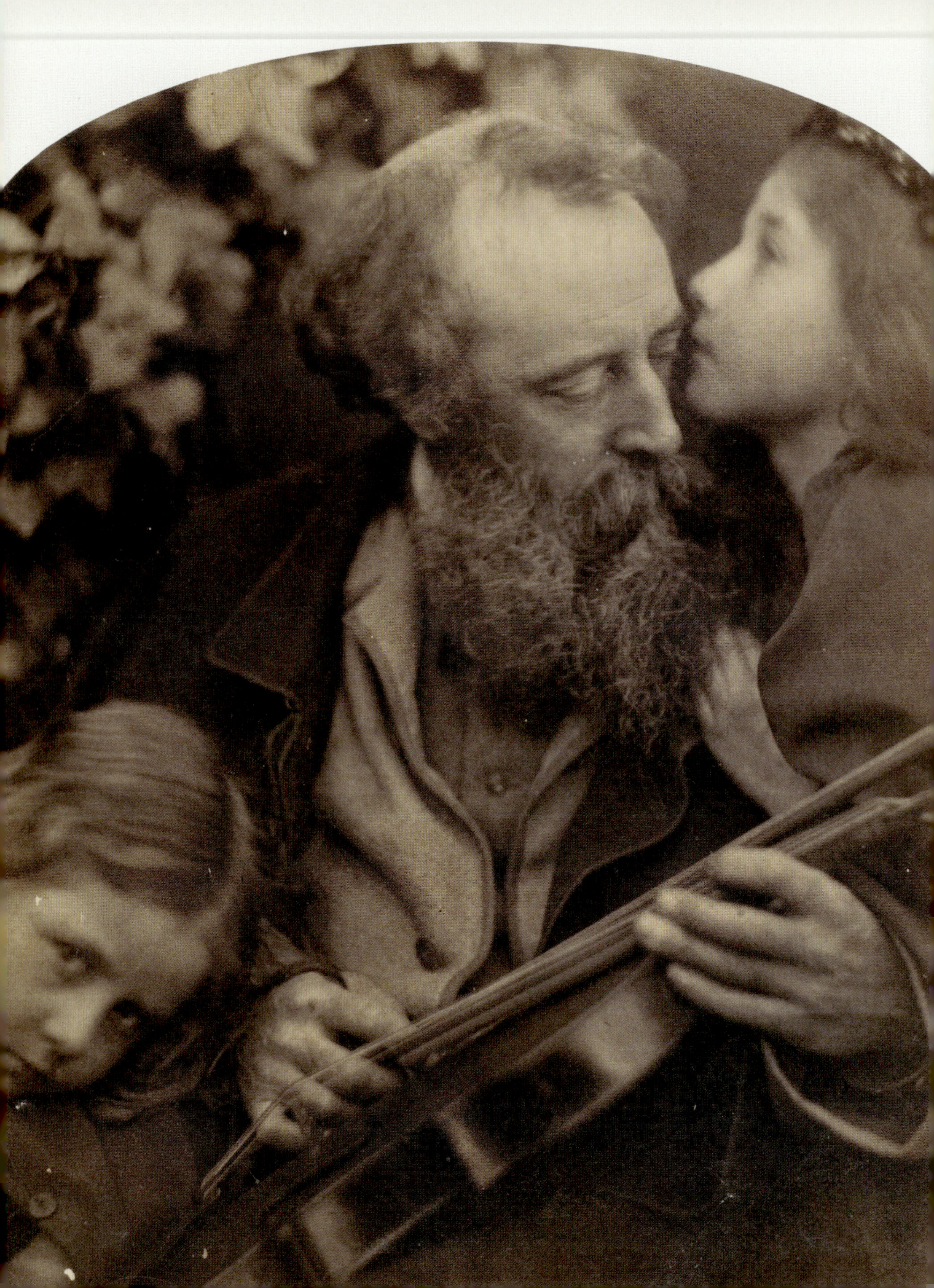

5 Whisper of the Muse

Carol Jacobi

From the 1840s a mix of artists and writers settled in Holland Park, west London and encouraged a coming together of the arts: music, literature, theatre and different pictorial practice. The Prinsep family, in particular, included the photographer Julia Margaret Cameron and entertained poets like Alfred Lord Tennyson, and painters such as George Frederic Watts and Dante Gabriel Rossetti. Cameron gave photographs to Watts and Rossetti and their reciprocal influence can be seen in several works. Watts and Cameron left a rich account of their close artistic collaboration and discussions in their correspondence.

The artists explored a new approach to art which became known as 'aestheticism'. One influence was the French critic Charles Baudelaire who argued that photographic exactitude left no room for imagination and that art should aim, instead, for 'intimacy, spirituality, colour, aspiration to the infinite'.[58] His ideas, aired during the 1860s in the writings of the poet Charles Algernon Swinburne, complimented the group's turn towards more mysterious imagery. Watts, Cameron and others rejected the sharp detail that had been the ambition of both earlier Pre-Raphaelitism and earlier photography in favour of sensual and elusive styles and subjects. In 1871 they were attacked as a 'fleshly school,' but they attracted followers and patrons and exhibited successfully at the new Grosvenor Gallery and other venues.[59]

Aesthetic artists chose subjects that dwelt on beauty, enchantment, love, loss and memory. From the late 1850s a newly intimate format, portraits made at close quarters in a shallow space, explored the emotions of sitters. The expressions, gestures and props that had communicated the dramas of earlier work were replaced by draped postures and dreamy expressions, representing psychological states. This intimacy was in keeping with the use of sitters who were of the circle; writers and fellow artists were shown as visionary figures, while young women and children became enquiries into beauty and spiritual states. These are combined in Cameron's *Whisper of the Muse* (left), taken at her Isle of Wight home in Freshwater and representing an allegory featuring Watts and two local children, Elizabeth and Kate Keown. The composition echoed paintings by Watts, such as *The First Whisper of Love* (1860–65, Walker Art Gallery, Liverpool).

Painters and photographers selected elements that appealed to the senses, attending to touch and the textures of cloth or loosened hair, for example, the sound of voices and music and the scent of flowers. The approach foregrounded formal effects and possibilities of art: colour and surface, composition and shape of the frame. Cameron achieved a photographic equivalent for Rossetti's colour and design with pattern and tone. She manipulated the light and focus of her photographs, and Watts and Rossetti employed chiaroscuro and broken brushstrokes to soften and blur their subjects. Where Rossetti enriched his hues to jewel-like intensity, Watts and Cameron discussed tonal drama and diffuse focus, which especially suited her monochrome photographic medium. Rossetti experimented with this more subtle approach in chalks which looked forward to softer, more monochrome oils such as *Proserpine* 1874 (no.114).

Julia Margaret Cameron
Whisper of the Muse
(portrait of G.F. Watts), 1865
Photograph, albumen print on paper
32.5 x 23.8
Wilson Centre for Photography

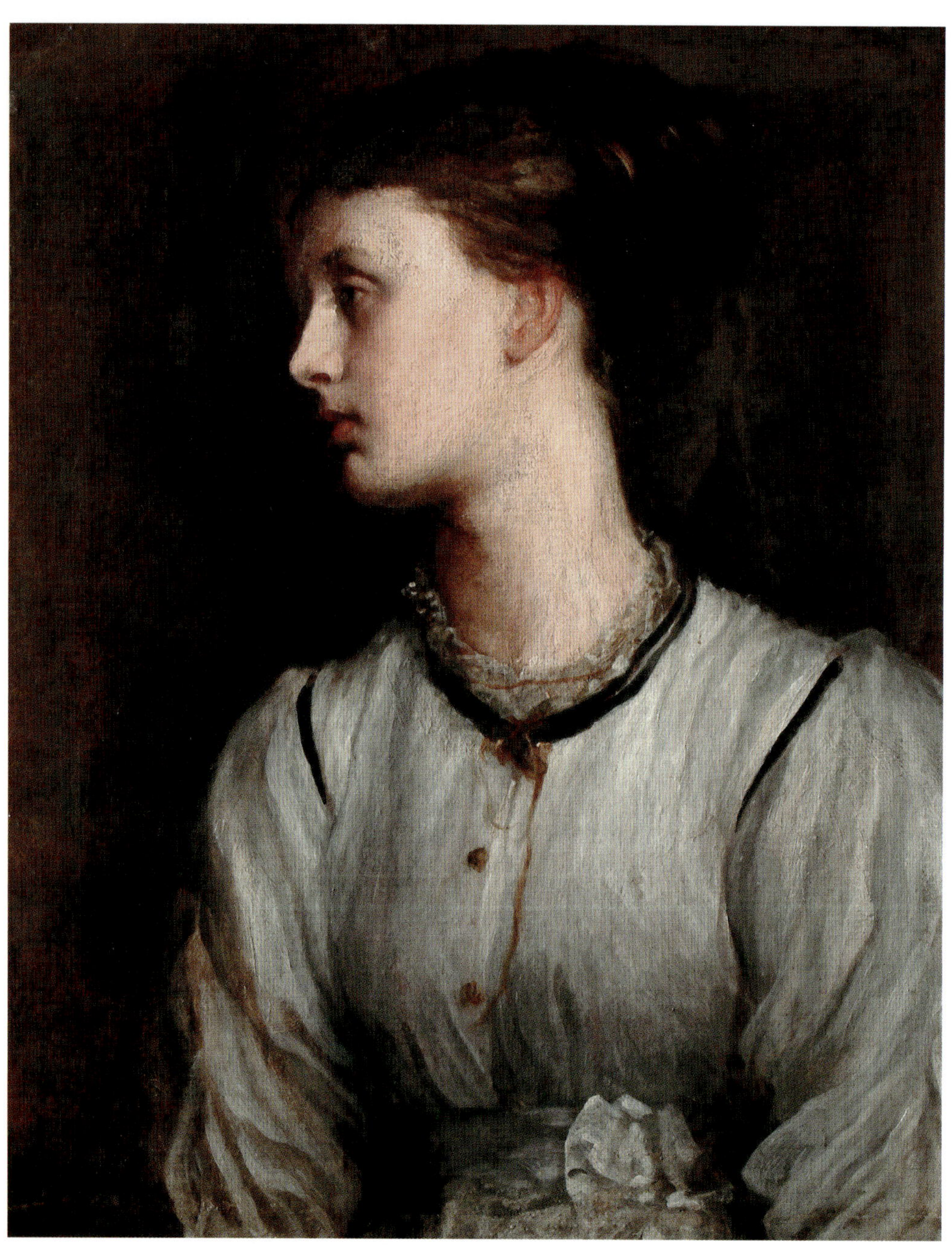

62 George Frederic Watts
***May Prinsep* c.1867–9**
Oil paint on canvas 66 x 53
Watts Gallery

These portraits of May Prinsep show an aesthetic sympathy between Watts and Cameron that played out across two media, many years and a vivid friendship of which Watts recalled: 'I had always to quarrel with Mrs. Cameron, that we might keep friends.'[60] They met at her sister Sara Prinsep's home, Little Holland House, where he had a studio from 1851. Once Cameron settled on the Isle of Wight in 1860, she and Watts saw each other during his frequent visits to their mutual friend and her Freshwater neighbour Alfred Tennyson.

Cameron's portrait of May was made at Freshwater in October 1870, one of sixteen studies in that month alone. There are four versions of this work; *Twilight* and an untitled variant feature a hanging lamp, its candle flame painted on the negative. Cameron inscribed this print *Study No.9*, similar to the simple title of Watts's own portrait of May. When in 1869 Watts showed the painting at the Royal Academy as *A Portrait*, he explained to a client: 'I rather dislike fanciful names for such occasions and would prefer calling it a study.'[61]

Cameron and Watts had access to wonderful sitters and made good use of them. As Coventry Patmore acknowledged in 1866, Cameron 'knows a beautiful head when she sees it – a very rare faculty; and her position in literary and aristocratic society gives her the pick of the most beautiful and intellectual heads in the world.'[62] HK

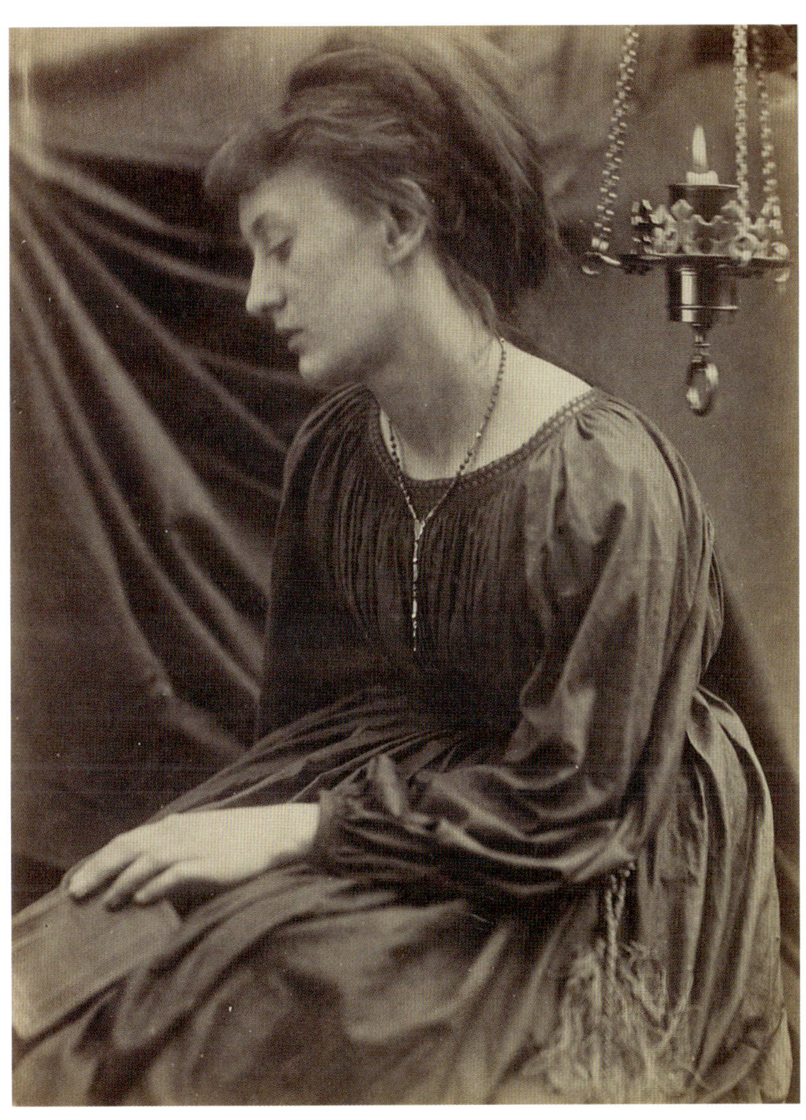

63 Julia Margaret Cameron
***May Prinsep, Study No.9* 1870**
Photograph, albumen print on paper 35.5 x 26.6
The Royal Photographic Society Collection
at the National Media Museum, Bradford

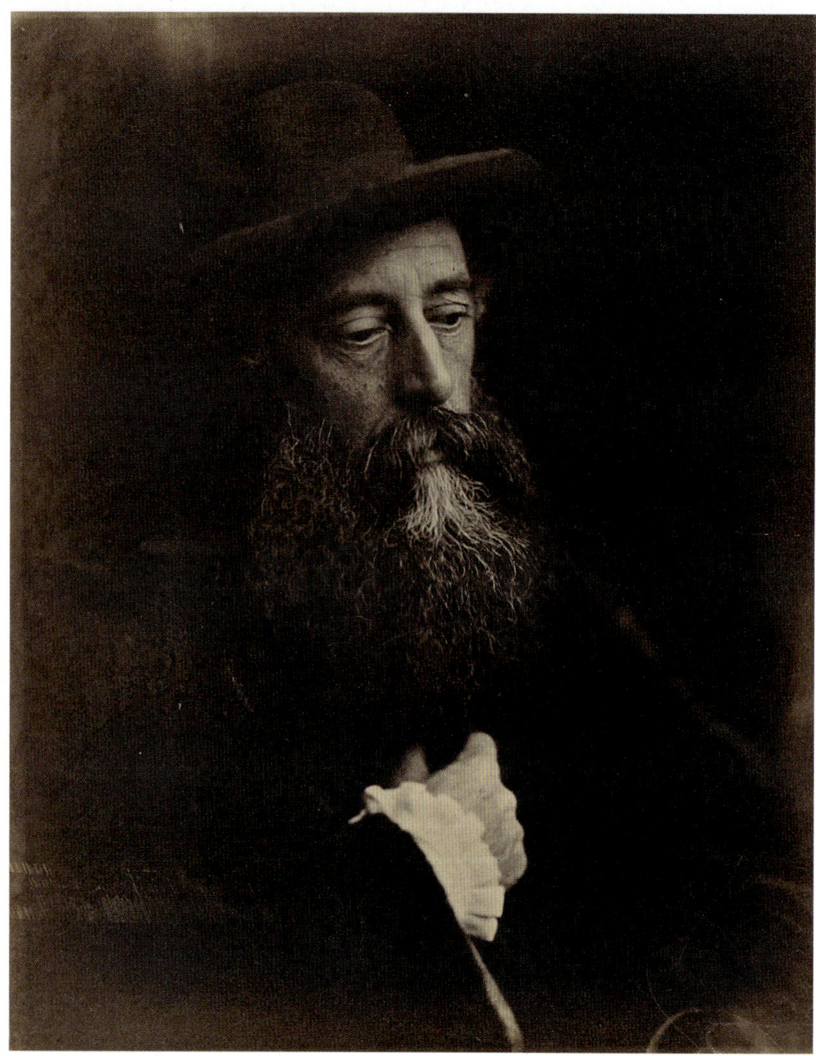

64 Julia Margaret Cameron
***G.F. Watts. R.A.* 1864**
Photograph, albumen print on paper 25 x 20
National Portrait Gallery, London

May Prinsep was not the only subject represented by both Watts and Cameron. There are visual similarities in their portrayals of a number of sitters, including Alfred Tennyson, Watts's bride Ellen Terry and May's uncle Thoby Prinsep. There is also a strong resemblance between Watts's self-portrait and Cameron's photograph of the artist made on the occasion of Watts's visit to Freshwater with Ellen Terry not long after their marriage in February 1864. The portrait was made out of doors; the right-hand edge shows a brick wall behind a dark draped backcloth, and exposure to the cold winter weather may explain Watts's hat and cloak. HK

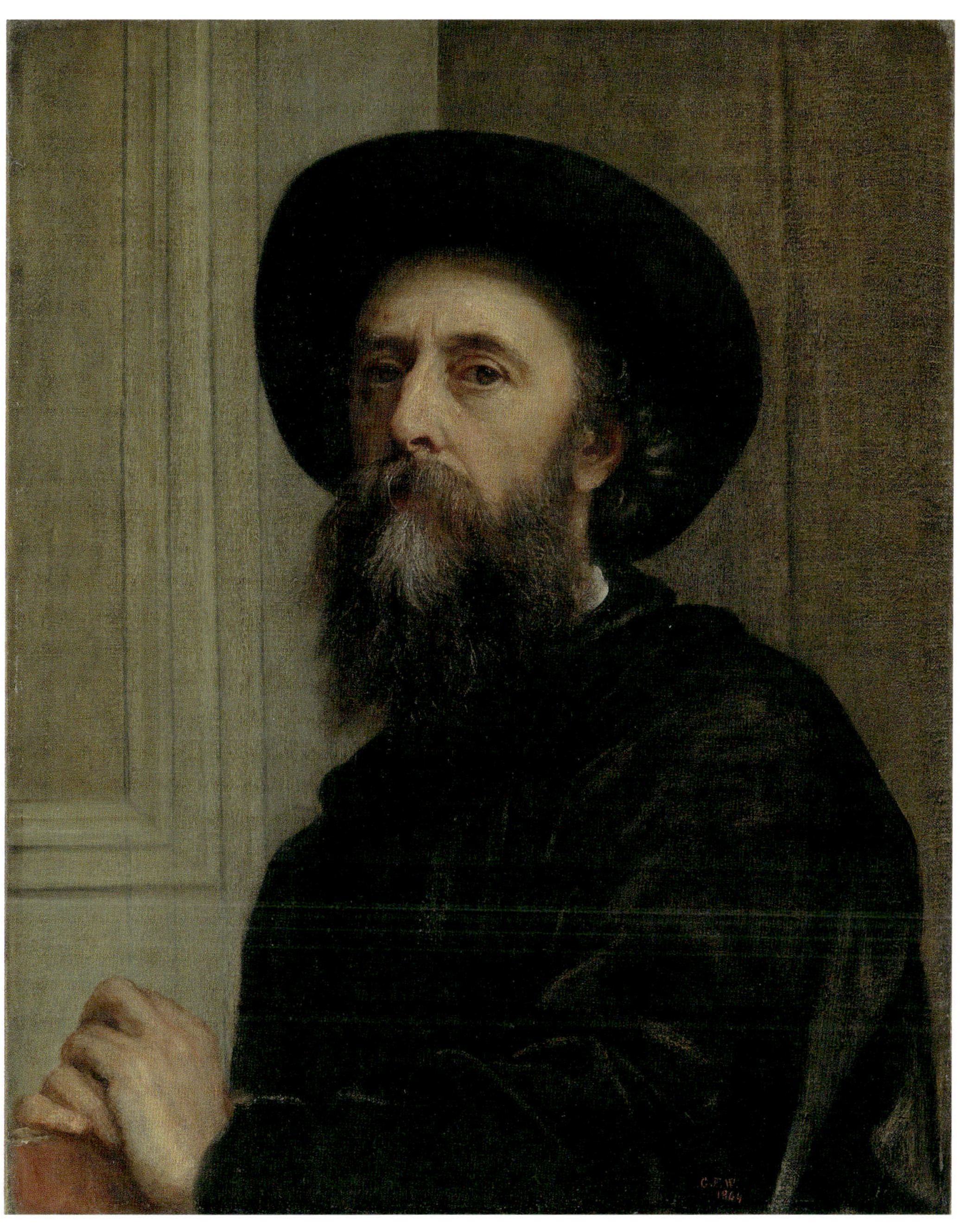

65 George Frederic Watts
***Self-Portrait* 1864**
Oil paint on canvas 64.8 x 52.1
Tate. Bequeathed by Sir William Bowman Bt 1898

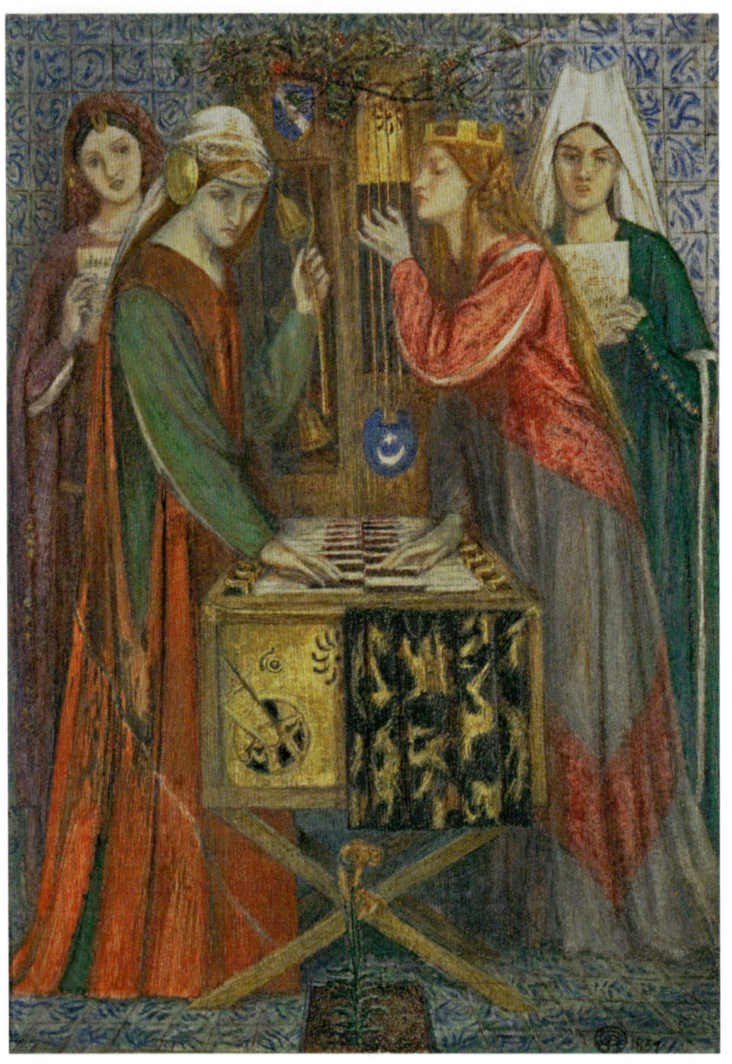

66 Dante Gabriel Rossetti
***The Blue Closet* 1857**
Watercolour on paper 35.4 x 26
Tate. Purchased with assistance from Sir Arthur Du Cros Bt and Sir Otto Beit KCMG through the Art Fund 1916

Rossetti described the subject of *The Blue Closet* as simply 'some people playing music'.[63] The focus on the abstract beauty of colour, arrangement and pattern, as well as music, looks forward to the aestheticism of the next decade. Its history exemplifies the convergence of the arts and the sharing of ideas between them. *The Blue Closet* was inspired by Tennyson's *Poems* and in turn gave rise to a poem by William Morris (1858):

Alice the Queen and Louise the Queen,
Two damozels wearing purple and green
Four lone ladies dwelling here
From day to day and year to year[64]

The watercolour was one of a series that Rossetti painted for Morris. The coloured tiles and fabrics are an early expression of that circle's interest in medieval arts and crafts, which Morris would realise in the form of his design company. The symmetrical composition evokes geometrical arrangements of angels in medieval paintings and presents a vertical pattern centred on the crossing of the instrument's legs. The likenesses are based on the artist and model Elizabeth Siddall.

Cameron's last and most important project was a photographically illustrated edition of Tennyson's *Idylls of the King and Other Poems*. This plate illustrates the following lines from *The Princess* (canto III 1847):

She stood
Among her maidens, higher by the head,
Her back against a pillar, her foot on one
Of those tame leopards.

The compressed vertical composition bears some resemblance to that of Rossetti's painting. Unusually, Cameron staged the photograph in a narrow windowed space rather than in her glass 'hen house' studio. Inspired incongruities abound: the 'maidens' are in fashionable aesthetic dress, while Princess Ida rests a retouched slipper on an ottoman covered with a leopard skin.

CJ & HK

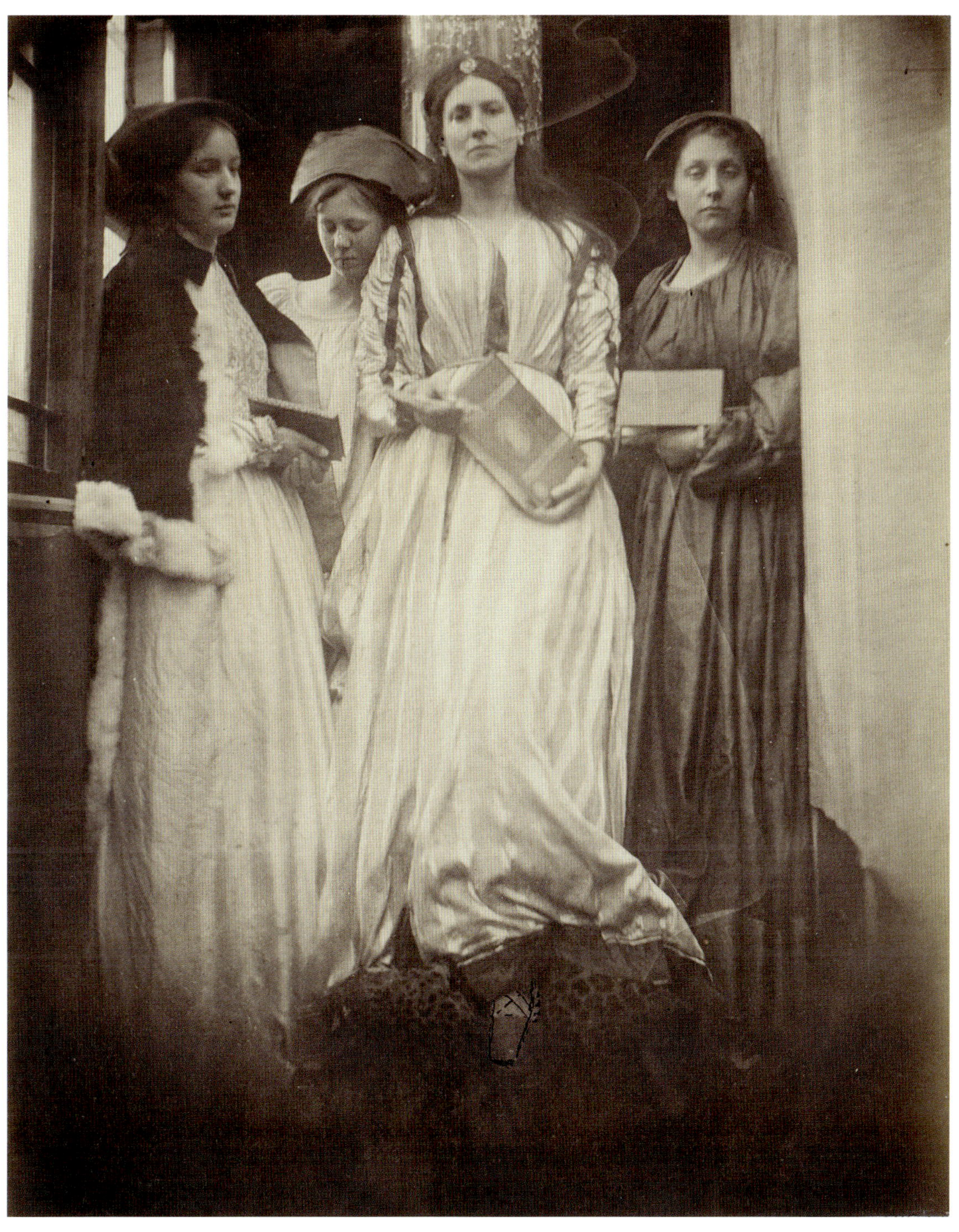

67 Julia Margaret Cameron
The Princess **(Miss Johnson, Miss Johnson, unknown woman, Mary Hillier), from *Idylls of the King and Other Poems*, vol.2, 1875**
Photograph, albumen print on paper 31.5 x 24.5
Wilson Centre for Photography

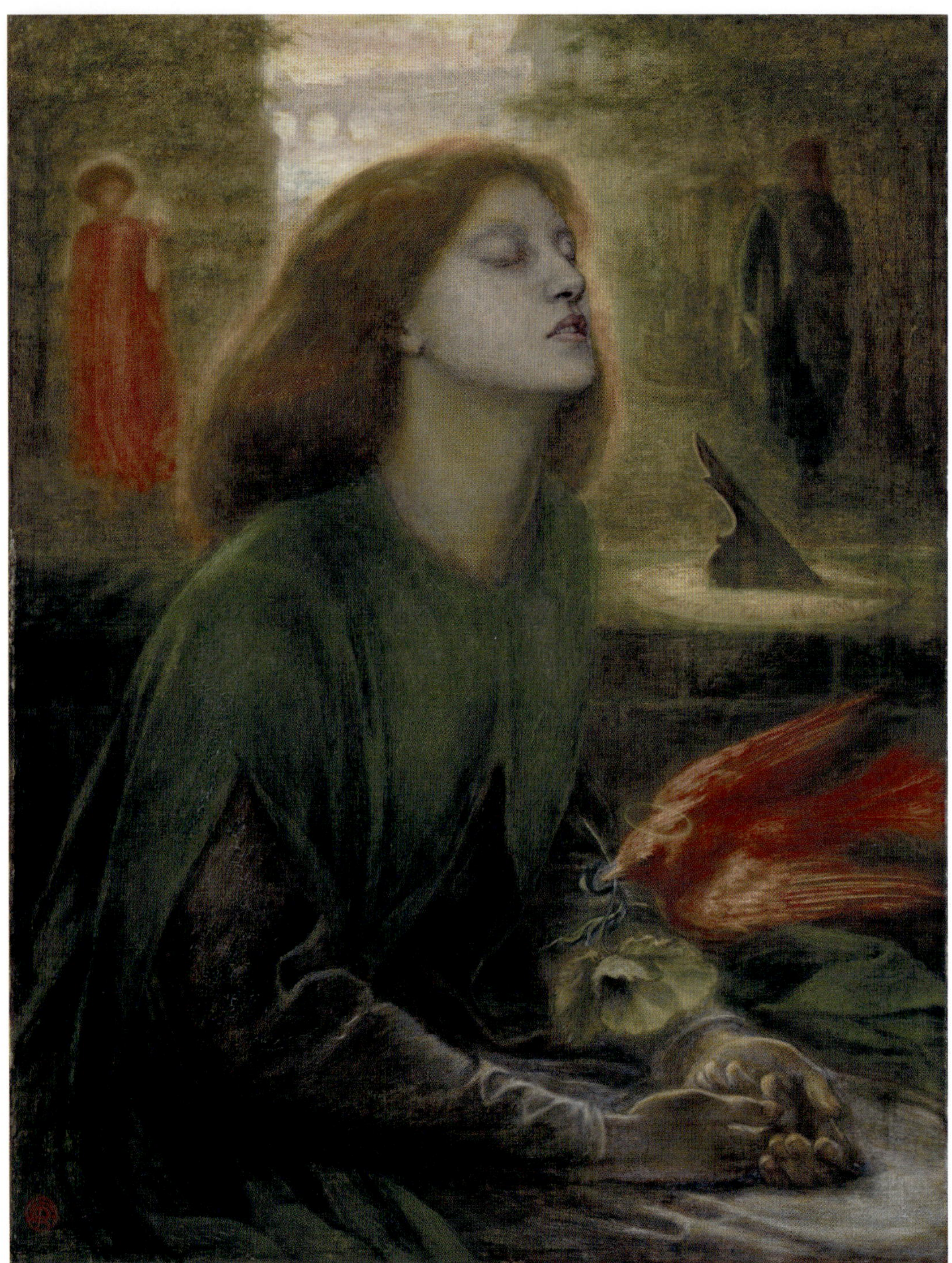

68 Dante Gabriel Rossetti
***Beata Beatrix* c.1864–70**
Oil paint on canvas 86.4 x 66
Tate. Presented by Georgiana, Baroness Mount-Temple in memory of her husband, Francis, Baron Mount-Temple 1889

Beata Beatrix was begun by Rossetti in the 1860s as a portrait of his wife, the artist Elizabeth Siddall, but set aside after her death in 1862. It haunted his studio, increasingly dusty, through the 1860s until it was rescued and re-lined by a friend. Cameron's 1867 photograph adapts a similar pose and theme. Mary Hiller is represented as Tennyson's heroine *Elaine* dying for longing for the knight Lancelot. It recalls Rossetti's painting as it appeared at that time, described by Swinburne as 'Her beautiful head lies back, sad and sweet, with fast-shut eyes in a death-like trance that is not death; over it the shadow of death seems to impend, making sombre the splendour of her ample hair and tender faultless features.'[65] Cameron's soft treatment may, in turn, have informed Rossetti's *sfumato* finish of the work, not completed until 1870.

Beata Beatrix was finished from memory. Rossetti was aware of Baudelaire's suggestion that art made from memory could be more potent than art made from life, and memory and memorial were central themes of his circle, explored in Tennyson's *In Memoriam*, for example. Memorial was an inherent characteristic of photography, which by its nature caught a moment in time that was almost instantly past. Memory was, moreover, understood as a response to associations or abstract characteristics, such as colour or sound, previously imprinted on the mind. CJ

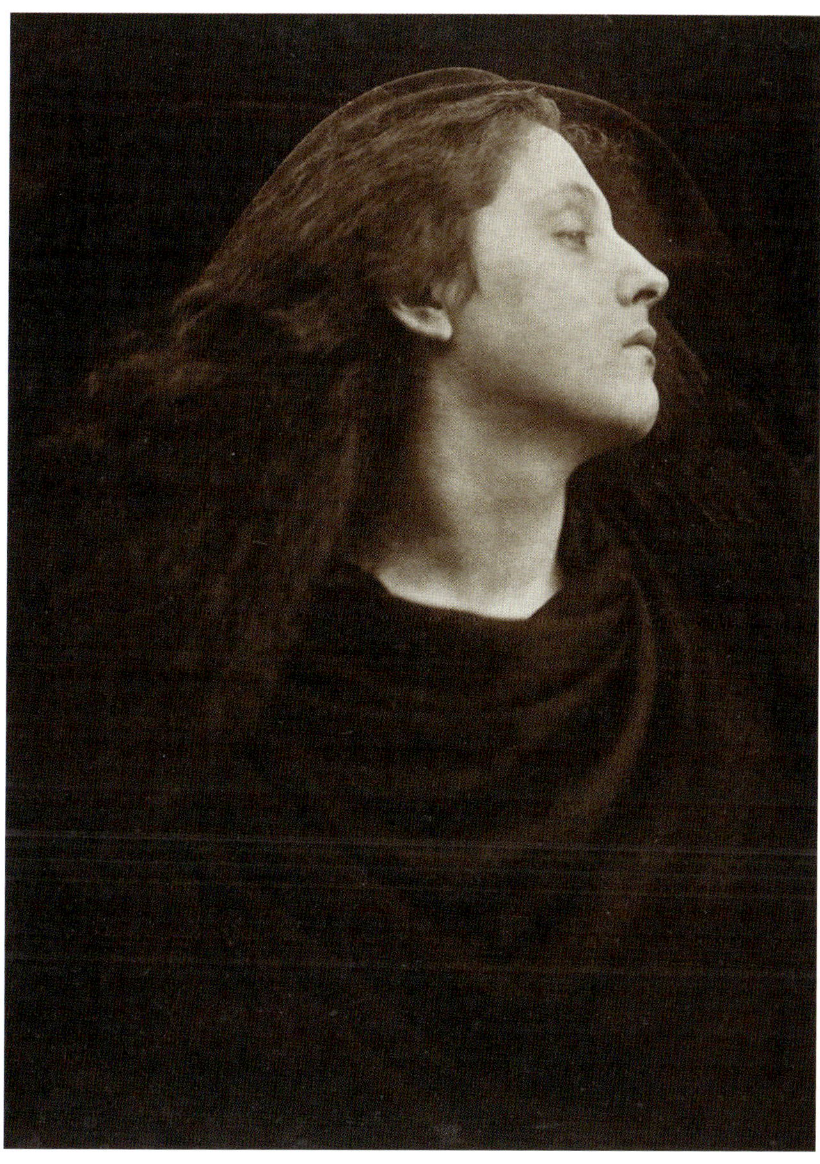

69 Julia Margaret Cameron
Call, I Follow, I Follow, Let Me Die
c.1867, printed c.1870–75
Photograph, carbon print on paper 37.2 x 26.6
The Royal Photographic Society Collection at the National Media Museum, Bradford

In 1865 Rossetti collaborated with the portrait painter, photographer and art dealer John Robert Parsons in creating eighteen full- and half-length photographs of Jane Morris posed in his house and garden. They were set against flat backgrounds to accentuate the effect of the folding drapery and set off the dark hair and profile. The focus emphasises Morris's large dreamy eyes, and her attitude recalls Watts's advice to Cameron that relaxed poses would create more beautiful impressions. The photographs were sources for both the compositions and the natural detail of a series of related paintings of Morris undertaken by Rossetti over the succeeding years, including *Mariana*. Their fidelity to Morris's distinctive physique advanced a new model of beauty; her full lips, sensuous fingers and strong, exposed brow, chin and neck suggest force and sensuality. Despite its title, *Mariana* dispenses with the narrative devices of earlier versions of the poem by Millais but retains the searing blue with which Millais animated his earlier oil version (1851; Tate). CJ

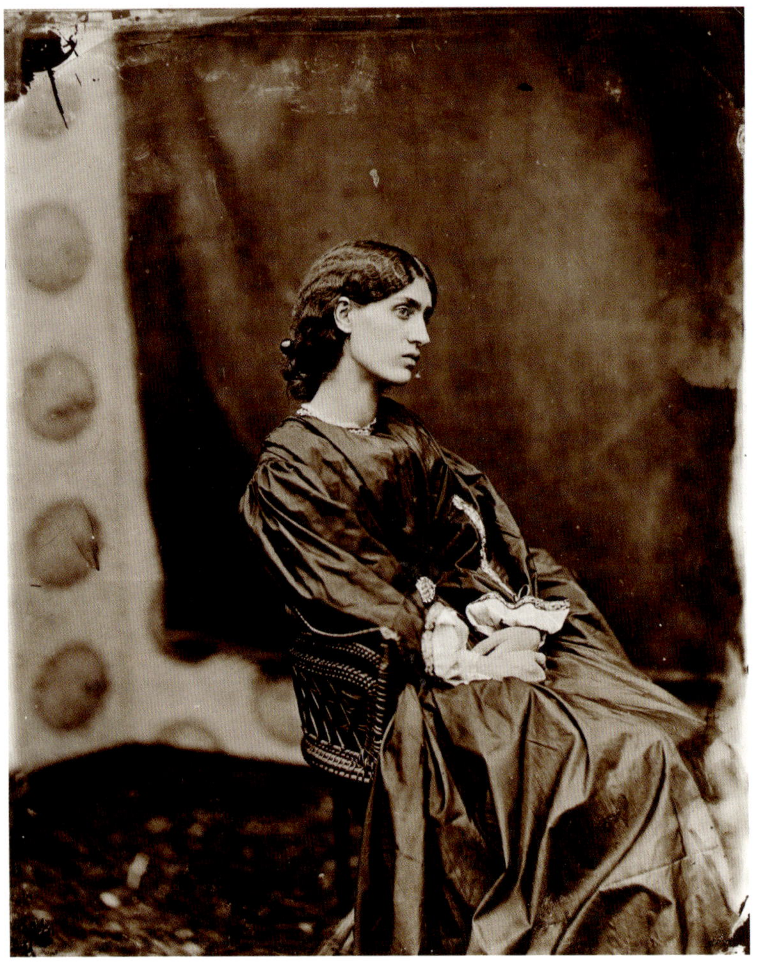

70 John Robert Parsons
***Jane Morris* 1865**
Photograph, albumen print on paper 39 x 33
Victoria and Albert Museum

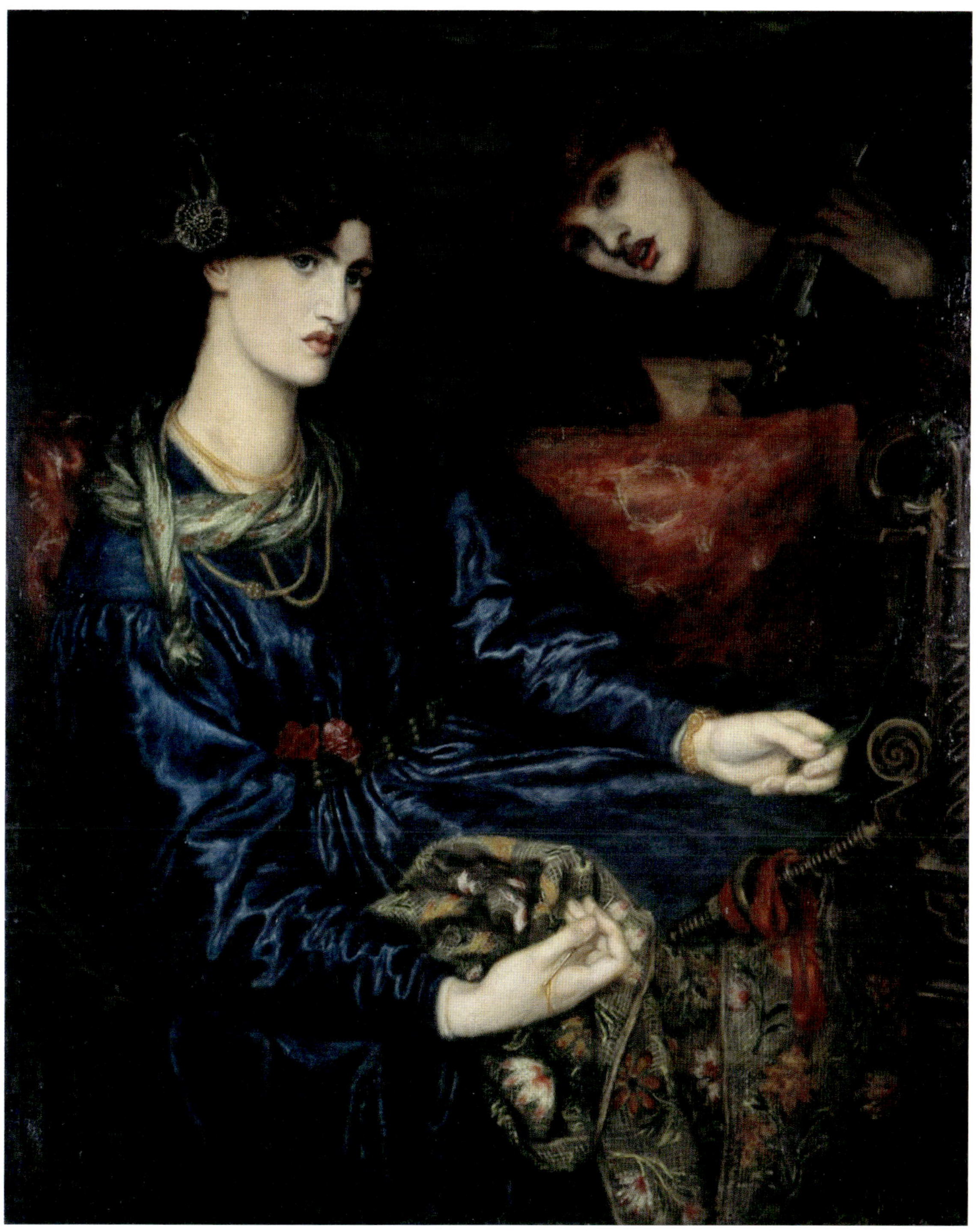

71 Dante Gabriel Rossetti
***Mariana* 1870**
Oil paint on canvas 109.8 x 90.5
Aberdeen Art Gallery & Museums Collections

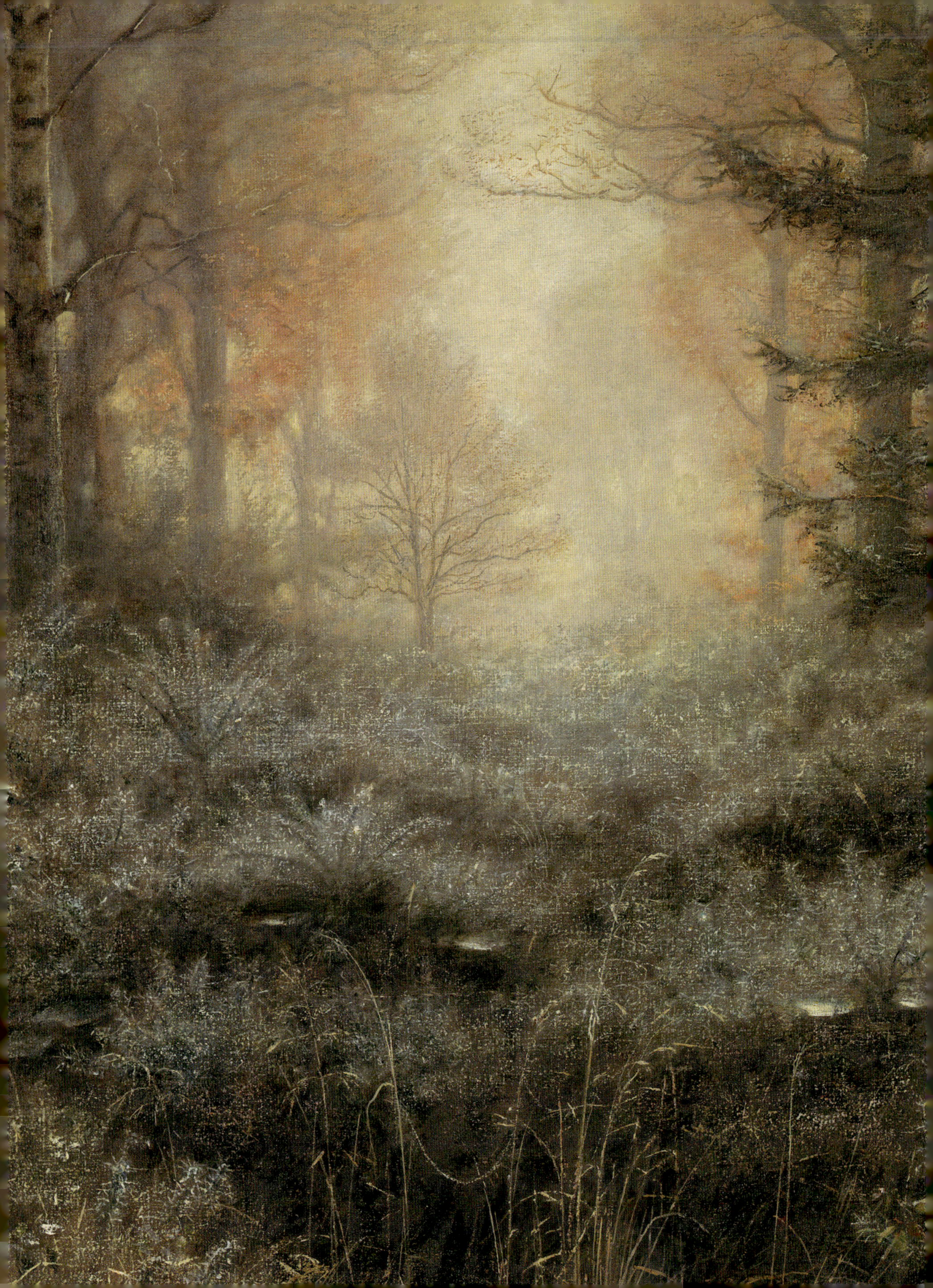

6 Life and Landscape

Carol Jacobi

In the later years of the nineteenth century, landscape came to the fore in modern art. From the end of the 1860s, poor and everyday characters and scenes, urban and rural, provided clear common ground, practice and critical language for painters and photographers. Both challenged the Academy hierarchy that marginalised landscape and genre scenes and sought a new dignity for naturalism. At the same time, and outside the Academy, the circle of the Pre-Raphaelites and James McNeill Whistler developed associative and aesthetic approaches to evolve the symbolist landscape.

French realism and impressionism were introduced to Britain by artists who had studied in Paris – Whistler, John Singer Sargent and younger painters like George Clausen and Henry La Thangue. The new Slade School of Art, founded in 1871, and exhibition venues such as the New English Art Club (NEAC), offering an independent forum in the spirit of the Grosvenor Gallery, provided an alternative to the Royal Academy exhibition and Schools, and photography flourished through new artistic groups such as the Brotherhood of the Linked Ring.

In the 1880s improved photomechanical processes abetted the spread of publications illustrated by engravings and photogravures, which were vehicles for artists and photographers. Studies of Romantic landscape painting of the past, notably Constable and Turner, were facilitated by printed and photographic reproductions. In turn, painters such as Whistler and Sargent found photographs useful in developing the naturalism of their works. New ready-to-use plates and cameras encouraged more artists to take their own photographs: Clausen began in 1883 and Sargent in 1890. Photographers like Peter Henry Emerson engaged with Clausen, La Thangue, Thomas Goodall and Whistler, seeking beauty in authentic records of rural countryside and industrial London. Painters and photographers tried out selective focus thought to be closer to the way the eye sees. Dynamic effects were investigated in the use of blur and bravura brushing.

Whistler inspired photographers to explore the poetry of atmospheric, indistinct views. In 1885 Ernest Chesneau noted that NEAC artists were dispensing with the figure, their aim directed at 'arousing our emotions only by the sentiment which natural scenery awakens in us' through the representation of nature as 'a magical spectacle, exhibiting ... splendid effects of light, colour, and form'.[66] Photographers, too, explored unpeopled landscapes to try, as Frederick Evans advised, 'for a record of an emotion rather than a piece of topography'.[67] Such exchanges underpinned the distinctively aestheticist approach of British painters and photographers to 'naturalism', and a sophisticated attention to composition, tonal values and atmosphere.

By the turn of the century, impressionist and symbolist landscape styles were admired, and 'pictorialist' photographers exhibited at the Linked Ring salons. In 1904 Clausen returned to the Royal Academy and became Professor of Painting, to a younger generation in the Academy Schools. His second lecture considered photography:

> *Until the invention of photography, there was only one way of seeing things – through the human eye ... Yet the painter, for a time, tried to rival the camera in minuteness and detachment, forgetting that it is just this human quality of attention and selection that makes a painting a work of art ... and we find photographers occupied today in arranging the tones and concentrating the lights of their pictures.*[68]

John Everett Millais
Dew-Drenched Furze **1889–90**
(detail, no.97)

In 1887 Thomas Goodall presented two similar pictures in two very different media. *Setting the Bow-Net* was the second numbered plate in *Life and Landscape on the Norfolk Broads*, a book of platinotype photographs made in collaboration with the photographer P.H. Emerson. In the same year Goodall showed his painting, *The Bow Net*, at the New English Art Club. *Setting the Bow-Net* was one of several photographic studies Goodall used for the painting, in which he posed his fiancée, Nancy, with her father, pretending to catch small fish in a funnelled net baited with water lilies.

The painter and his subjects were local people: Nancy was from a Broadlands family and Thomas's father owned a house at Oulton Broad. They married in 1886, and Goodall's *Bow Net* may have been a tribute to his new wife. Goodall's artistic connections are also very much to the fore; the bright, strong palette of the painting echoes the work of his close friend, the NEAC artist Henry La Thangue. La Thangue and Goodall himself appear in several *Life and Landscape* photographs.

Goodall kept his copy of *Life and Landscape* on the houseboat that was his painting studio throughout his life. The album is rather battered, with frayed binding and edges. Several pages bear splashes of paint whose pigments can be matched to other Goodall paintings. Their subjects derive from those long-ago photographs, showing how deeply those works were embedded in Goodall's practice. HK

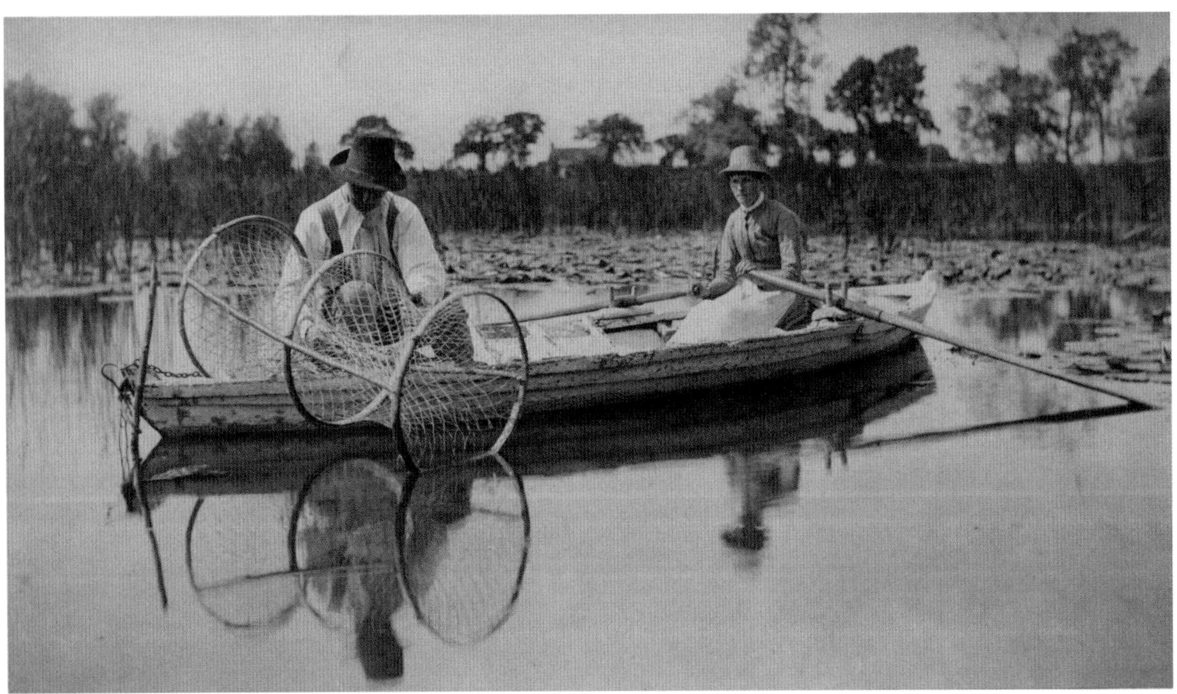

72 Peter Henry Emerson and Thomas Frederick Goodall
***Setting the Bow-Net* 1885, from *Life and Landscape on the Norfolk Broads*, London 1887**
Photograph, albumen print on paper 16 x 29
Private collection

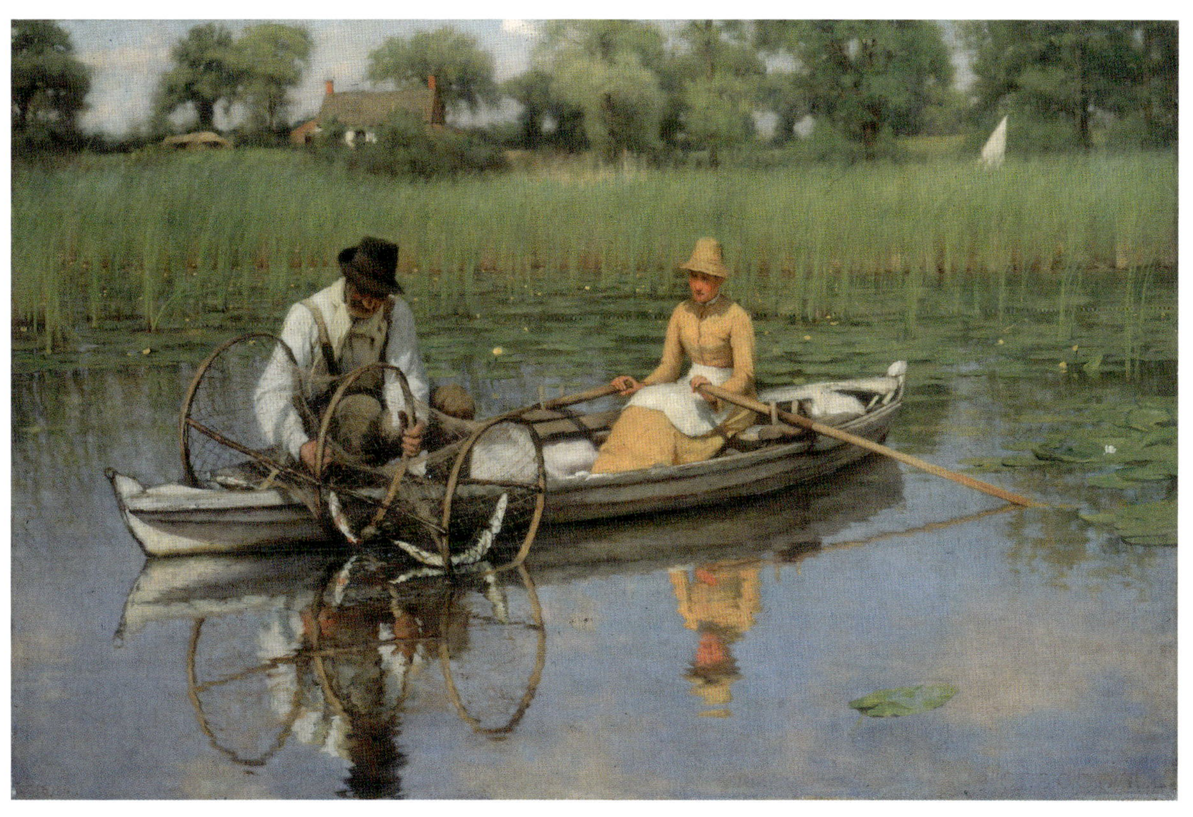

73 **Thomas Frederick Goodall**
The Bow Net **1886**
Oil paint on canvas 83.8 x 127
National Museums Liverpool, Walker Art Gallery

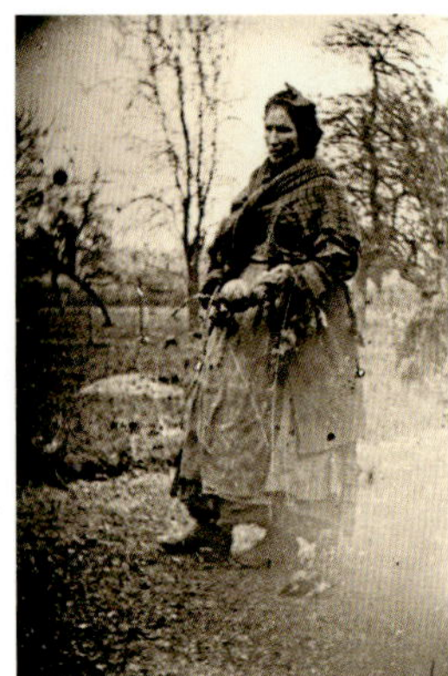

74 George Clausen
***Woman in Turnip Field* 1883, printed 2016**
Photograph, inkjet on paper, printed from the original negative 11.5 x 7.4
Museum of English Rural Life, University of Reading

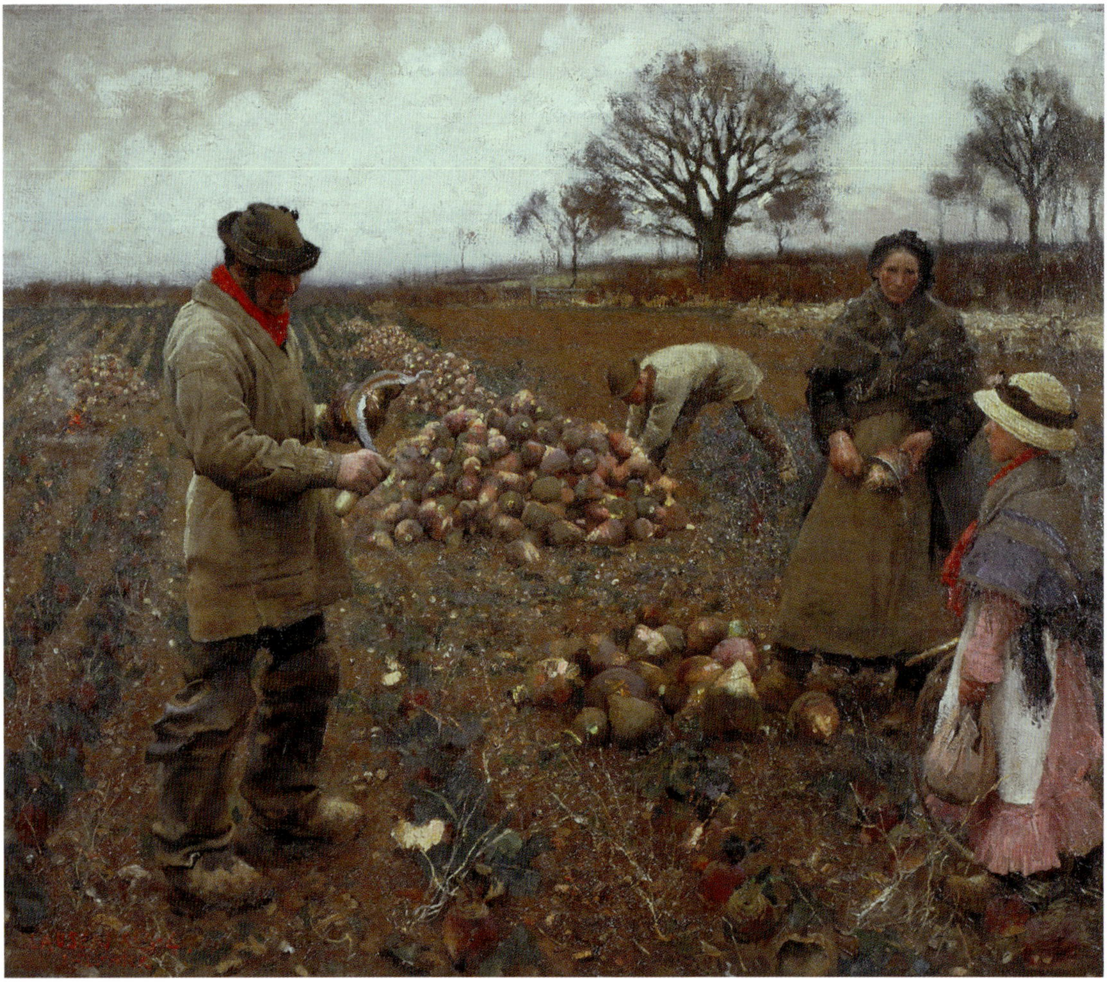

75 George Clausen
***Winter Work* 1883–4**
Oil paint on canvas 77.5 x 92.1
Tate. Purchased with assistance from the Friends of the Tate Gallery 1983

George Clausen pursued academic training in Paris and was later influenced by realist painters like Jules Bastien-Lepage. In the early 1880s he found inspiration in rural Hertfordshire: 'One saw people doing simple things under good conditions of lighting: and there was always landscape. And nothing was made easy for you: you had to dig out what you wanted.'[69] This new naturalism was showcased in *Winter Work*, for which Clausen made studies with a small 'Academy' plate camera.

Clausen's muted palette and suppressed tonal values are echoed in *Poling the Marsh Hay*, a photograph whose 'sombre grey tone' Goodall described as accurately representing that November day.[70] Goodall also discussed the sombre subject, the salvage of a flooded crop for animal litter, whose narrative echoes *Winter Work* in the harsh labour of pulling turnips for winter fodder.

Goodall and Clausen were founding members of the New English Art Club and Goodall introduced Clausen to Emerson, who bought one of the painter's small head studies in August 1886. Emerson subsequently corresponded with Clausen, debating perspectives on art and photography. HK & CJ

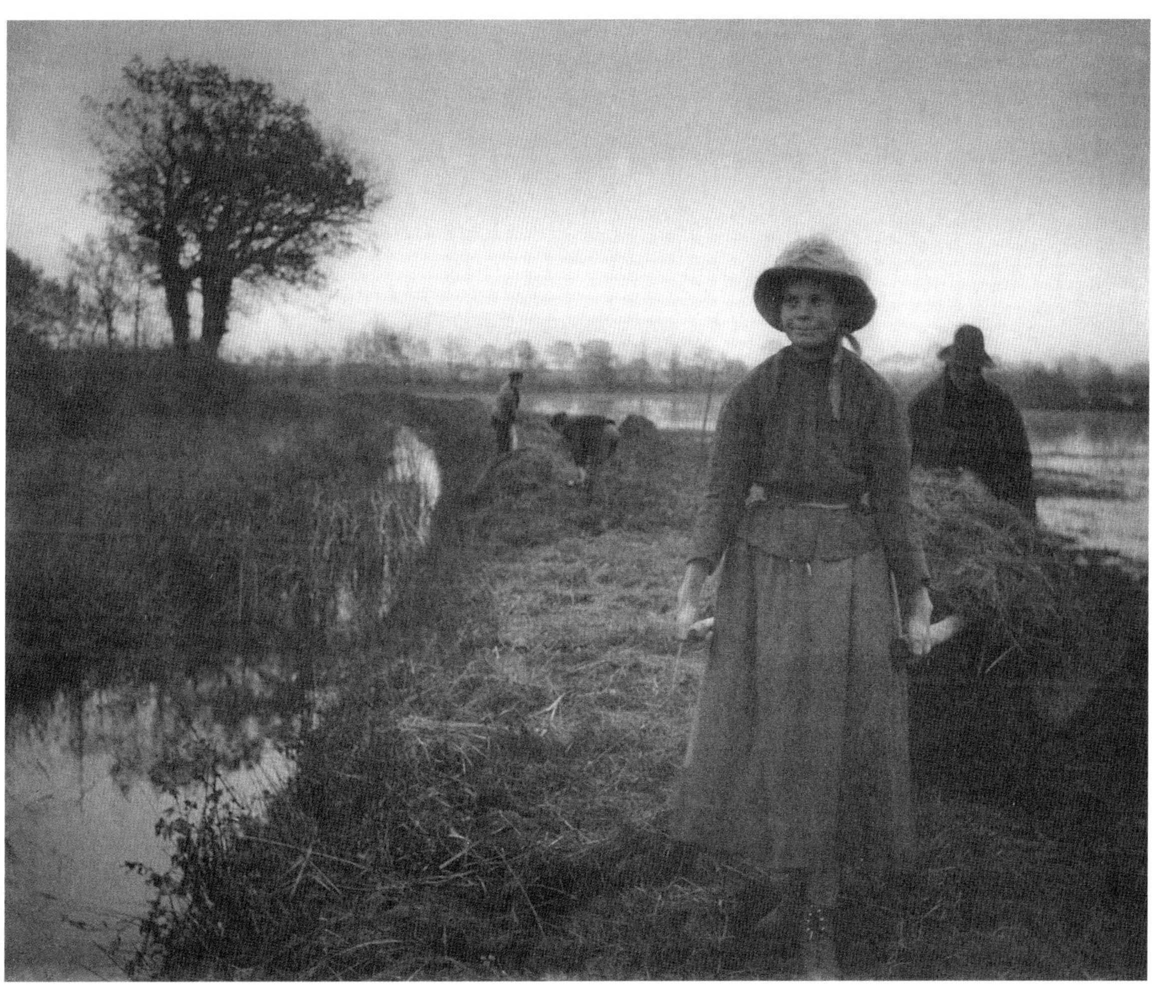

76 Peter Henry Emerson and Thomas Frederick Goodall
***Poling the Marsh Hay* 1885–6, from *Life and Landscape on the Norfolk Broads*, London 1887**
Photograph, platinum print on paper 23.2 x 28.8
Wilson Centre for Photography

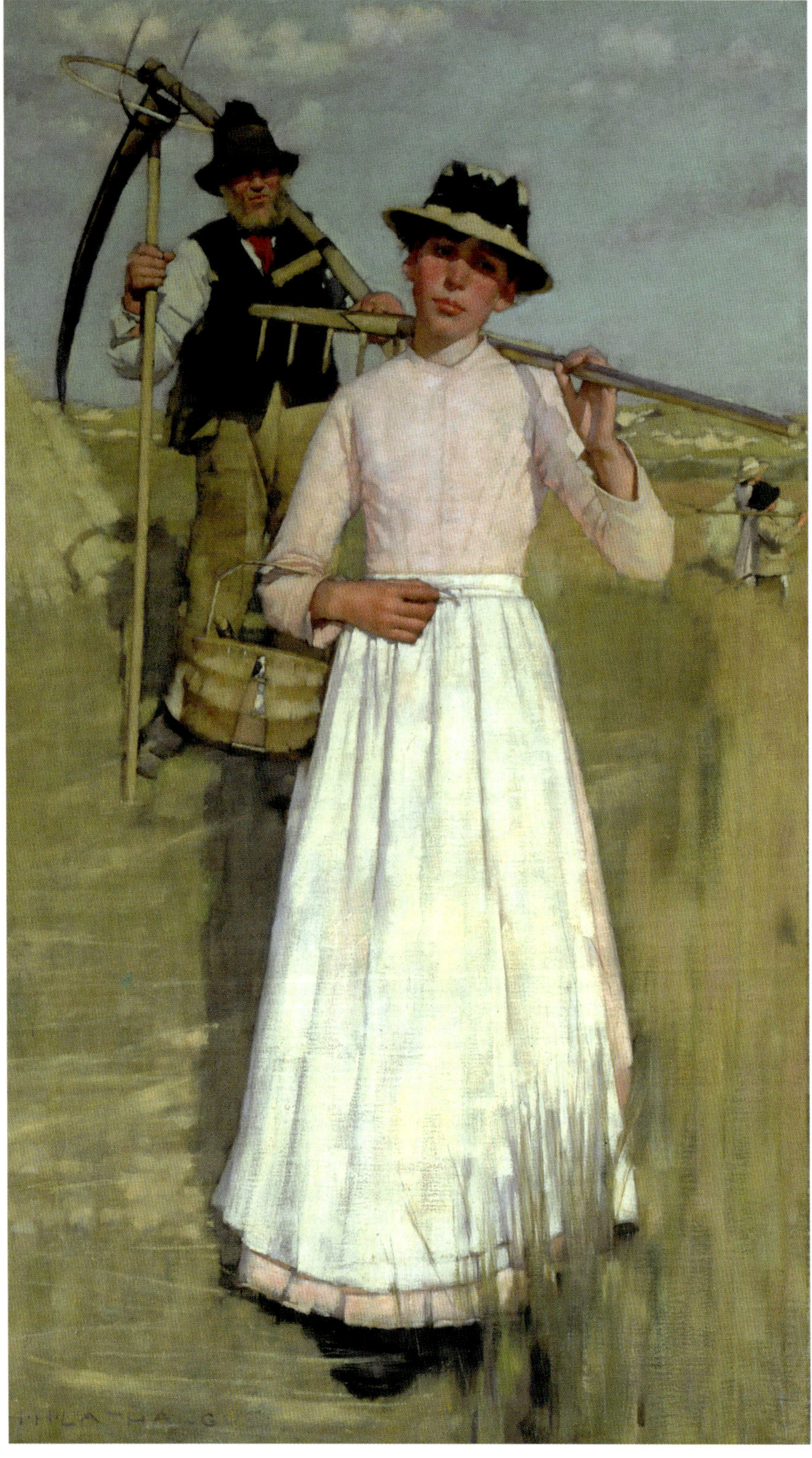

77 Henry Herbert La Thangue
The Return of the Reapers
1886
Oil paint on canvas 119 x 69.5
Tate. Purchased 1982

Emerson described the subjects of this photograph, 'these Norfolk peasants', as attentive to the natural world, 'a naturalist in his way every one of them'.[71] The photograph was itself 'naturalistic', presenting the landscape and its reed cutters with an immediacy that suggested a direct encounter. Emerson and Goodall's approach is very like that seen in La Thangue's painting: in both works the central figures are situated in a shallow foreground space at the front of the frame, at full height and eye level with the viewer. Each picture is carefully composed, right down to the counterweight of diagonals in the figures with the scythes. Indeed, the photograph is far from a candid snapshot, for an instantaneous exposure was not possible with Emerson's large-format camera.

The naturalistic motive and its pictorial structures derive from paintings by Jean-François Millet in the 1850s and Jules Bastien-Lepage in the late 1870s. Both were important influences on La Thangue, who studied at the École des Beaux Arts, Paris, in the early 1880s and painted in the French countryside in the summers of 1881–3. For his part, Emerson praised both Millet and Bastien-Lepage in *Naturalistic Photography* (1889). Goodall was the likely conduit, for he and La Thangue were old friends from their student days at the Lambeth School of Art and the Royal Academy, and Goodall introduced Emerson to La Thangue in 1885. HK

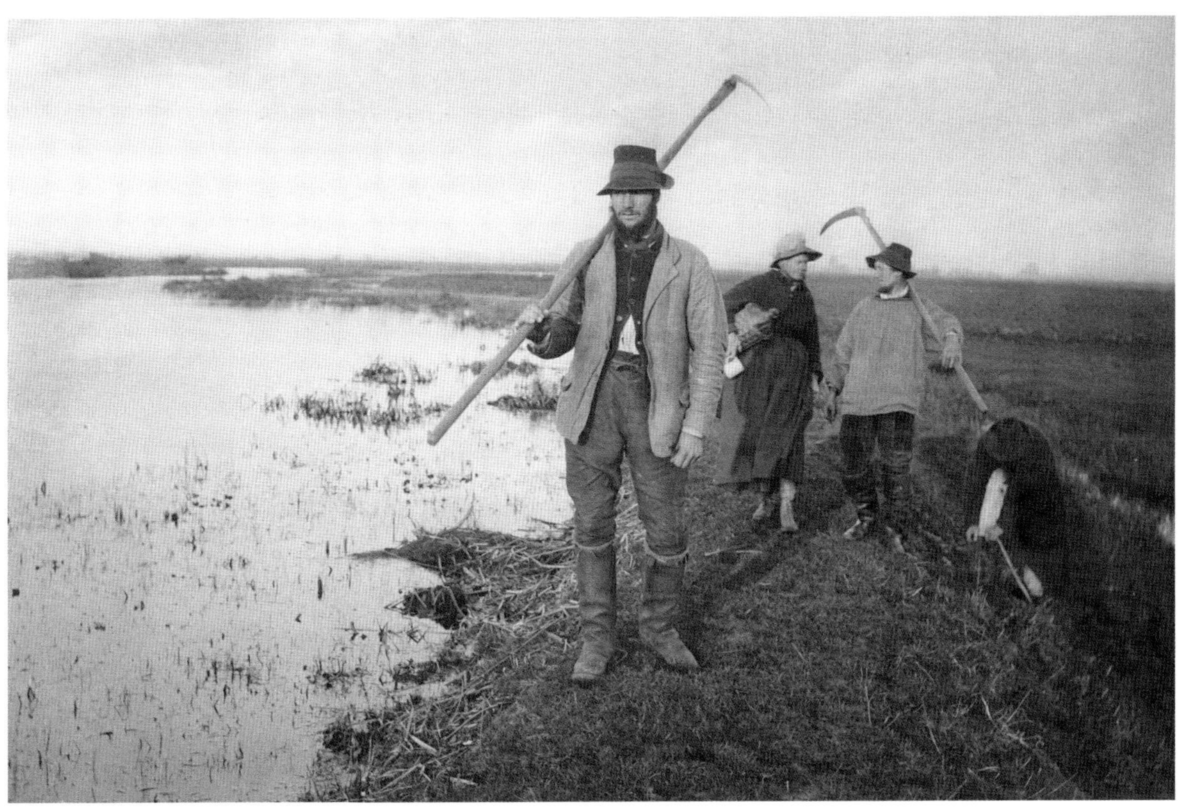

78 Peter Henry Emerson and Thomas Frederick Goodall
Coming Home from the Marshes 1885–6,
from *Life and Landscape on the Norfolk Broads,*
London 1887
Photograph, platinum print on paper 19.1 x 29.2
Wilson Centre for Photography

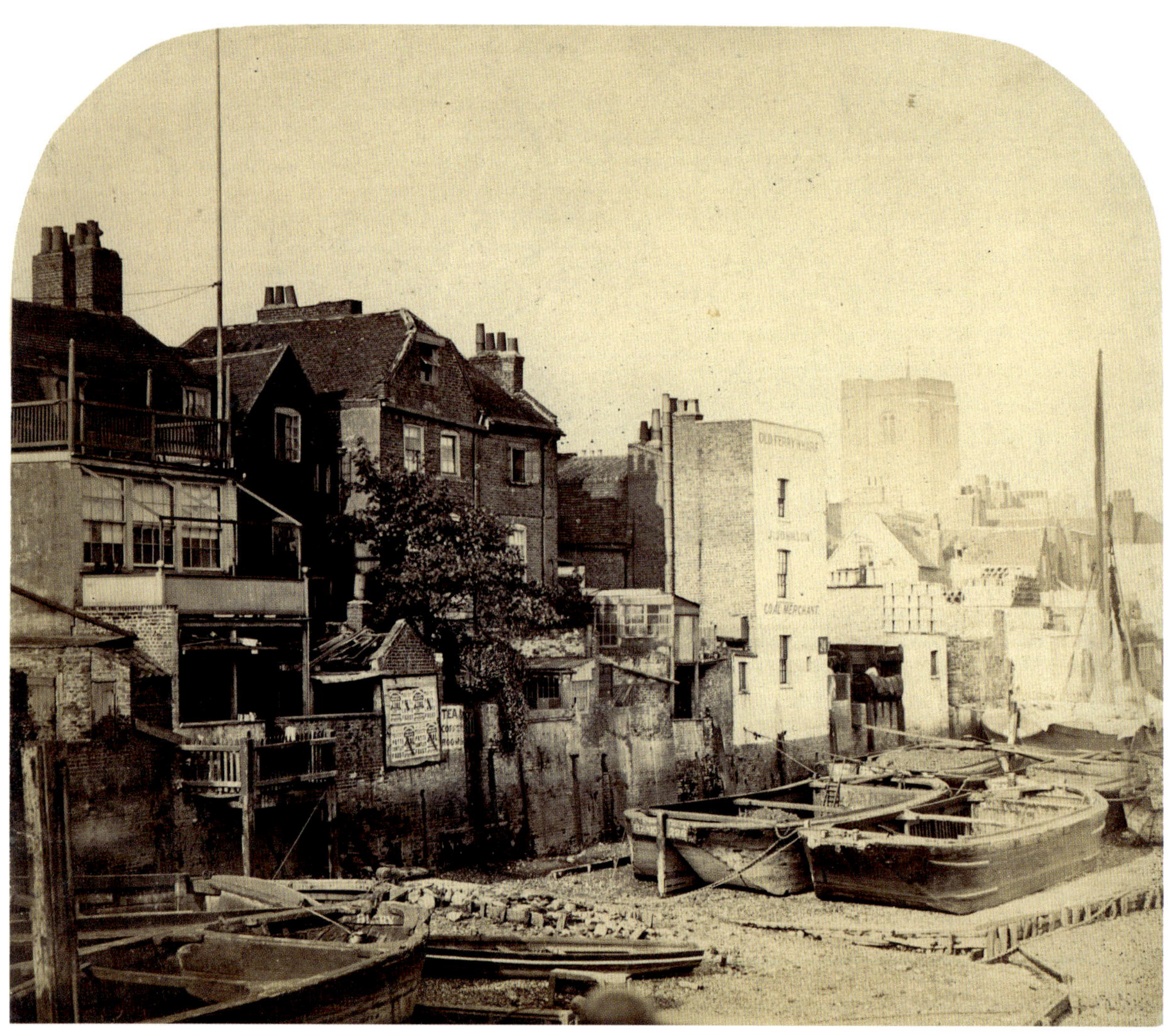

79 James Hedderly
***The Adam and Eve, Chelsea* c.1865**
Photograph, albumen print on paper 19.1 x 23.3
Royal Borough of Kensington and Chelsea

80 James Abbott McNeill Whistler
***The Adam and Eve, Old Chelsea* 1878**
Etching on paper 17.5 x 30
The Hunterian, University of Glasgow

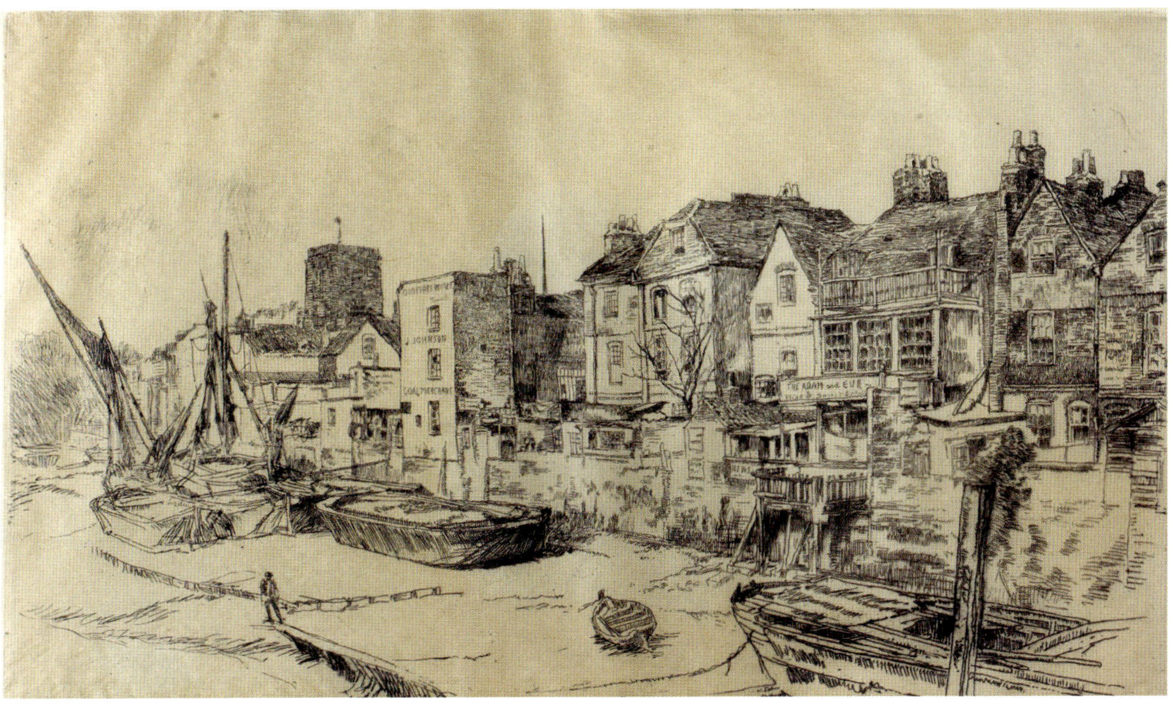

Whistler's etching is dated 1878, when the Adam and Eve tavern had already been demolished to allow for the new Chelsea Embankment. Whistler reconstructs the former view. It is thought that he used James Hedderly's photograph, taken around 1865, as an aide-memoire.[72] When a horizontally reversed image of Whistler's etching is compared to the photograph (reversal occurs during the printing process), the similarity of the viewpoints is clear. But there are differences, too: the etching includes a figure in the foreground, for instance. It has been noted that Whistler may have referred to other photographs of the site, not least those by Hedderly, with whom Whistler was well acquainted.[73] EJ

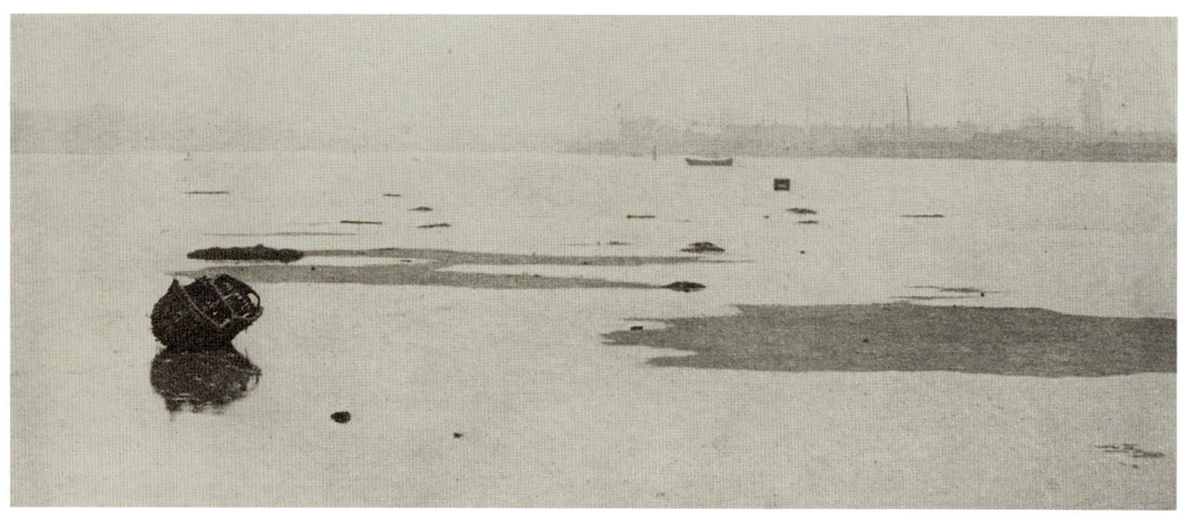

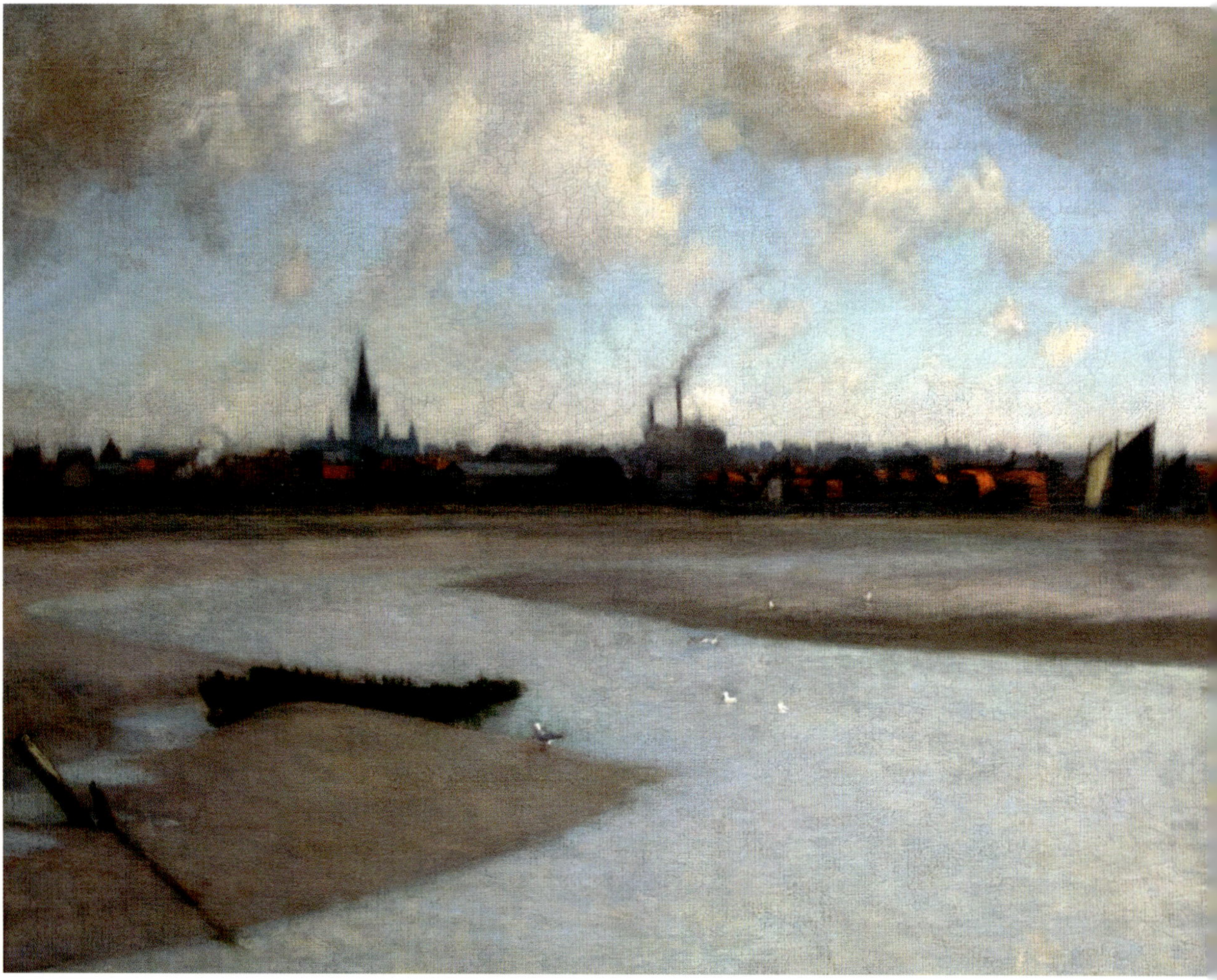

81 Peter Henry Emerson and Thomas Frederick Goodall
***Low Water on Breydon*, 1887 from *Wild Life on a Tidal Water*, London 1890**
Photogravure on paper 9.4 x 21.2
Wilson Centre for Photography

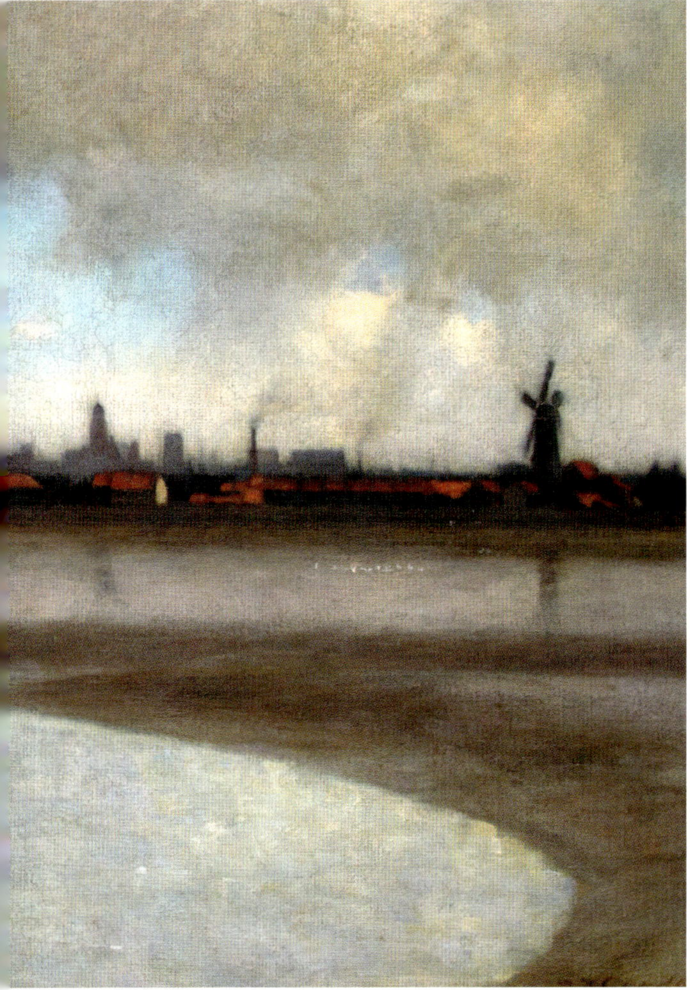

The photographs for *Wild Life on a Tidal Water* were made in the summer of 1887 from Goodall's houseboat at Breydon Water, where he was working on a painting, originally titled 'The Last of the Ebb' and destined for the Royal Academy in 1888. The canvas presents a formal arrangement of nearly abstract elements within a broad, horizontal format, a composition seen in its photographic counterpart, *Low Water on Breydon*, published in *Wild Life* as a subtle and delicate photogravure.

The painting was Goodall's focus during their time at Yarmouth, and he spotted his scene immediately, as Emerson recounted:

> *Even at the last of the ebb, standing in your punt, you can overlook the moist mud-banks on whose levels is reflected the blue sky ... We seem to float through a dreamy land of mists soaked with the most delicate dyes.*
> *'By God, it's wonderful!' I cried.*
> *'Ay,' said Dick* [pseudonym for Goodall], *holding up his punt with one hand and stroking his beard with the other, while his keen blue eyes drank in the landscape; 'there's my picture. Do you see, old chap? I shall take that fine old windmill on the right, that smoking factory chimney on the left, and start my foreground there, just this side of that decaying boat; and what a magnificent subject it is!' he added, as his punt swung slowly round with the flowing tide.*[74]

HK

82 Thomas Frederick Goodall
***View of Great Yarmouth, Norfolk* exh. 1887-8**
Oil paint on canvas 45.7 x 96.5
Private collection

83 James Abbott McNeill Whistler
***Nocturne: Blue and Silver – Cremorne Lights* 1872**
Oil paint on canvas 50.2 x 74.3
Tate. Bequeathed by Arthur Studd 1919

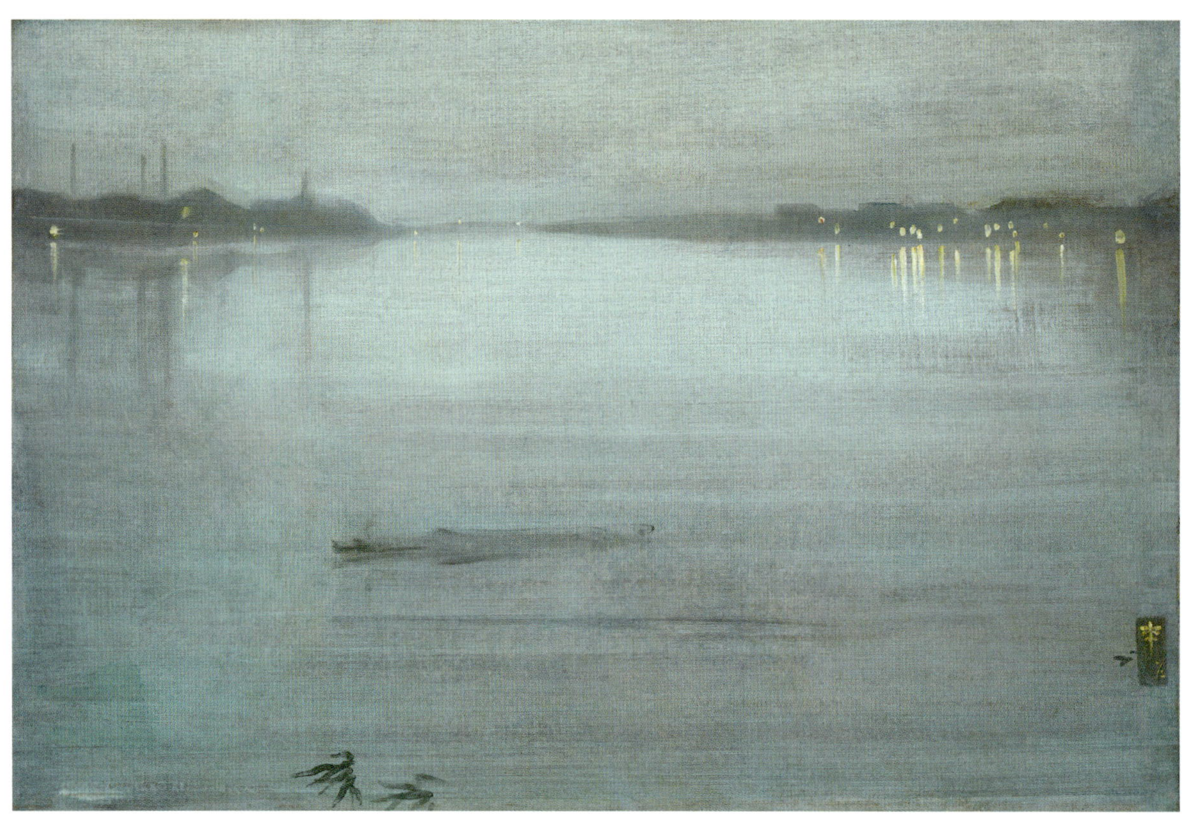

84 Peter Henry Emerson
***The Bridge*, from *Marsh Leaves*, London 1895**
Photogravure on paper
Wilson Centre for Photography

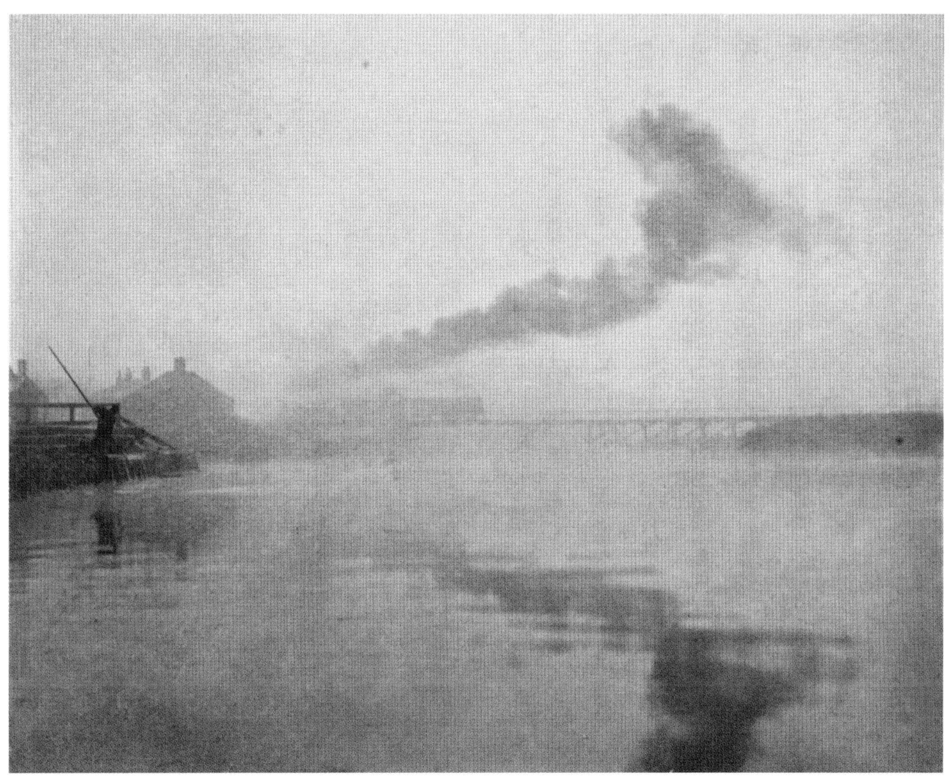

Emerson was initially resistant to Whistler's work, criticising the painter's 'evil nocturnes' in his 1889 book, *Naturalistic Photography for Students of the Art*.[75] But he soon reversed his opinion and sent a portfolio of photographs to Whistler in 1890, after which they met in Paris. Emerson later sent Whistler a copy of *Marsh Leaves*, whose photographs evoke the ethereal, schematic effects of that artist's paintings, as Emerson understood the aesthetic in 1892: 'Whistler … holds pure and simple that the whole aim & subject of a picture is to seek a *decorative scheme or pattern* either of line or colour.'[76]

Emerson's tribute extended from pictures to words, as the text accompanying *The Bridge* is titled 'A Nocturne': 'Grey wreaths of mist began to rise and float over the dusky river … As the afterglow paled in the western sky, the pale round silver disk of the moon, quaintly marked, shone brighter in the pale blue sky, and burnished the clouds of white mists now floating over the brimming waterways and gliding softly over the marshes.'[77] HK

David Young Cameron described James Craig Annan's photogravure of Venice as 'a dream in the softest tones dedicated in loving homage to the Bride of the Sea lying enchanted and far away across the long low lines of grey lagoons'.[78] Annan's print was also a homage to Whistler, whose well-known 'Venice Set' etchings may have inspired the 1894 trip from which these works arise.[79] Annan and Cameron worked side by side, as their results show. Both use the horizon line as the dominant compositional element. Annan's photograph, made with a small hand-camera, is tightly cropped, whereas Cameron allows the verges to disappear, as in Whistler's treatment of the subject. Cameron has left out the gondola mooring posts that provide vertical counterweights for Whistler and Annan. Annan has gently enhanced the edges of the buildings outlined against the sky, mirroring an effect seen in Cameron's pencil drawing.

Such hand-work was possible with photogravure, a fine photomechanical process that Annan had learned from its Viennese inventor, Karel Klíč, when Annan's father Thomas bought the British rights to the process for his printing company, T. & R. Annan. The firm made gravure reproductions for artists, and James became close to 'the circle of young Glaswegian artists like James Guthrie, John Lavery, E.A. Walton, [and] D.Y. Cameron, now known as the Glasgow School'. Annan added: 'The constant communication with these men and the most careful studies of the old masters were the only art education I received and I regard it as extremely valuable.'[80] HK

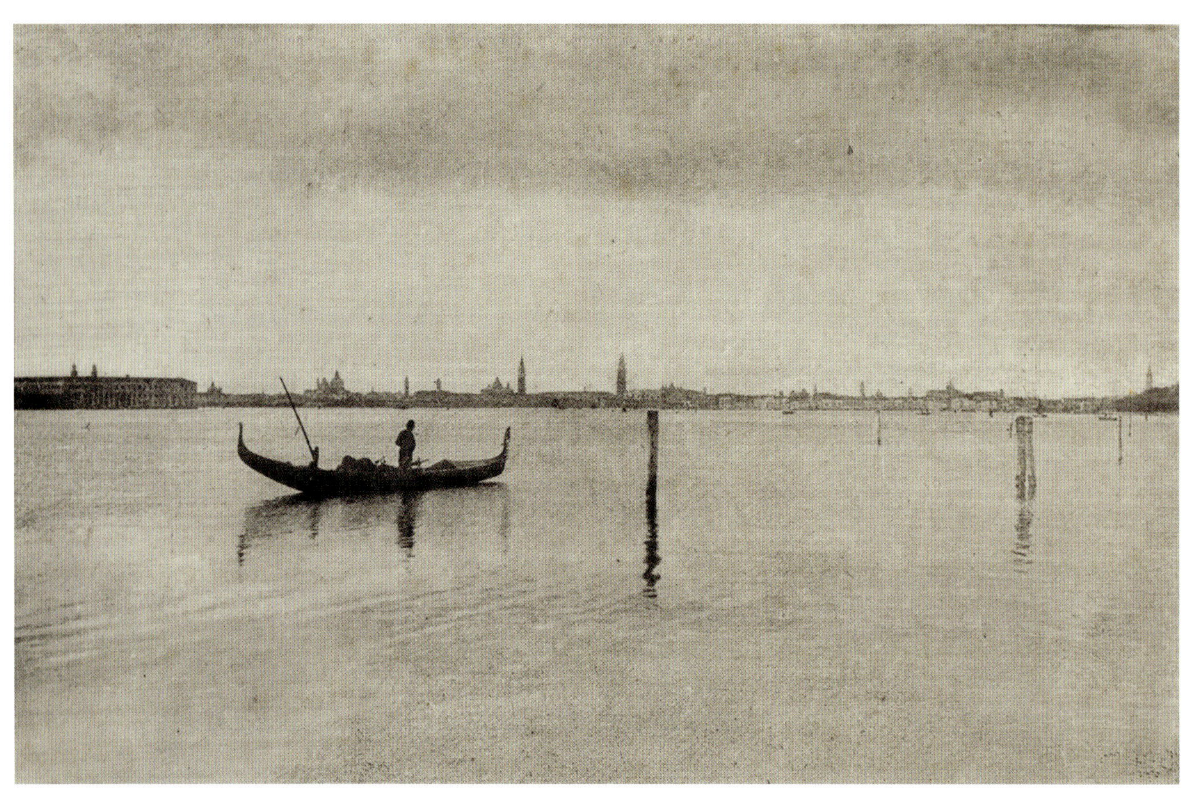

85 James Craig Annan
***Venice from the Lido* c.1894, published 1896**
Photogravure on paper 9.6 x 15
Private collection courtesy of Bernard Quaritch Ltd

86 James Abbott McNeill Whistler
***Little Venice* 1880**
Etching on paper 18.6 x 26.4
The Hunterian, University of Glasgow

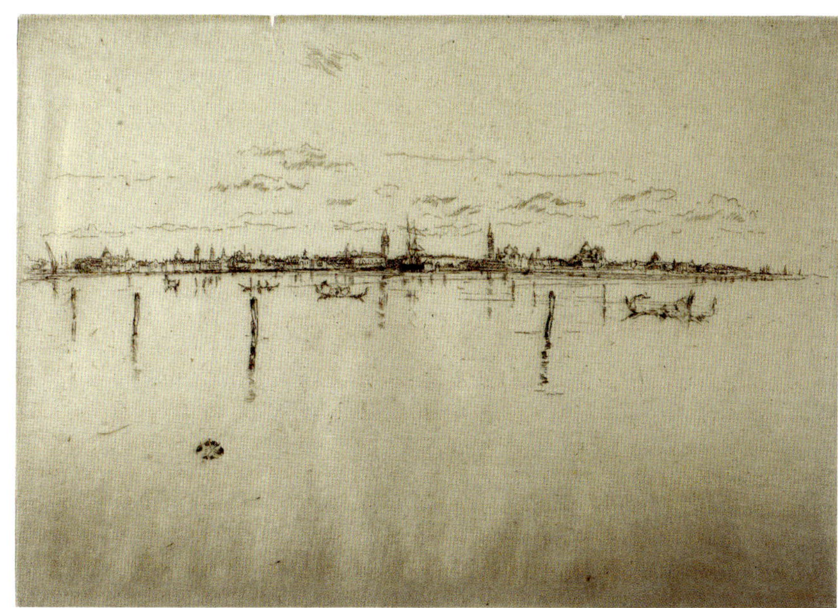

87 David Young Cameron
Pencil study for the etching,
***Venice from the Lido: San Giorgio Maggiore, Santa Maria Della Salute and Entrance to the Grand Canal* c.1894–6**
Pencil on paper 17 x 35
Private collection

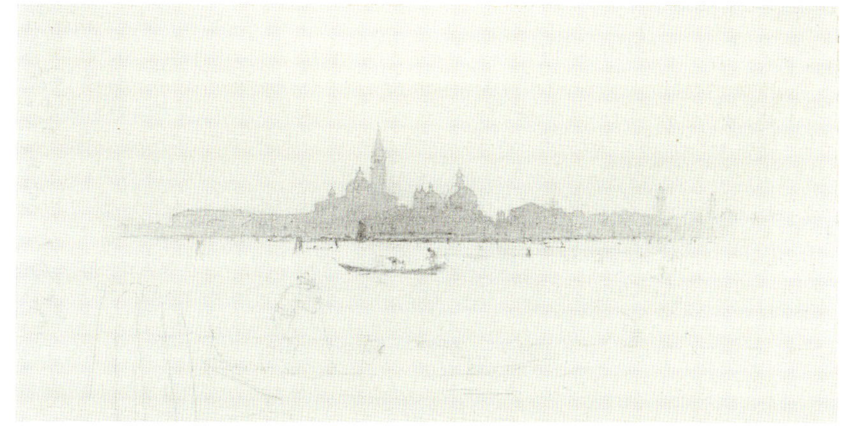

88 David Young Cameron
***Venice from the Lido* 1896**
Etching on paper 17.5 x 35
Private collection

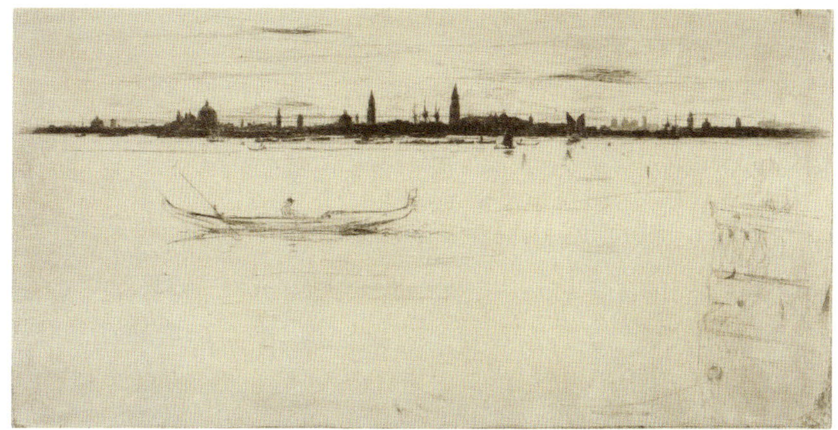

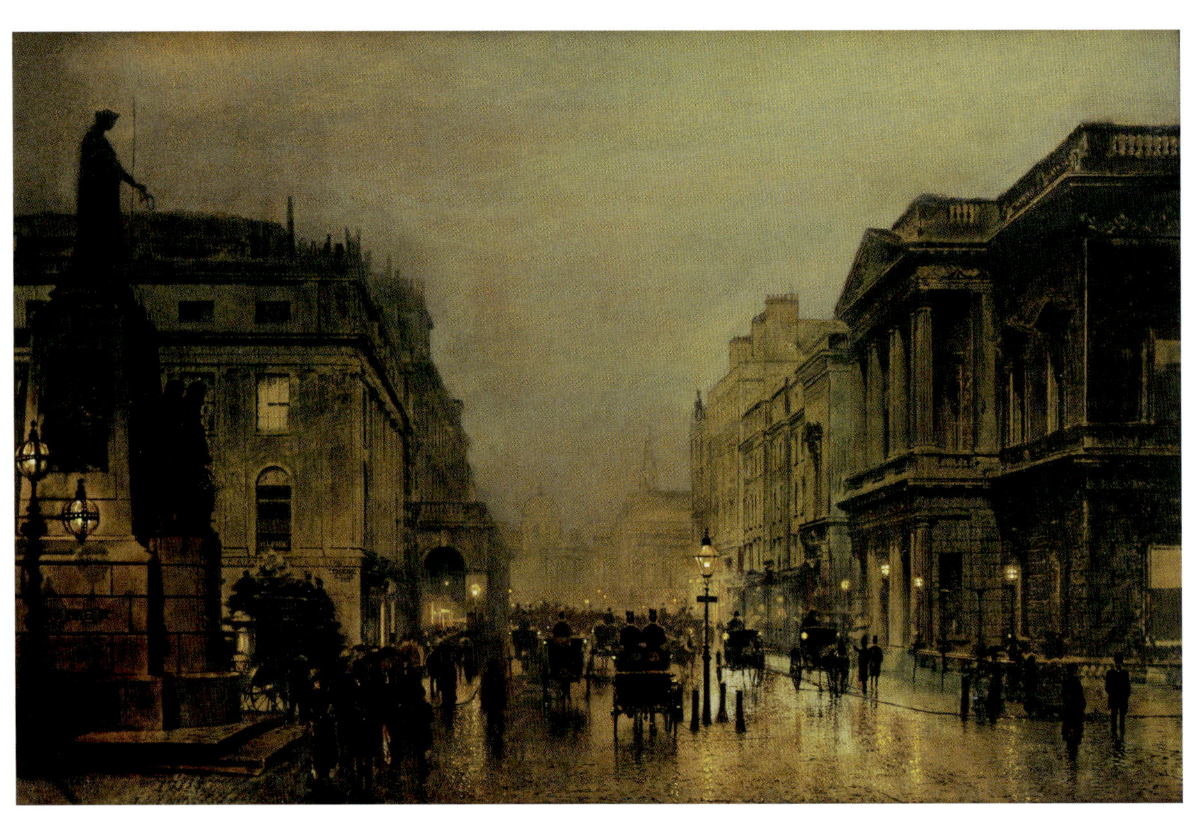

89 John Atkinson Grimshaw
Pall Mall c.1880s
Oil paint on photograph 30.5 x 45.2
Private collection

90 George Davison
***Oxford Street: A Wet Day* exh. 1897**
Photogravure on paper 10 x 7
Private collection

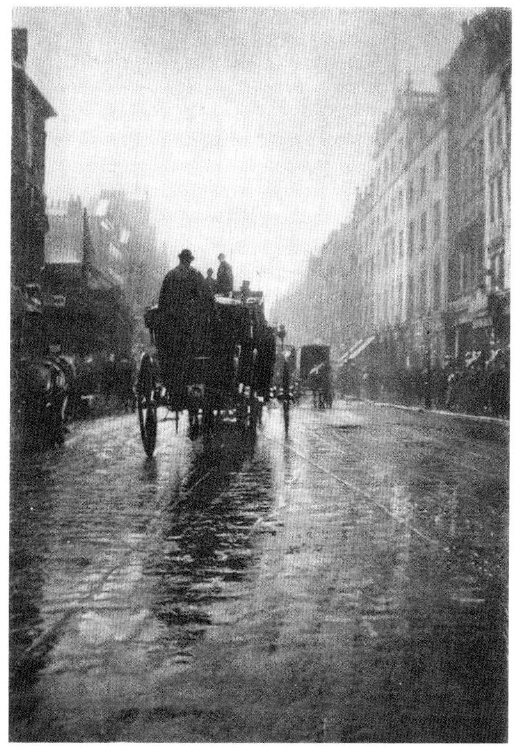

In the late 1870s Grimshaw turned from bright Pre-Raphaelite studies of the natural world to industrial and urban scenes of streets glowing with new gas and electric lighting. His clients lived in cities like Liverpool, Leeds and London, where from 1885 to 1887 he had a studio near Whistler at Manresa Road, Chelsea. Whistler apparently told Grimshaw that he had thought himself the inventor of 'nocturnes' until he saw Grimshaw's 'moonlit pictures'.

Grimshaw's London nocturne was painted directly onto a photograph, using his established technique of thinly applied paint coated with quick-drying copal oil varnish. This was a valuable short cut for an artist who produced quantities of canvases to sustain precarious finances. Grimshaw would have used a daytime view, for night-time photographs were not feasible until the mid-1890s. He could have purchased commercially published views of London streets from photographers such as Francis Bedford.

Some photographers did shoot 'day-for-night'; here George Davison made a short exposure to deepen the tones of the image and emphasise the *contre-jour* effect of the cab silhoutted against the light. He explained that this turned a 'prosaic' photograph into one whose 'special atmospheric conditions' made 'very pictorial effects'.[81] Grimshaw effectively used the same approach, darkening the scene and painting in areas of artificial light. HK

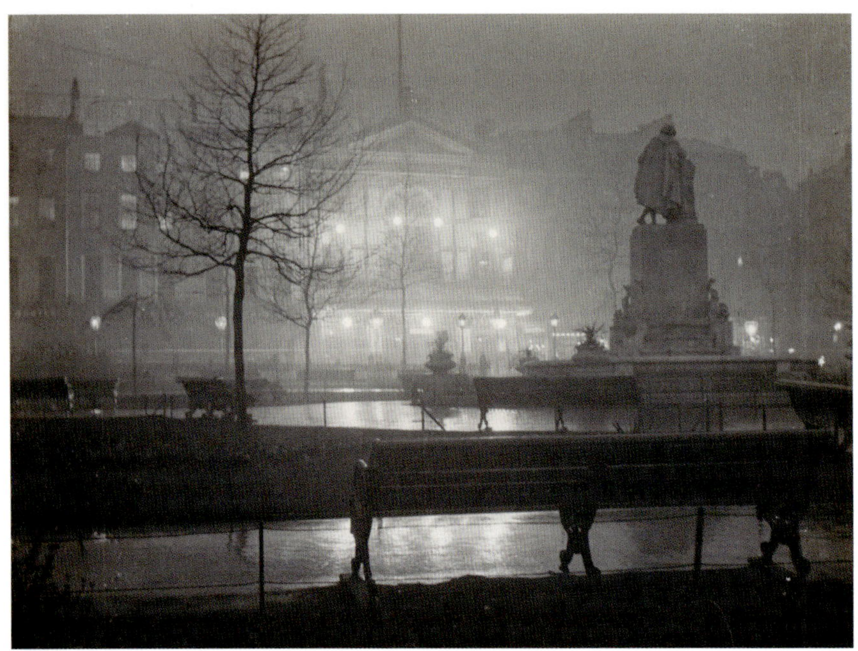

91 Paul Martin
***The Old Empire Theatre in Leicester Square, London* 1895**
Photograph, platinum print on paper
17.5 x 23.5
Victoria and Albert Museum

92 Arthur Hacker
***A Wet Night at Piccadilly Circus* 1910**
Oil paint on canvas 71 x 91.5
Royal Academy of Arts, London

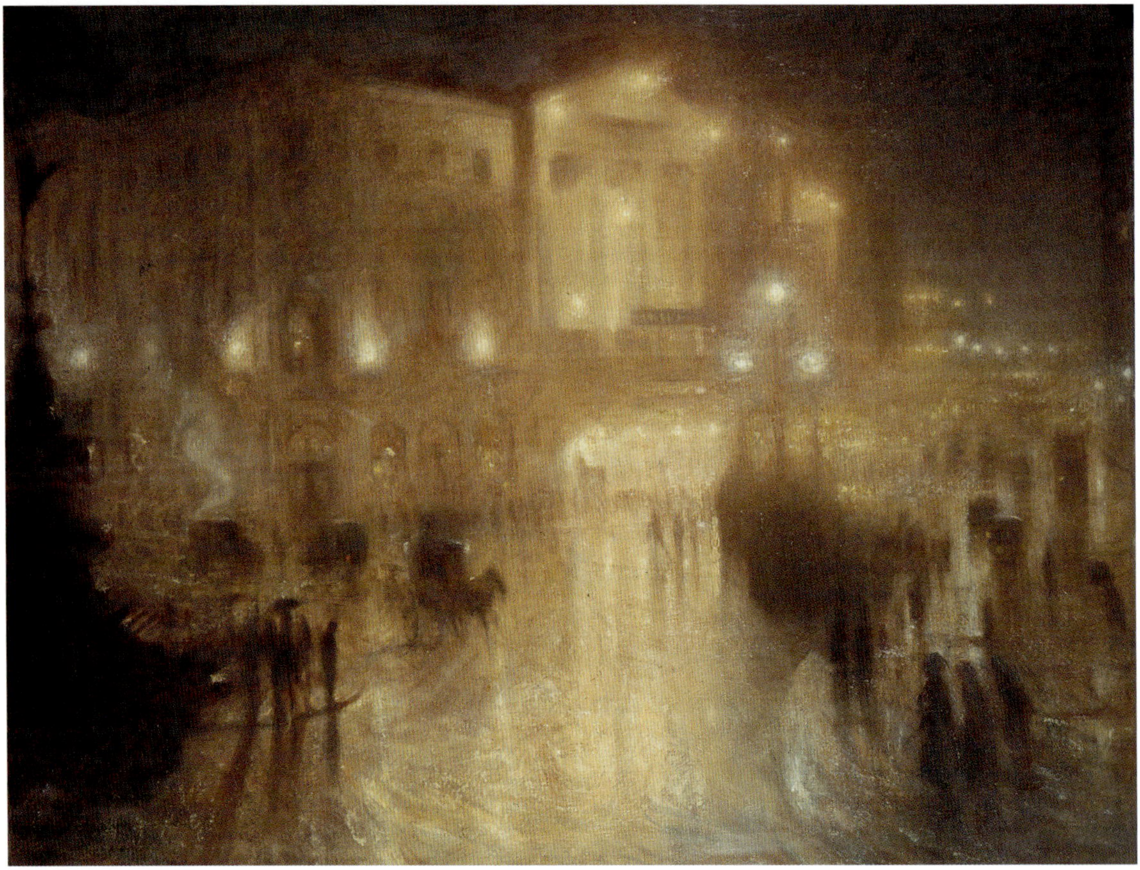

Paul Martin's innovative nocturnes were made at a time when city nights were getting brighter, as gaslights gave way to brighter electric lighting and faster photographic plates registered lower levels of natural and artificial light. Martin incorporated reflected light off rainy streets to shorten his exposure time. He also experimented with halation, in which the source of illumination – here the lamps of the Empire Theatre – refracts outwards in a halo of scattered light.

Martin was a member of the Linked Ring, and in 1896 he exhibited this and other 'London by Gaslight' photographs at the Photographic Salon and the Royal Photographic Society. The work was acclaimed and imitated, spawning 'Night-Hawks' groups at photographic clubs.

A decade later, Martin's technical challenges had largely been addressed. But Coburn used many of the same devices for pictorial effect; in *Leicester Square* the theatre lights reflect onto the wet pavement, balancing out the composition. Gaslight had largely gone, yet the enchantment of its glow could be recreated through halation. Coburn's London photographs arose from a collaboration planned with the writer Arthur Symons to respond to the city in pictures and words. Each published in 1909: Coburn's *London* included *Leicester Square*, while Symons described the extravagance of artificial lighting in *London: A Book of Aspects* – 'footlights are the flaming stars between world and world' and 'every row of gas lamps turns into a trail of fire'.[82]

In *A Wet Night at Piccadilly Circus* Hacker paints the effect of halation. It spills outwards, suffusing the scene in a blaze of light that evokes Symons's description of the Circus as 'like a whirlpool … The lights glitter outside theatres and music-halls and restaurants; lights coruscate, flash from the walls, dart from the vehicles.'[83] HK

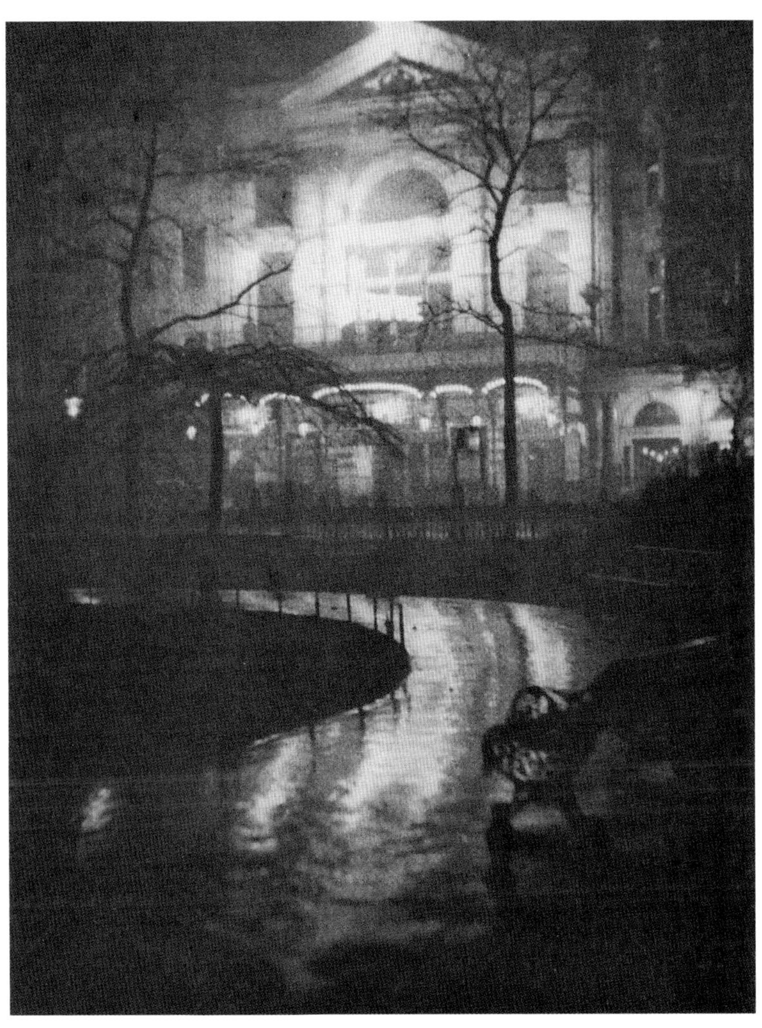

93 Alvin Langdon Coburn
Leicester Square (The Old Empire Theatre)
1908, published 1909
Photogravure on paper 20.6 x 17.2
Wilson Centre for Photography

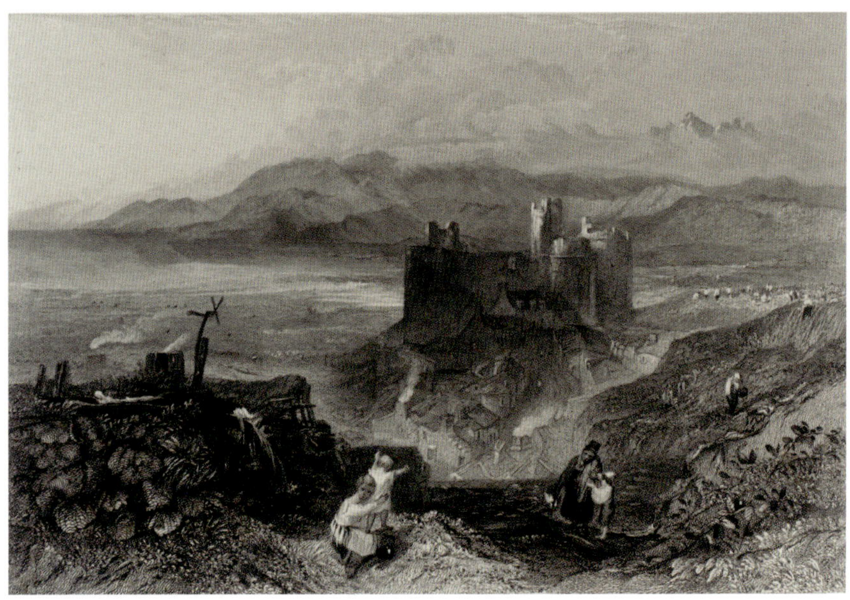

94 After J.M.W. Turner
***Harlech Castle, North Wales* 1836,**
from *Picturesque Views in England and Wales*
Line engraving on paper 16.2 x 24.4
Tate. Purchased 1986

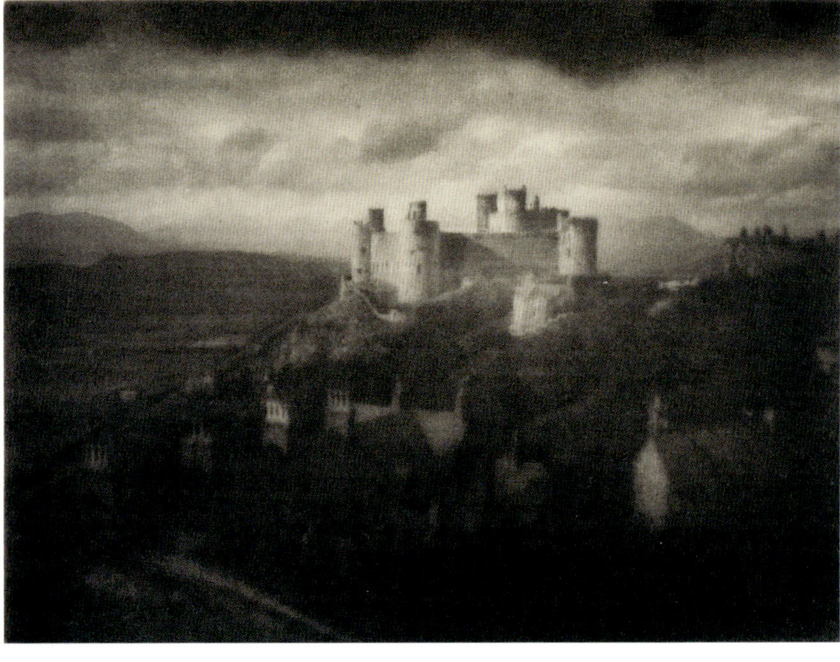

95 George Davison
***Harlech Castle* 1903**
Photogravure on paper 15.5 x 21
Wilson Centre for Photography

In the later nineteenth century photographers began to show 'pure' landscapes without figures. George Davison credited an interest in atmospheric effects, which were now more accurately represented with new orthochromatic plates: 'landscapes with marked character call for no figures, nor do the wide range of subjects in which the sky makes the chief attraction with its delicate gradations and forms fanciful or reposeful.'[84] In this photogravure Davison's composition and expressive clouds suggest Turner's *Harlech Castle*.

When, in 1908, Davison's socialist politics led to his resignation from Eastman Kodak's board, he settled in Harlech, where he gathered activists, musicians, artists and Linked Ring brothers like James Craig Annan and Alvin Langdon Coburn. In 1918 Coburn and his wife built a house nearby; they settled permanently in Wales in 1930.

This is one of Dudley Johnston's best-known works, a Turneresque study that illustrates his ethos that 'subordination of detail [is] the chief means to an imaginative end'.[85] It is a splendid example of gum platinum printing, in which a platinum print is overprinted by the gum bichromate process, here providing a blue-grey tint and deepening the shadows.

Johnston became Curator of the Royal Photographic Society in 1924 and built the society's pictorial collection, largely through donations from his old Linked Ring compatriots like Henry Peach Robinson, Frederick Evans and Alvin Langdon Coburn. HK

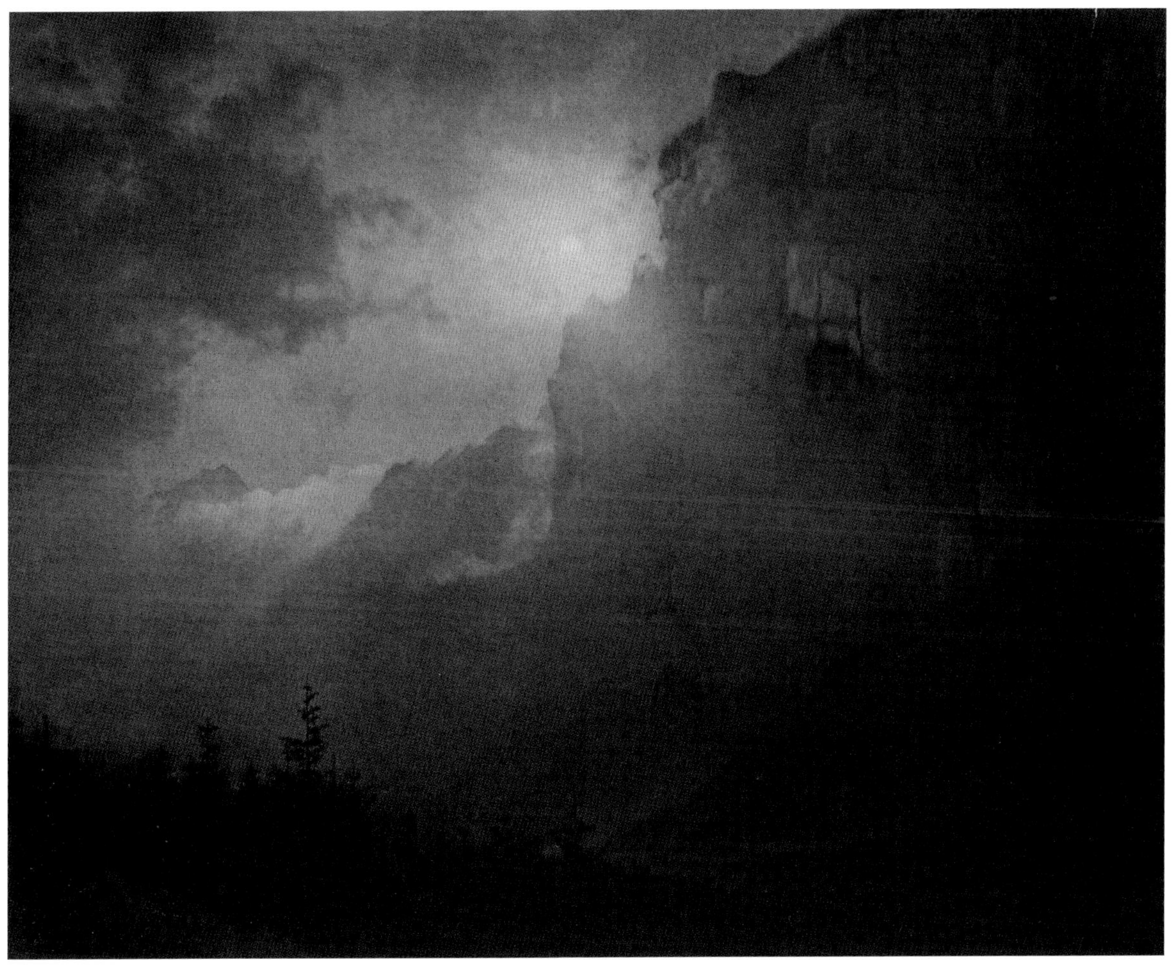

96 John Dudley Johnston
***The Valley of the Dragon* 1909, printed 1910**
Photograph, gum platinum print on paper 28 x 35.5
Courtesy of Bernard Quaritch Ltd

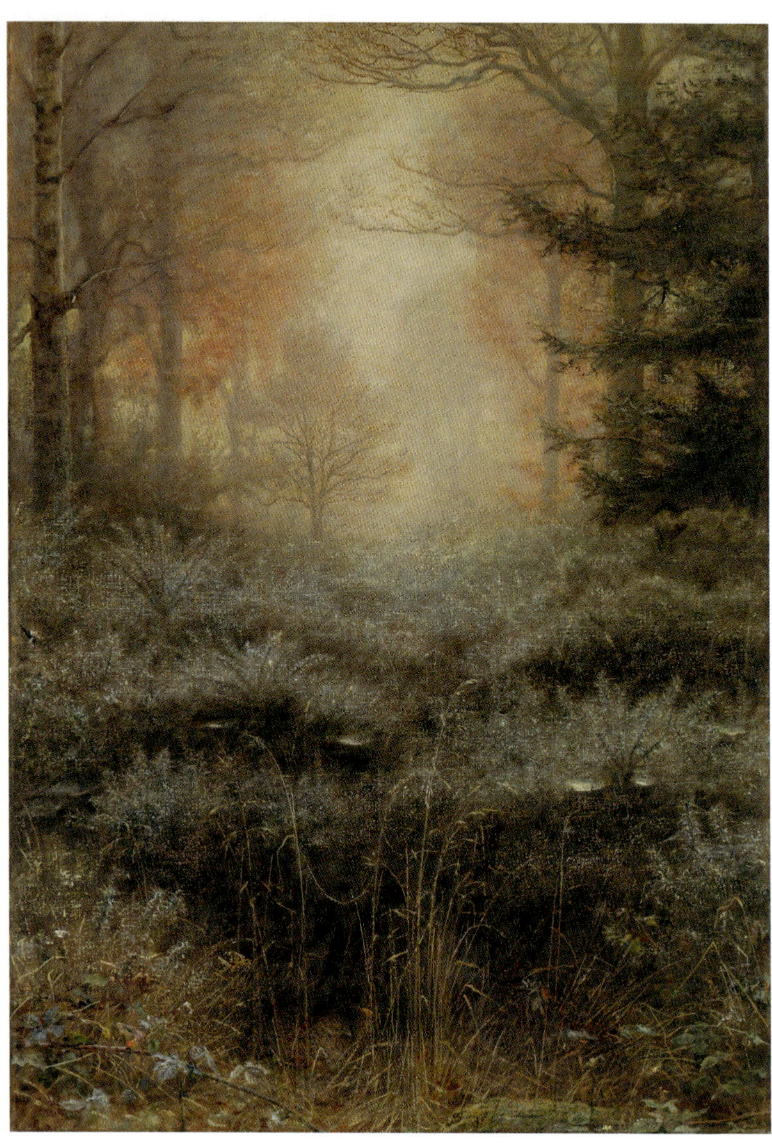

97 John Everett Millais
***Dew-Drenched Furze* 1889–90**
Oil paint on canvas 173.2 x 123
Tate. Presented by Geoffroy Millais in memory of his late father, Sir Ralph Millais Bt, 2009

In the 1870s Millais began exhibiting elegiac Scottish landscapes worlds away from his Pre-Raphaelite work twenty years before (no.18). The landscapes were empty and evoked their emotional effect through formal characteristics and technique, a development of aestheticism. *Dew-Drenched Furze* was perhaps Millais's most abstract work. It was painted on location in the Murthly estate, and the title quotes Tennyson's *In Memoriam* (section 11, 1850):

> *Calm and deep peace on this high wold,*
> *And on the dews that drench the furze,*
> *And all the silvery gossamers*
> *That twinkle into green and gold.*

Broken brushwork, chalky scumbled surface and scattered highlights (a development of Constable's 'snow') dissolve the surface of the painting and the forms in the landscape, which melt not into darkness but into light. The photographer H.P. Robinson commended Millais's late landscapes in 1888, noting that his effects of light and silhouette, subdued colour and narrowed frame, echoed photography.[86] This overlapping vision is underlined in a contemporary photograph by Millais's son (Tate Archive), the photographer Geoffroy Millais, of his father in a nearby location and against a similarly abstract area of the image burnt out by overexposure. CJ

98 Frederick Henry Evans
***Dirge in Woods (Meredith's Poem)* 1894**
Glass lantern slide 7 x 5.7
Private collection

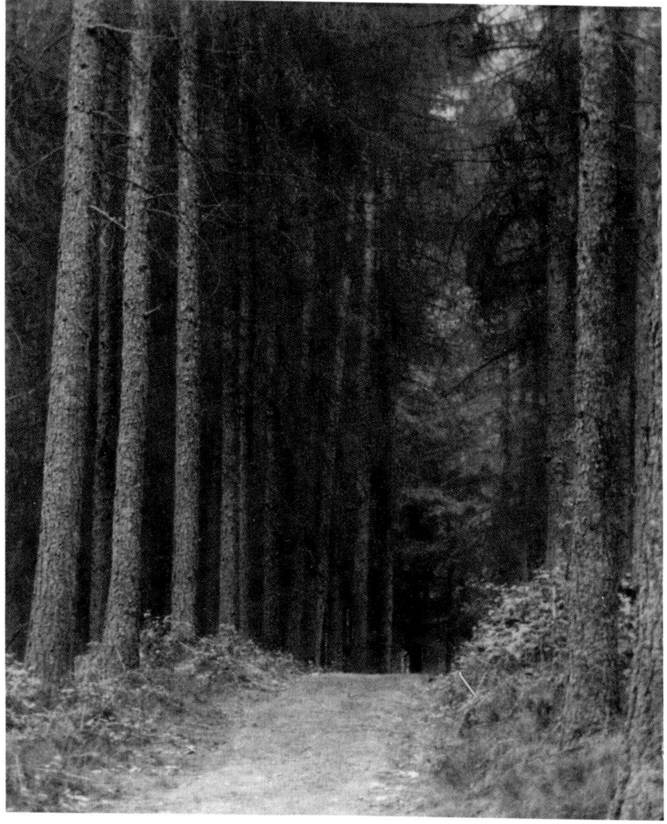

Evans made the original negative for this work in 1894 and exhibited it as a platinum print titled *Redlands Woods*. Redlands Woods was a favourite haunt of the poet George Meredith, and Evans contributed a gravure of this image to the memorial edition of Meredith's works (1909). At the 1909 Photographic Salon Evans showed a print he had made for Meredith. The poet had died before receiving the gift, and in tribute, Evans included the following lines from Meredith's poem 'Dirge in Woods':

A wind sways in the pines,
And below
Not a breath of wild air;
Still as the mosses that glow
On the flooring and over the lines
Of the roots here and there.
The pine-tree drops its dead;
They are quiet, as under the sea,
Overhead, overhead
Rushes life in a race,
As the clouds, the clouds we chase;
As we go,
And we drop like the fruits of the tree
Even we
Even so.[87]

The negative was later lost, and Evans made this lantern slide from the platinum print. Evans showed the slide during lectures; his note on the rebate instructs 'see Meredith's poem'. HK

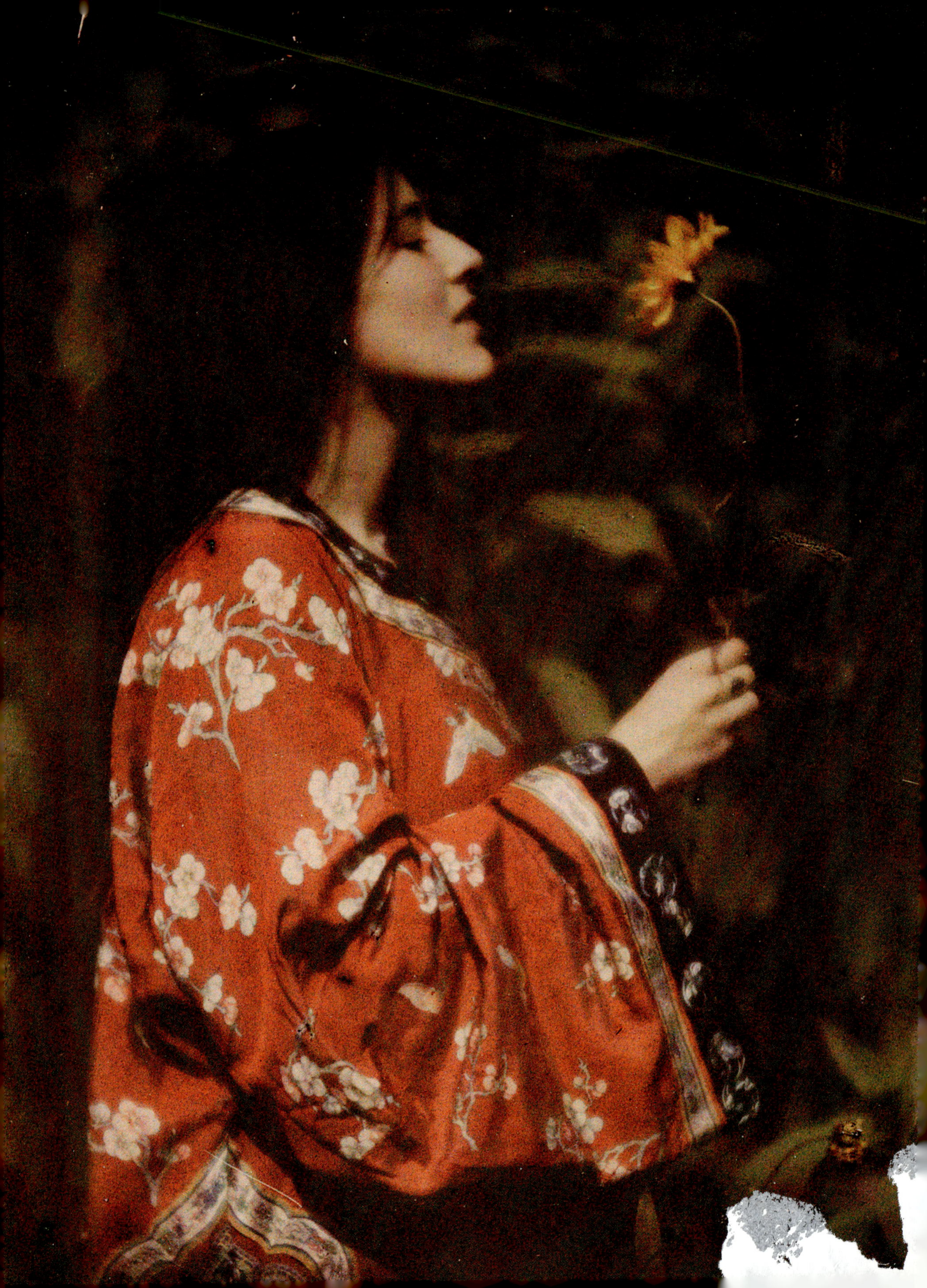

7 Out of the Shadows

Carol Jacobi

By the end of the century, the arts in Britain enjoyed a confident, cosmopolitan, eclectic outlook. Thriving cities such as London, Birmingham and Glasgow became centres for painters and photographers with global exposure and careers. These were reflected in international exhibitions, publications and organisations. The Linked Ring's regular London salons and publications were influential, connecting with similar groups and exhibitions in Europe, North America and the British Empire. Photography exhibitions looked more like art exhibitions, with works artfully mounted and framed and in shared venues such as the Dudley Gallery, London, which hosted the Linked Ring salons and the New English Art Club (NEAC).

Writers, painters and photographers enjoyed close connections such as that between Frederick Evans and Aubrey Beardsley. Copeland & Day, the publishing firm of the photographer Fred Holland Day, brought the writings of Dante Gabriel Rossetti, Walter Pater and Oscar Wilde to America. Illustrated publications circulated bodies of work by past and contemporary artists and photographers alike, and facilitated sophisticated, interdisciplinary dialogues. Sargent and Whistler collected photographs of old masters, for example, while Day advised fellow photographers to study old masters along with Whistler and Sargent. Subject matter and motifs were freely exchanged across literature, the pictorial arts and design. Critics saw a special sympathy between the intimate subjects and flattened, asymmetrical compositions of impressionism and Japonism and photography.

From the 1870s Pater's influential text *The Renaissance: Studies in Art and Literature* brought aestheticism to wider notice and proposed a modern Renaissance embracing all the arts: 'All periods, types, schools of taste are in themselves equal.'[88] He proposed an analogous, creative relationship between periods, and the chapter 'The Poetry of Michelangelo' discussed the influence of the sculptor on the late work of Rossetti and Frederick Leighton. His suggestion that the ancient Greeks, Michelangelo and Leighton each remade the athlete according to their own age and individual vision was reflected in Day's Michelangelo-esque *Nude in Shadow* (no.113).

Pater's description of sculpture as a struggle between fact and art (answering earlier debates about the nude) was pertinent to photography, and his solution of dematerialising matter by interrupting surfaces with movement, shadow or light looked forward to the glimmering contours of Leighton's bronzes and Day's platinum prints. By the end of the century, symbolism was an international movement in the arts and poetry. Painters and photographers applied mystery, dematerialisation and diffusion to allegorical and mythical subjects, addressing the inner rather than the outer eye.

Pater argued that the distinctiveness of the arts lay in the inherent qualities of their different media, but that these were united in their address to the mind through the senses. Arts and crafts principles based on a shared formal language of line, tone and colour became a feature of art-school syllabuses. Formal handling became more idiosyncratic and expressive. The dialogue between art and photography and the focus on formal aspects found striking expression in colour, available after 1907. Photographers experimenting with this new format looked to painting and design, often introducing colour in the form of aesthetic artefacts and fabric.

Alvin Langdon Coburn
***Elsie 'Toodles' Thomas* c.1907–8**
Autochrome glass plate 50 x 60
The Royal Photographic Society Collection at The National Media Museum, Bradford

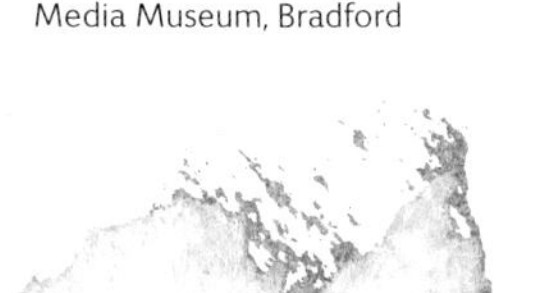

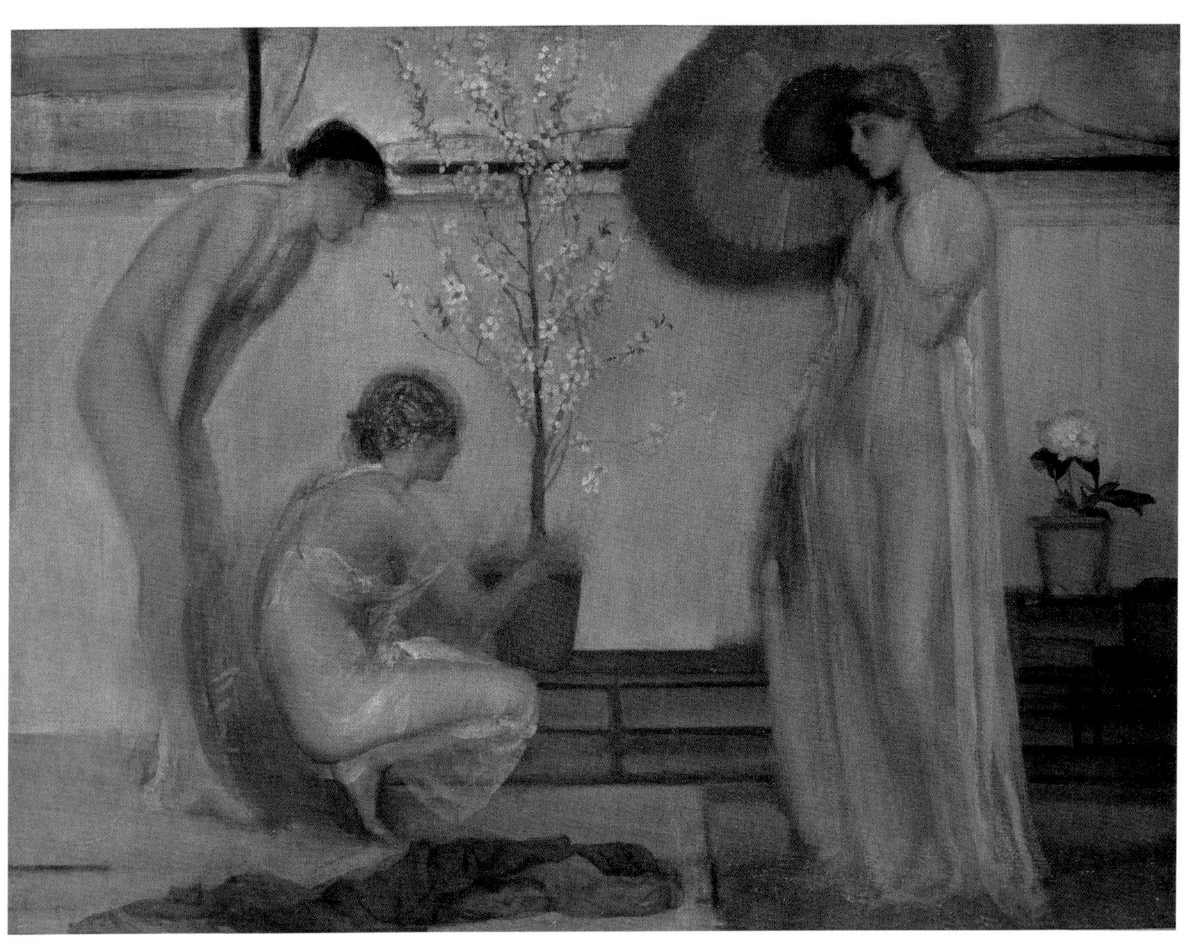

99 James Abbott McNeill Whistler
***Three Figures: Pink and Grey* 1868–78**
Oil paint on canvas 139.1 x 185.4
Tate. Purchased with the aid of contributions from the International Society of Sculptors, Painters and Gravers as a Memorial to Whistler, and from Francis Howard 1950

The aesthetic and arts and crafts movements brought the arts into closer relationships. In 1868, Whistler planned rooms that united art, design, poetry and music for the mansion of the shipping magnate Frederick Leyland. Only the dining room was completed, but *Three Figures: Pink and Grey* represents one of the compositions intended for a music room, reworked at a later date. Its frame was to be decorated with musical extracts. Whistler drew on *ukiyo-e*, Japanese prints and design widely collected in the arts and crafts movement, and on the rhythmic drapery of Greek Tanagra figures in the British Museum. This seamless synthesis of sources was facilitated by photographs, and a photograph of a Tanagra statuette and Whistler's drawing from it (1894) are now in the Hunterian Museum and Art Gallery, Glasgow.

In 1907 the Lumière Brothers launched a new photographic process that produced full colour images on glass plates. As the critic Dixon Scott explained in *The Studio*, autochrome plates mobilised a 'fabulous army' of 'starch-grains' coloured green, violet and orange, 'densely and adroitly marshalled, some four million to the square inch'.[89] This 'army' provided the coloured filter for a panchromatic emulsion, recently developed to be sensitive across the colour spectrum. The final product was the glass plate itself, reverse-processed to give a positive image viewed through the coloured filter layer. Each exposure yielded a unique photograph, which was displayed like a lantern slide or reproduced as an expensive four-colour printed illustration.

A number of London photographers took up the process, including John Cimon Warburg, who was a member of the Royal Photographic Society and exhibited at the Photographic Salon. Warburg was most interested in the decorative aspect of a photograph, which he felt took precedence over narrative. He overexposed this plate to produce a paler palette, mitigating the intensity of the autochrome colours. CJ & HK

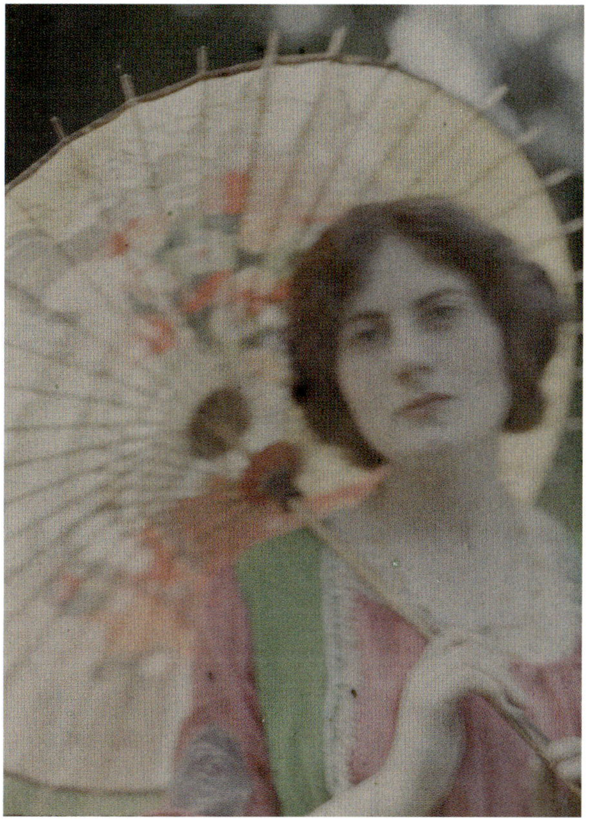

100 John Cimon Warburg
***The Japanese Parasol* c.1909**
Autochrome glass plate 10.8 x 8.2
The Royal Photographic Society Collection at The National Media Museum, Bradford

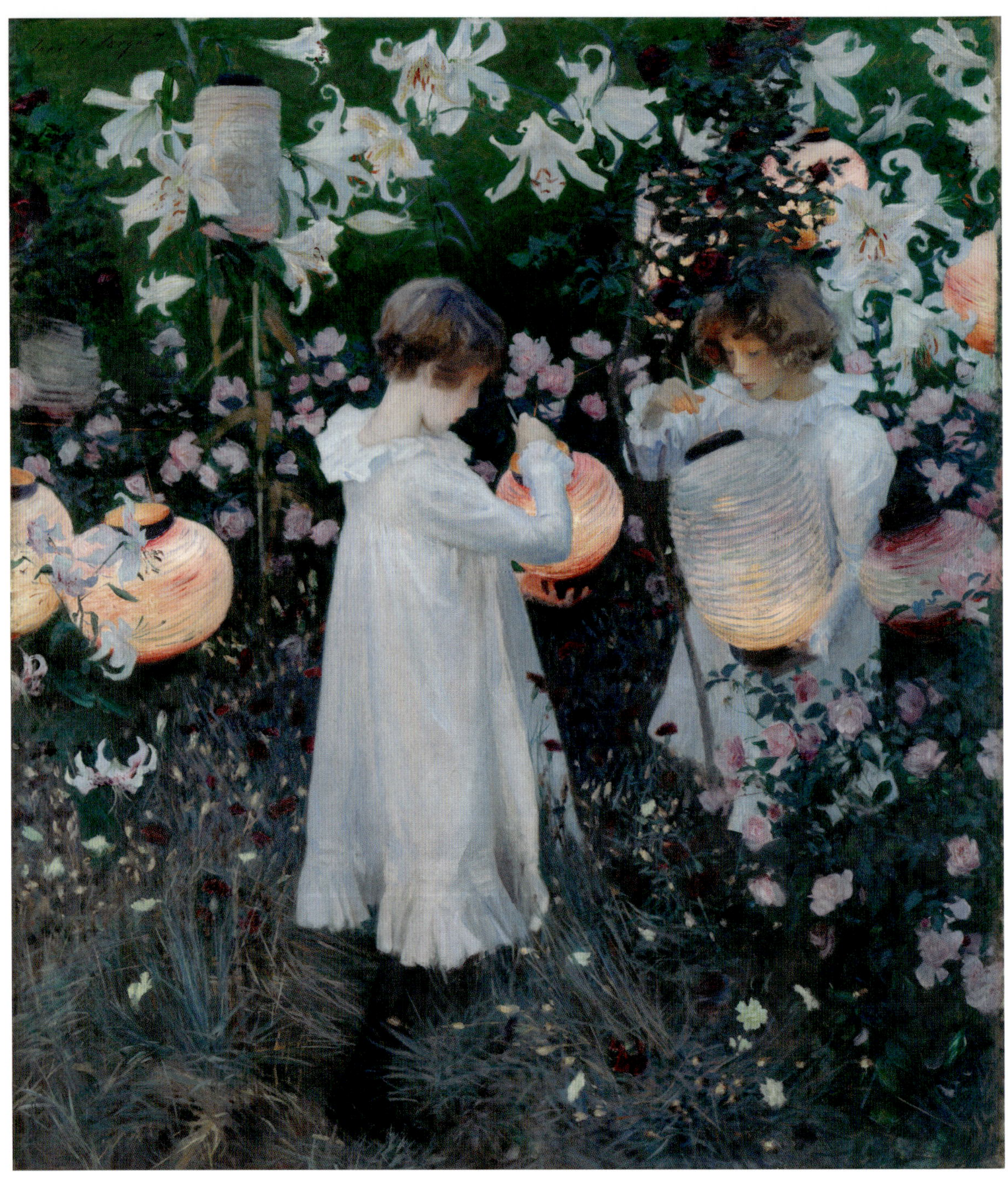

101 John Singer Sargent
***Carnation, Lily, Lily, Rose* 1885–6**
Oil paint on canvas 174 x 153.7
Tate. Presented by the Trustees of the Chantrey Bequest 1887

British painters enjoyed international celebrity and certain works acquired iconic status, which broadened their influence. Their fame generated variations by the artists themselves, by admirers and in reproductions of all kinds. Sargent's *Carnation, Lily, Lily, Rose* was a triumph at the Royal Academy in 1887; it was bought for the nation, placed on permanent display and reproduced in the *Art Journal* in 1888 and in a deluxe edition of photogravures in 1903.[90] It entered the vocabulary of motifs in British art, illustration and photography. The impact and success of Sargent's painting were due to its confident adaptation of the NEAC's aestheticised impressionism to the scale and medium of Academy painting, including Japonist motifs, fleeting light effects and an immersive, photographic composition lacking a horizon. This tipped-up view frequently reappeared in later Sargent paintings known to be based on photographs that he owned.

Warburg made this autochrome portrait of his young daughter Peggy, posed in the shady orchard of the family's Riviera garden. The autochrome plate was a largely automatic process: the depth of colour responded to exposure time, but the hues could not be adjusted. Warburg would have pre-visualised the striking complementary colours in the oranges, the gold of Peggy's bracelets and her blue-white dress. The relatively long exposure time – several seconds in midday sunlight and up to thirty seconds indoors – explains the blurred outlines of a small girl standing still for many seconds.

CJ & HK

102 John Cimon Warburg
***Peggy in the Garden* 1909**
Autochrome glass plate 10.8 x 8.2
The Royal Photographic Society Collection at The National Media Museum, Bradford

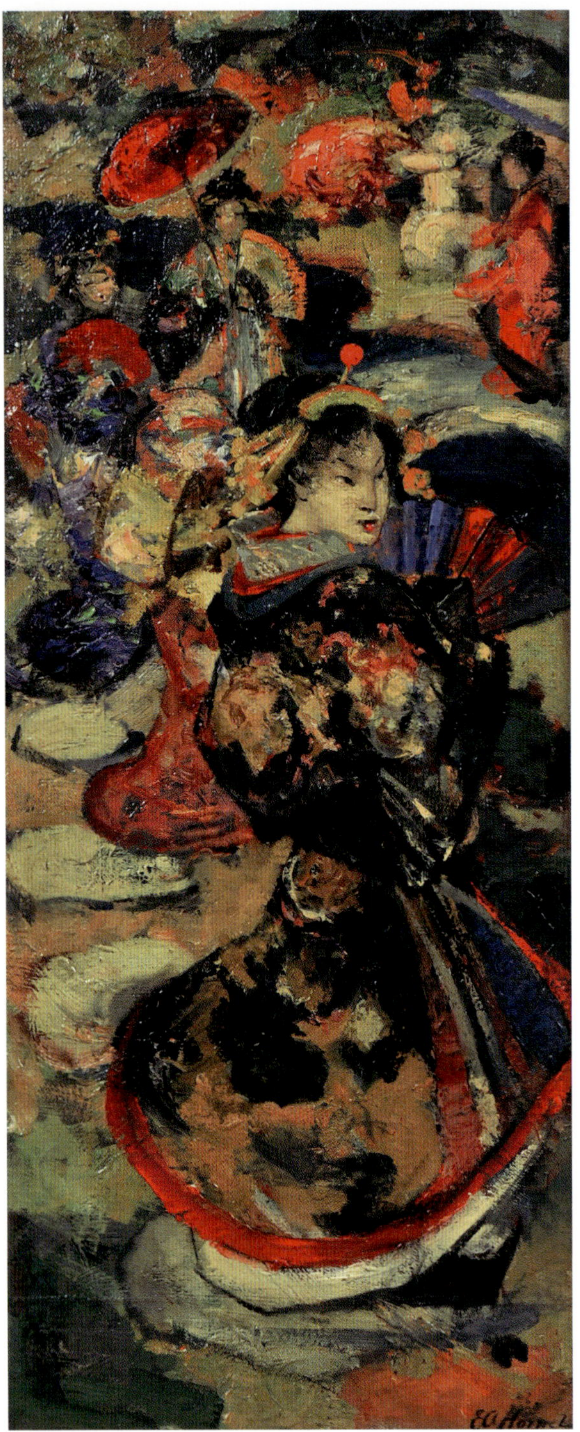

103 Edward Atkinson Hornel
***Two Geishas* 1894**
Oil paint on canvas 75.6 x 32.5
National Trust for Scotland, Broughton House and Garden

In 1893 Edward Atkinson Hornel and George Henry, associates of the avant-garde 'Glasgow Boys', a group of progressive artists who took inspiration from Impressionist and post-impressionist artists on the continenent, travelled to Japan. Elected members of the Photographic Society of Japan, they purchased Japanese souvenir photographs known as *shashin* and took photographs of their own. Hornel amassed over a hundred prints, now in the collection of Broughton House & Garden (National Trust for Scotland).

On returning to Scotland, Hornel moved away from French-inspired naturalism towards a more decorative style. His genre subjects recall those of *ukiyo-e* such as playing shuttlecocks or music as shown in the Japanese photographs, but he assembled these into different designs. The paintings lack the graceful contours and modelling of Japanese precedents and are translated into a flat, colourist tapestry of impasto, post-impressionist brushstrokes. Here the figure wears hair ornaments like those in the photograph, and the hem of the formal kimono appears to have suggested the patchwork colours of that in the painting. CJ

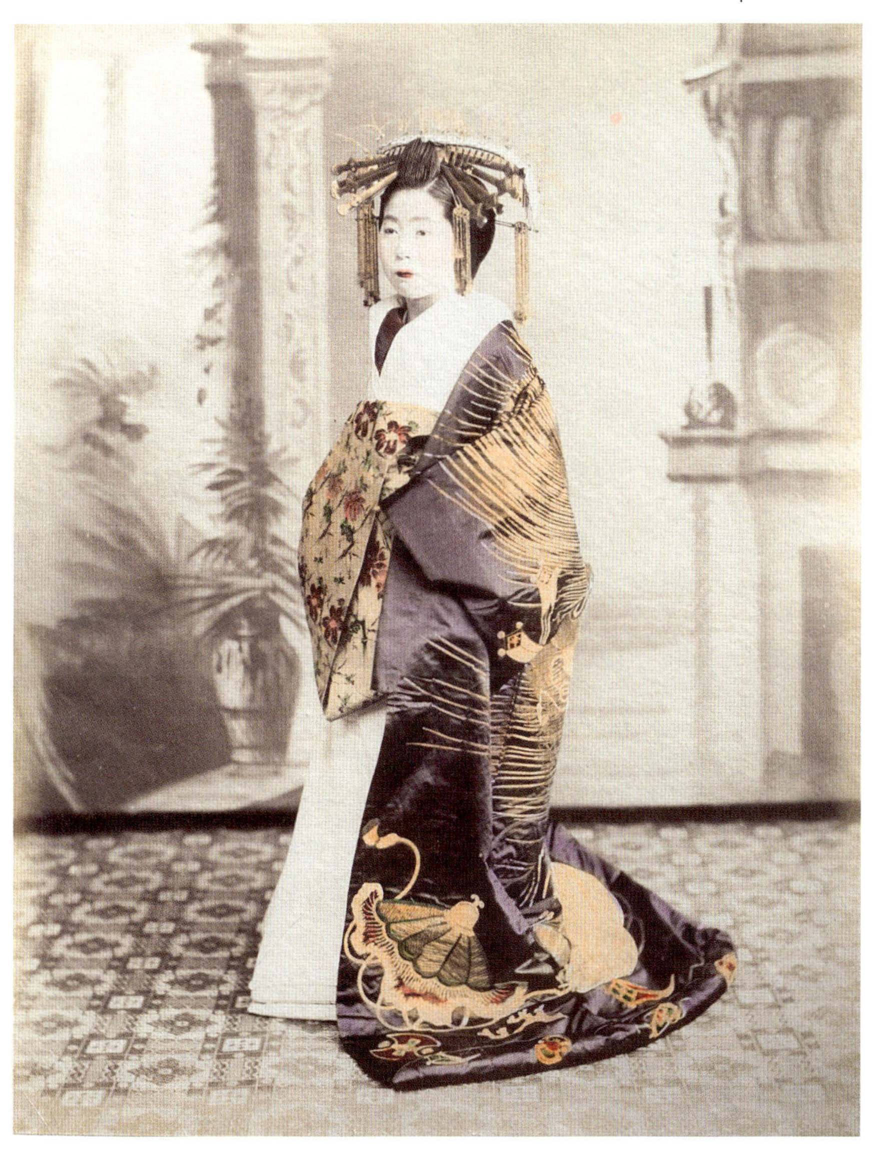

104 Photographer Unknown
***Geisha* c.1890**
Photograph, albumen print on paper
National Trust for Scotland, Broughton House and Garden

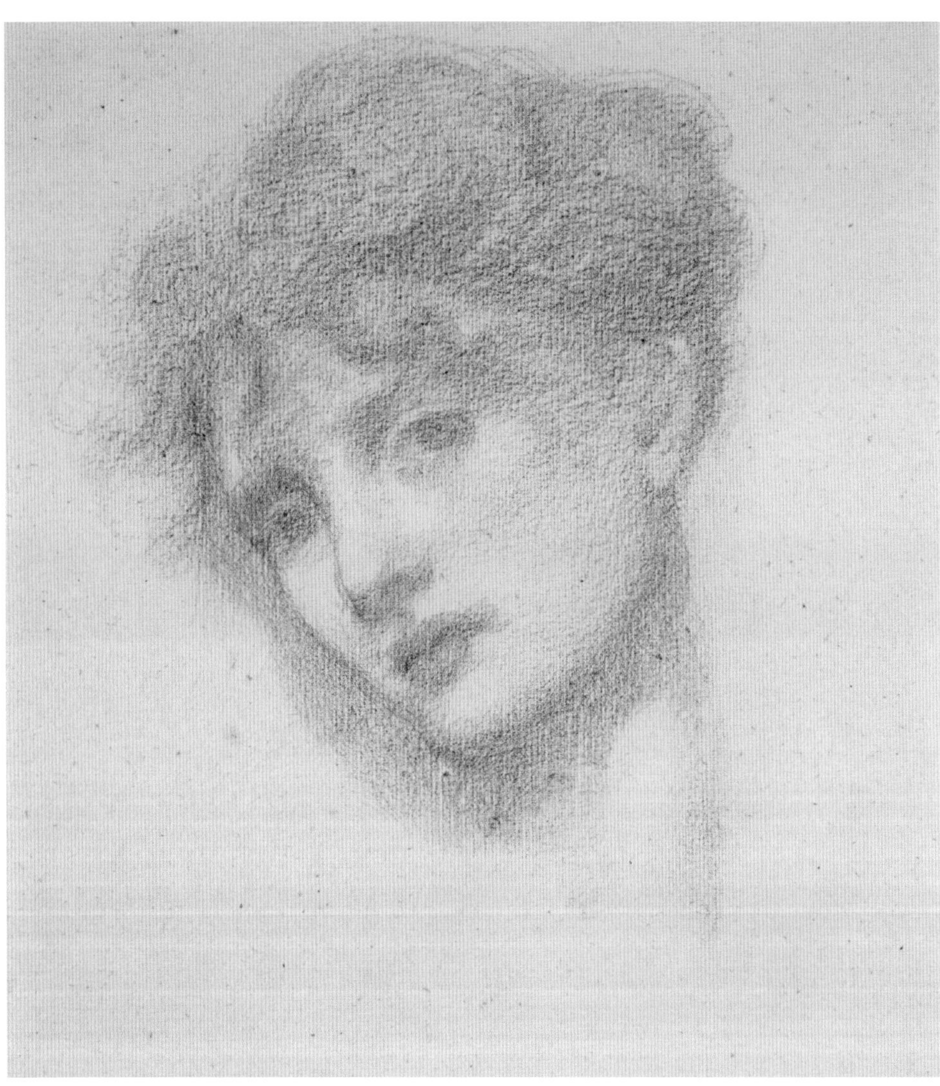

105 Edward Coley Burne-Jones
***Study of a Woman's Head* 1870**
Graphite on paper 20.3 x 18.4
Tate. Bequeathed by A.N. MacNicholl 1916

The Birmingham painter and designer Edward Coley Burne-Jones was a close associate of Rossetti and Morris and a leading figure in the aesthetic movement. In the late 1860s Rossetti and Burne-Jones became increasingly interested in the powerful sculptural forms and beautiful colour of Renaissance art. *Study of a Woman's Head* employs the technique of *sfumato* – a smoky dissolving contour most associated with Leonardo da Vinci – to introduce softness and mystery to this drawing.

Croft was a Birmingham photographer and a member of the Royal Photographic Society. His portraits are deceptively simple: there is little visible beyond the darkest tones. He argued that 'every picture should tell its own tale, but in such a manner as leaves a considerable amount of the details of the story to be furnished by the beholder … in accordance with his own varying moods and inclinations'.[93]

What tale might this portrait tell? A passage from a George Egerton story suggests possibilities in a neat synthesis of psychology and photography: 'The paleness of some strong feeling tinges her face … Her inner soul-struggle is acting as a strong developing fluid upon a highly sensitised plate; anger, scorn, pity, contempt chase one another like shadows across her face.'[94]

This pigment print was made by the gum bichromate process, which used a mixture of gum arabic, watercolour pigment and potassium bichromate sensitiser coated on paper. The coated paper was exposed to light through a negative and 'developed' by soaking in warm water to remove unexposed areas. The softened gum could be brushed away, and this was Croft's approach, picking out small areas of the face while allowing the rest of the image to sink back into shadow. CJ & HK

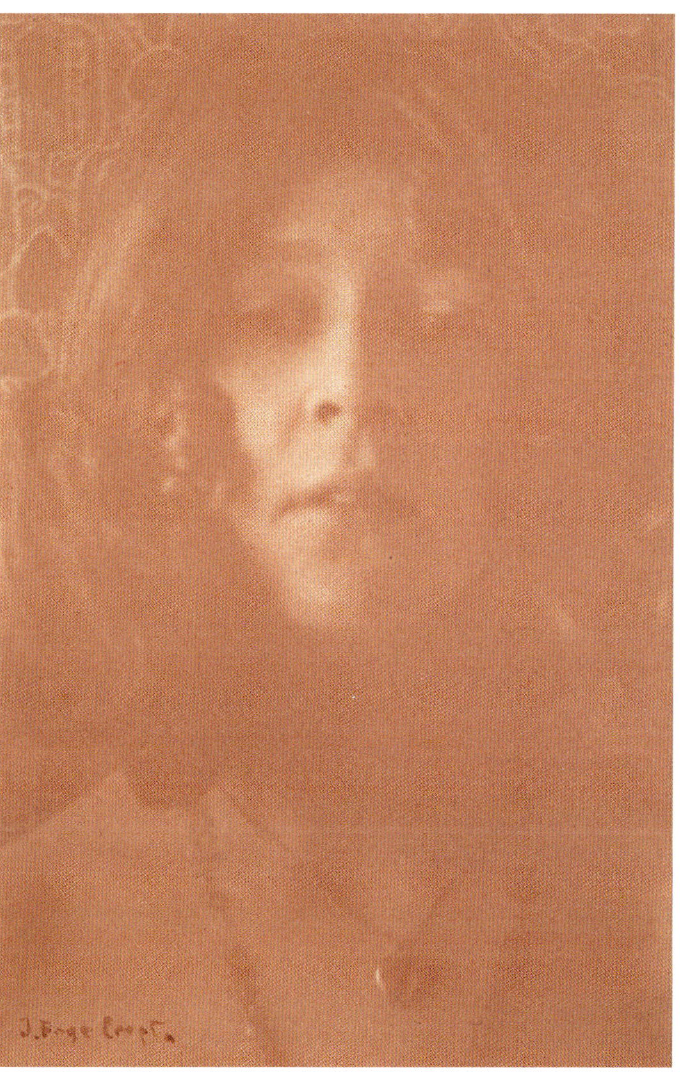

106 John Page Croft
***Insensibility* 1904**
Photograph, gum bichromate print on paper 20.2 x 13.4
The Royal Photographic Society Collection
at the National Media Museum, Bradford

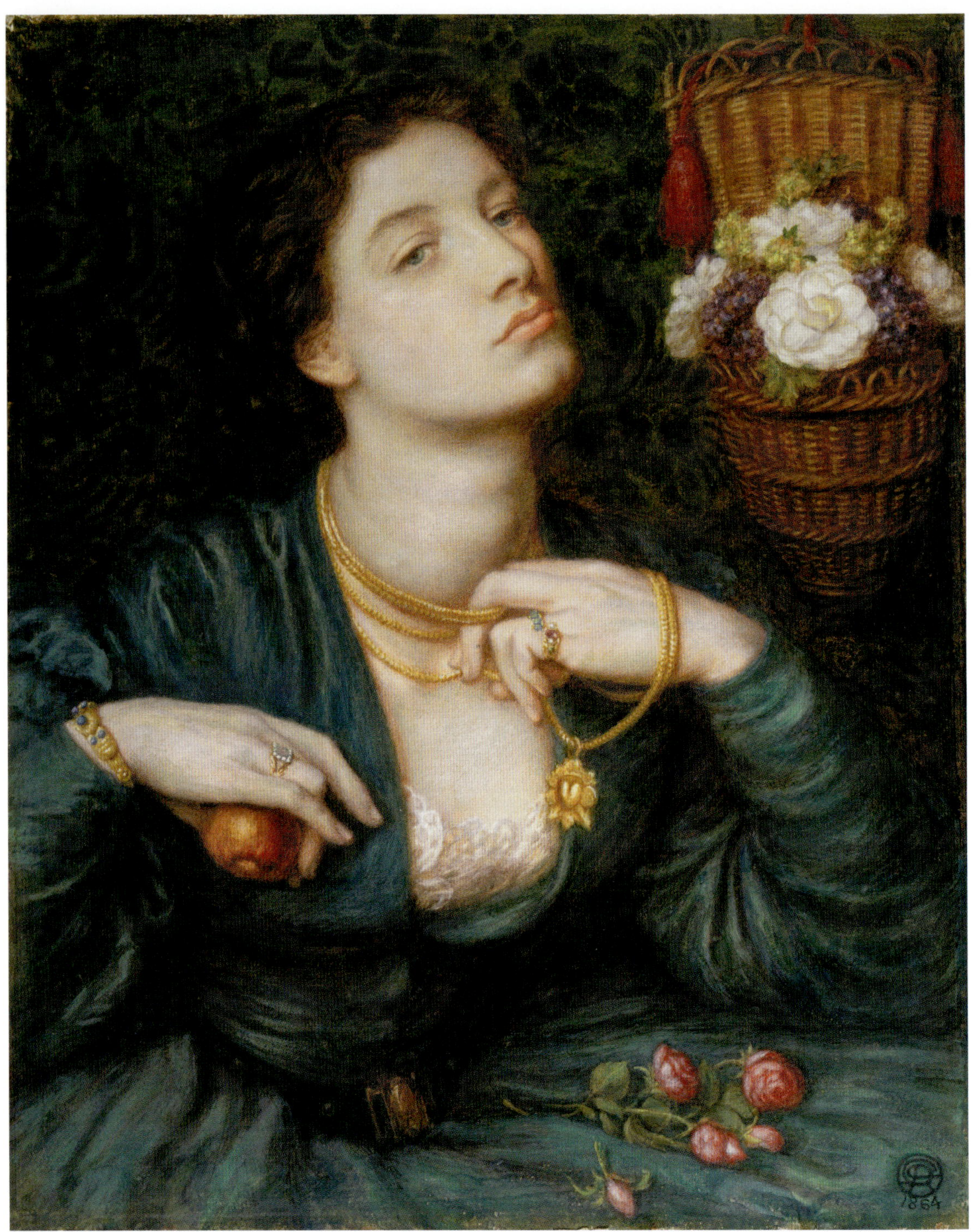

107 Dante Gabriel Rossetti
***Monna Pomona* 1864**
Watercolour and gum arabic on paper 47.6 x 39.3
Tate. Presented by Alfred A. de Pass 1910

Dixon Scott praised de Meyer's autochromes, for the elements within each picture were chosen and arranged so that it becomes 'distinctly a piece of creation ... Its beauty has been deliberately captured, the product of a decisive effort of "imaginative reason"; and it is a beauty recondite and remote, very different from the rather distracting and insouciant beauty which would emanate from the actual flowers, the actual bowl and drapery.' He could have been describing this portrait of Ottoline Morrell when he added that in autochrome portraits 'the picture has been prepared as one prepares a stage-picture; the Camera has merely been used to perpetuate it'.[95] De Meyer would become a celebrated fashion photographer, and the picture shows his ability to stage Morrell as a painter would; the languorous tilt of her head, throat and bust resemble aesthetic portraits such as Rossetti's *Monna Pomona*.

De Meyer collaborated with Alvin Langdon Coburn on several photographic exhibitions, beginning with *An Exhibition of Modern Photography* at the New English Art Club in 1907. They showed European and American photographers, including Fred Holland Day. The exhibition was praised for its Whistlerian design, the 'walls hung with pale brown canvas ... divided by panels of deep brown oak – toplight [sic] tempered à la Whistler by white muslin'.[96] They mounted a second and third show at the Goupil Gallery in 1908 and 1910. HK

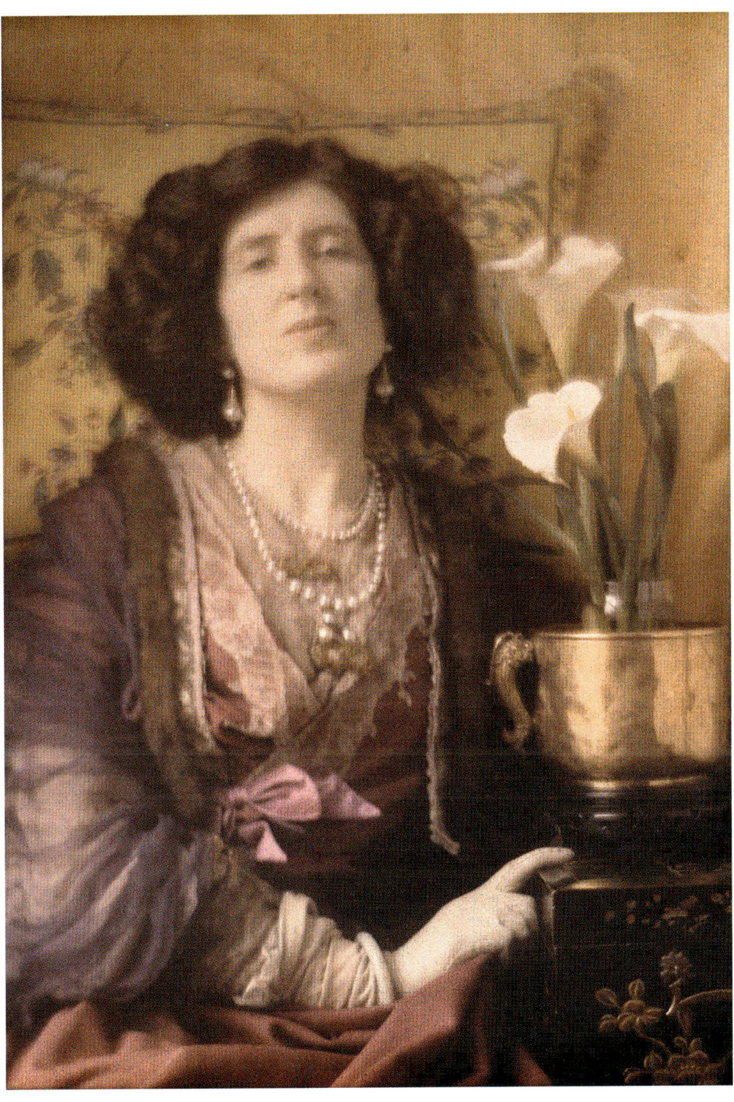

108 Baron Adolph de Meyer
***Lady Ottoline Morrell* c.1907**
Half-plate autochrome 16.5 x 10.8
National Portrait Gallery, London. Purchased with help from the Friends of the National Libraries and the Dame Helen Gardner Bequest, 2005

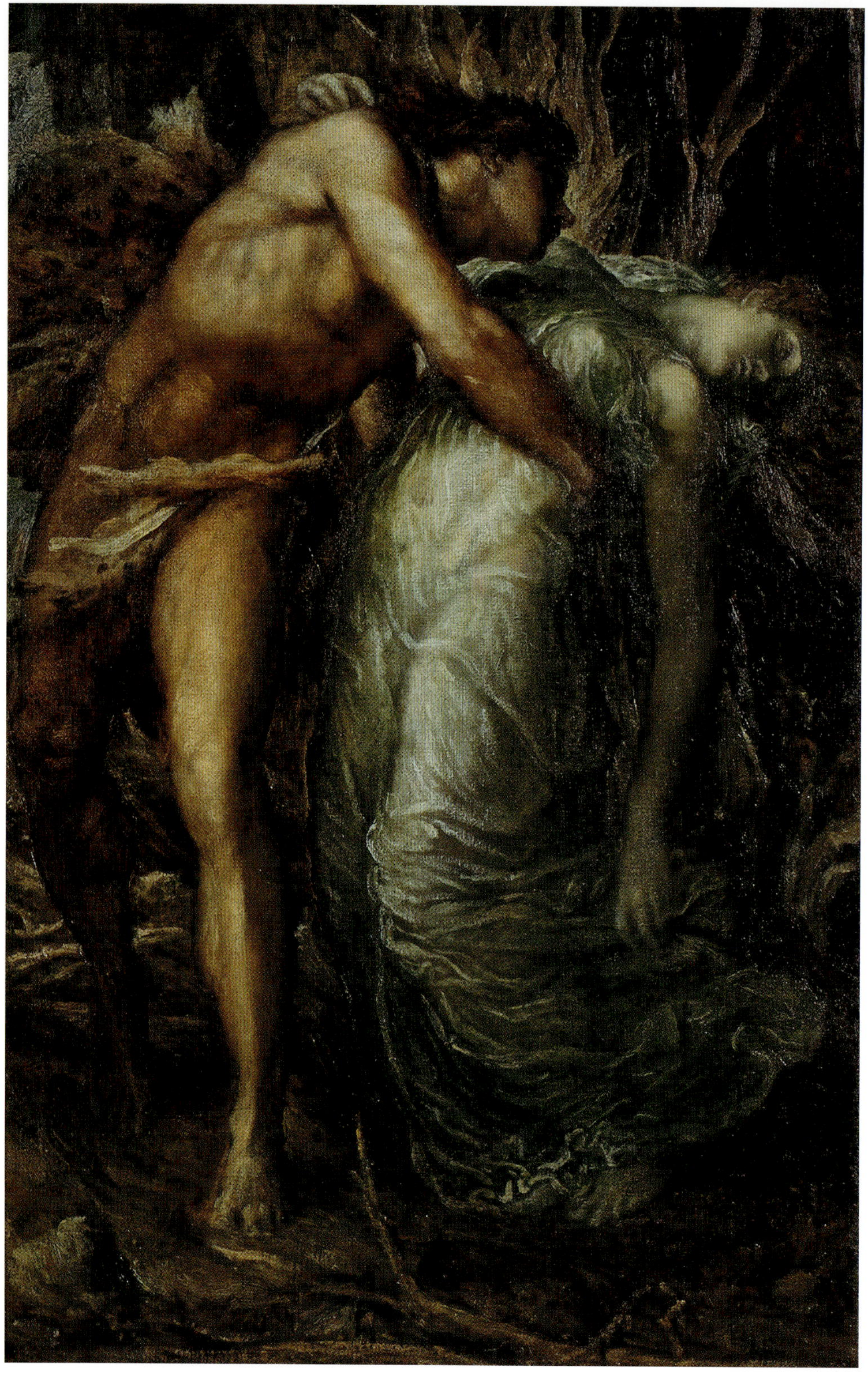

109 George Frederic Watts
***Orpheus and Eurydice* 1869**
Oil paint on canvas 71.8 x 48.1
Aberdeen Art Gallery & Museums Collections

110 William A. Stewart
***Ex Umbris* 1908**
Photograph, platinum print on paper 23.9 x 25.6
National Media Museum, Bradford
The Royal Photographic Society Collection
at the National Media Museum, Bradford

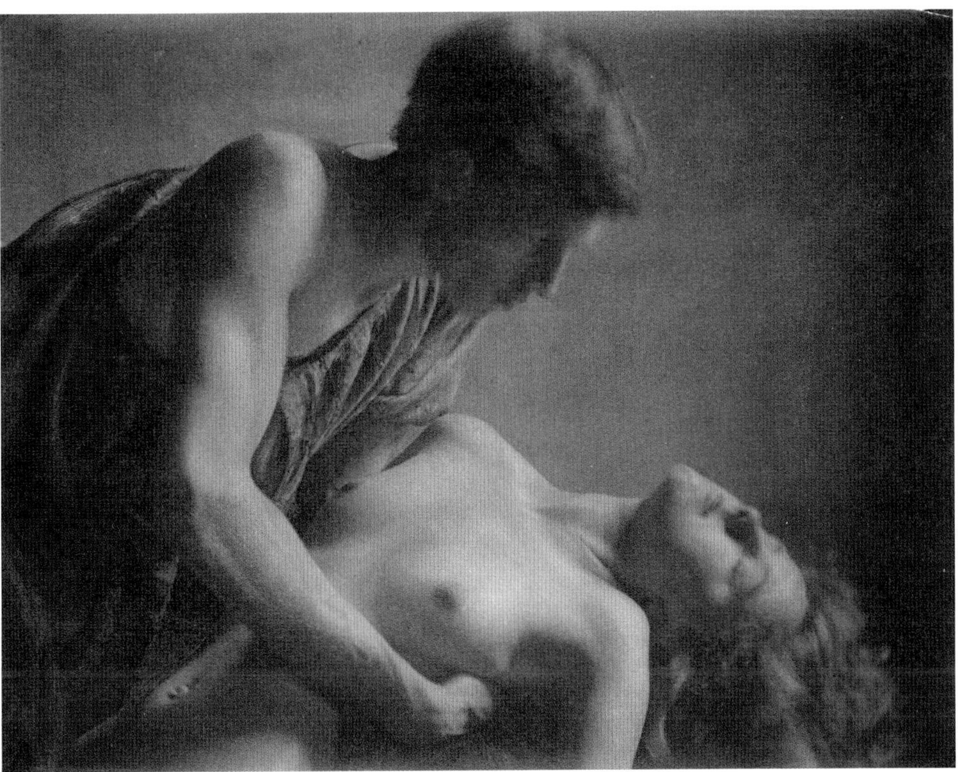

As George Bernard Shaw noted, aesthetic nudes appeared more frequently on the walls of exhibitions, transformed into art by exquisite composition and lighting.[97] The myth of Orpheus and Eurydice was one of a number of nude motifs with symbolist overtones that enjoyed creative re-treatments in art.

Watts's first version explored the aesthetic themes of mourning current in the Holland Park circle in the 1860s. Orpheus, son of Apollo, seeks Eurydice in the underworld and persuades Hades to let her go. He is instructed not to look back at her as they leave, but she stumbles and, as he twists to catch her, she returns to the shadows. Watts represented the turn and the last embrace. He returned to the subject repeatedly and also commissioned many photographs of his paintings. In 1880 he tried out new modifications on a print by Frederick Hollyer (Watts Gallery). The motif was well known through exhibitions and prints and was reprised in a sculptural version by Charles Ricketts in 1906. Watts's death two years before gave the mourning theme an extra significance.

Stewart's title *Ex Umbris* translates as 'out of the shadows'. The Orpheus and Eurydice narrative of emerging from shadow to light and back into shadow suited the aesthetic interests in indistinctness and was resonant for photographers. Both versions play on the way light and shadow reveal and dissolve the human form. CJ

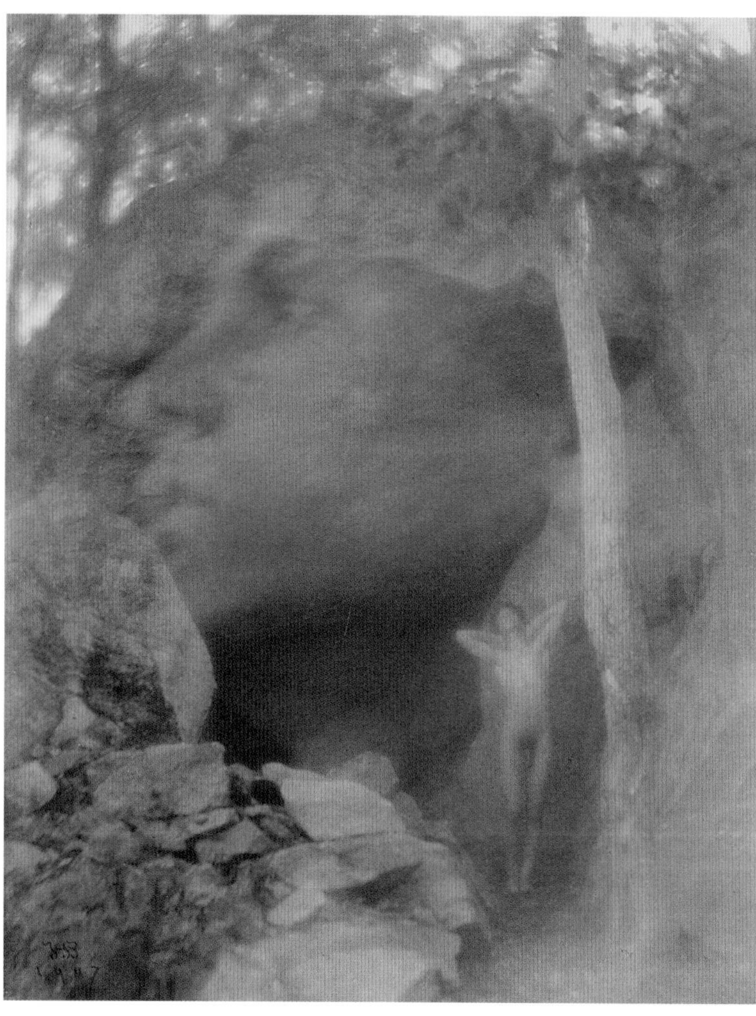

111 Fred Holland Day
***The Vision* 1907**
Photograph, platinum print on paper 24.4 x 18.4
The Royal Photographic Society Collection
at the National Media Museum, Bradford

Day's composite photograph incorporates a full-length figure from another Orpheus study, while the disembodied head – which may refer to Orpheus's beheading by the Maenads – is cropped from a photograph later exhibited as *Study for Endymion*. The shadow under the jaw suggests the entrance to the underworld.

In portraying a male nude, Day transmuted the camera's naked realism into an ideal beauty set within a timeless Arcadia. He described this 'Antique Vision' in 1900: 'In taking the ... figures out-of-doors, [the] photographer has gone back to antique life.'[98] Reality was further veiled by Day's soft-focus lens (made to an old British design), while aged platinum printing paper gave a lower contrast and more delicate tonal values.

The Orpheus photographs were made near Day's Massachusetts home, but they reflect his British connections, including his passion for John Keats, whose *Endymion* reconsiders the Orpheus myth. Day's obsession with the poet inspired his first trip to London in 1889, his remarkable collection of Keatsiana and his financing of the Keats memorial bust for the Hampstead Parish Church, whose 1894 presentation was attended by Aubrey Beardsley and the publisher John Lane. Lane subsequently contracted Day's Boston imprint, Copeland & Day, to publish ten titles including Oscar Wilde's *Salomé* and *The Yellow Book*.

Day gave the prints illustrated here to Frederick Evans, who introduced him to Beardsley and Lane and was his entrée to the Linked Ring, Day's most compatible photographic cohort. Evans also supported Day's signal exhibition, *The New School of American Photography*, at the Royal Photographic Society in 1900, featuring nearly 400 works by forty-one photographers.

Day owned a reduced-scale copy of Michelangelo's *The Dying Slave*. It may have influenced the pose of *Nude in Shadow*, as it did Leighton's *Sluggard*. HK

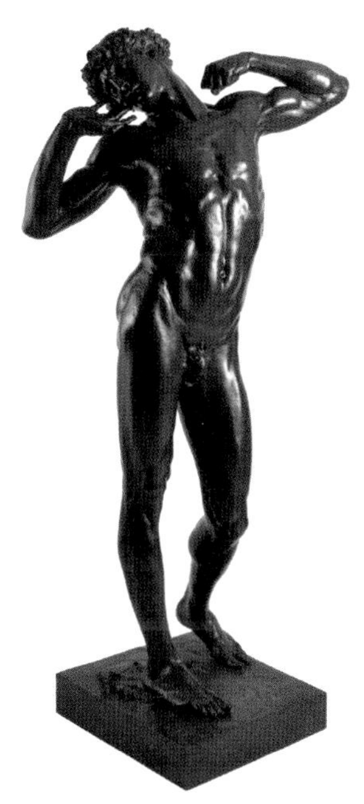

112 Frederic Leighton
***The Sluggard* 1885**
Bronze 191.1 x 90.2 x 59.7
Tate. Presented by Sir Henry Tate 1894

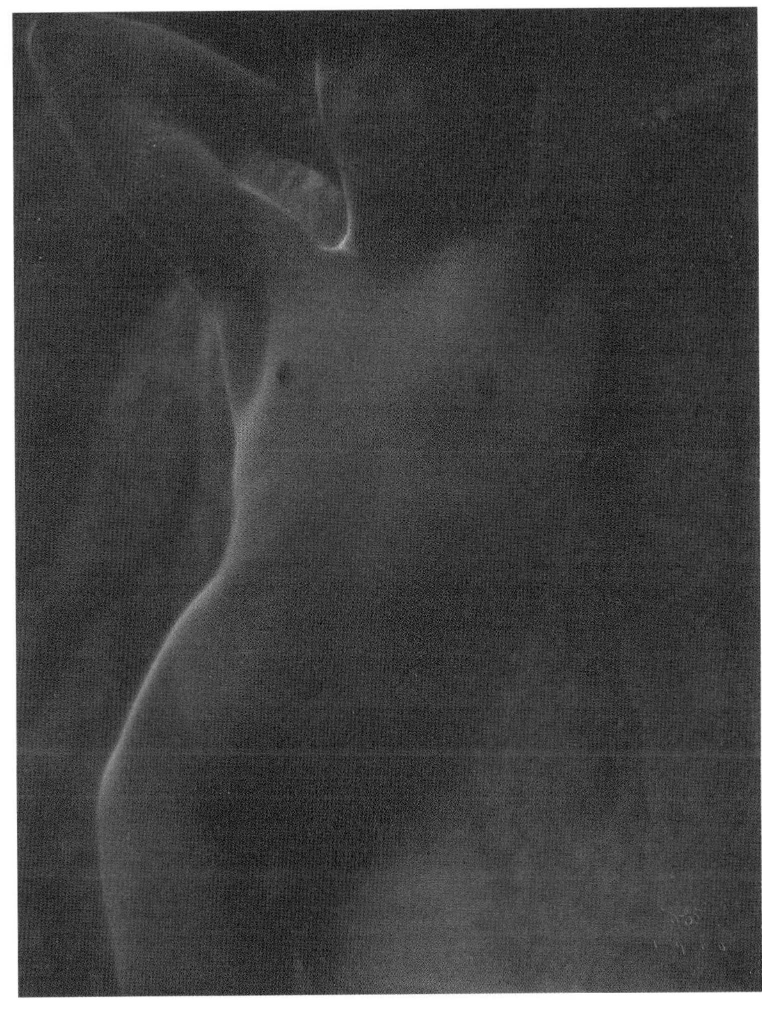

113 Fred Holland Day
***Nude in Shadow* 1910**
Photograph, platinum print on paper 32.9 x 21.3
The Royal Photographic Society Collection
at the National Media Museum, Bradford

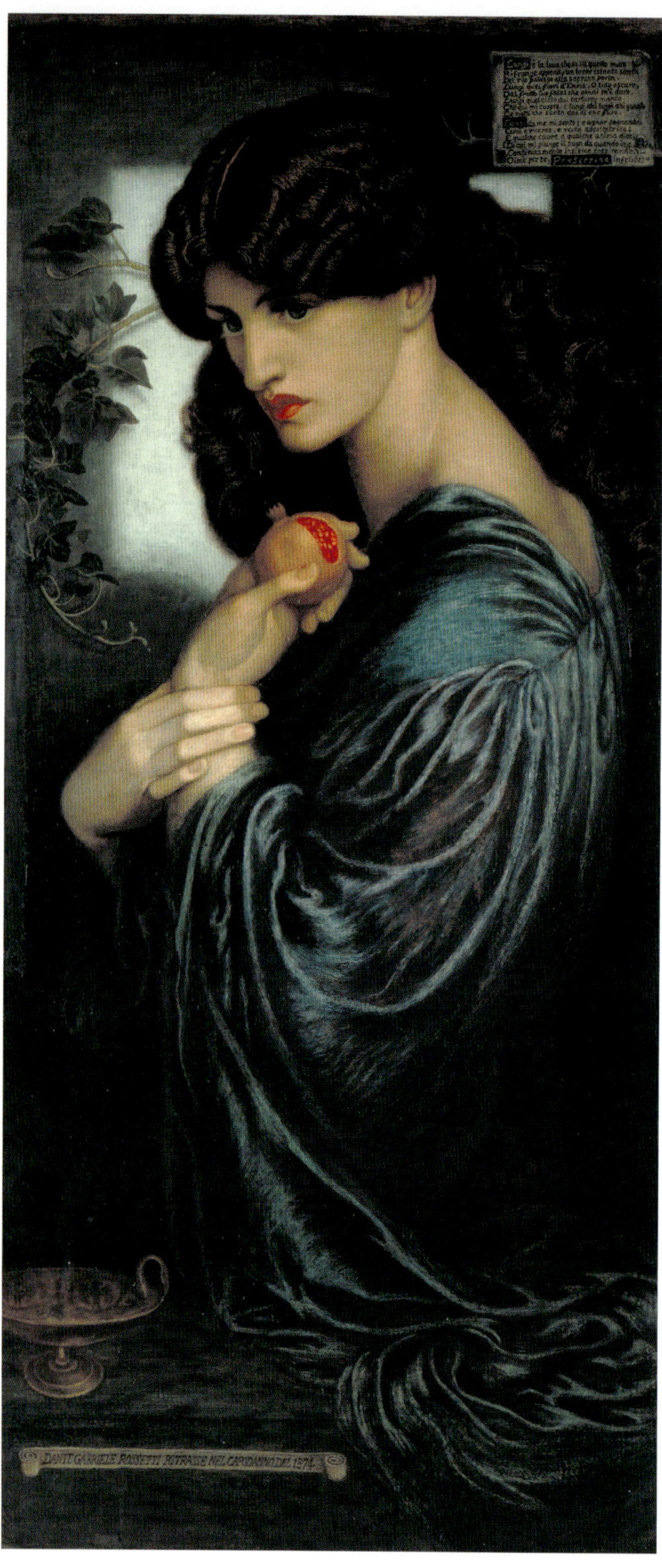

114 Dante Gabriel Rossetti
***Proserpine* 1874**
Oil paint on canvas 125.1 x 61
Tate. Presented by W. Graham Robertson, 1940

The tale of Proserpine was closely related to Eurydice and equally redolent of the aesthetic theme of mourning and mystery. Proserpine was the consort of Hades. Like Eurydice, she was allowed to return to the world, the provision being that she would not take any of the fruits of Hades, but she had eaten one grain of a pomegranate. Rossetti's first version of Jane Morris in this guise was rendered in chalk and the painting inaugurated his later style, in which a dryer, more broken surface further softens outlines and a narrower palette enhances the emotional impact of colour. A rectangle of light from the world above contrasts with Proserpine's shadowy tresses and the underwater hues of her heavily draped robe. The ivy represents memory.

Rossetti's distinctive female poetic figures were widely emulated in Britain and abroad. *Proserpine* was remade in eight versions, the last in 1881 shortly before Rossetti's death and represented in the form of a sonnet and an ecphrasis, circulated from 1875.[99] Rossetti's death in 1881 catalysed reissues of these and publications of the painting in accounts of his work, notably Henry Marillier's *Dante Gabriel Rossetti: An Illustrated Memorial* (1899), illustrated with photogravures.[100] The motif found its way into printmaking and photography.

Charles Ricketts's design for *A House of Pomegranates*, a collection of fairytales by Oscar Wilde, featured a pomegranate picker between each story whose basket is filled by the end of the book. Wilde located the 'artistic beauty' of his book in the formal language of 'Ricketts's delicate tracing and arabesques.'

Zaida Ben-Yusuf's celebrated photograph *The Odor of Pomegranates* was exhibited in 1900 in the important exhibition, *The New School of American Photography*, at the Royal Photographic Society, organised by Fred Holland Day. Born in London, Ben-Yusuf ran a successful photographic studio in New York. Her portraits emulated those of Whistler and Sargent and her departure into mythical subject matter was inspired by her friendships with Day and George Davison. The model for *The Odor of Pomegranates* was of Jane Morris's type with a wing of dark hair shadowing her eyes. The composition echoed the elongated shape and pose of *Proserpine* and the descending curves of drapery, which melt into the background. CJ

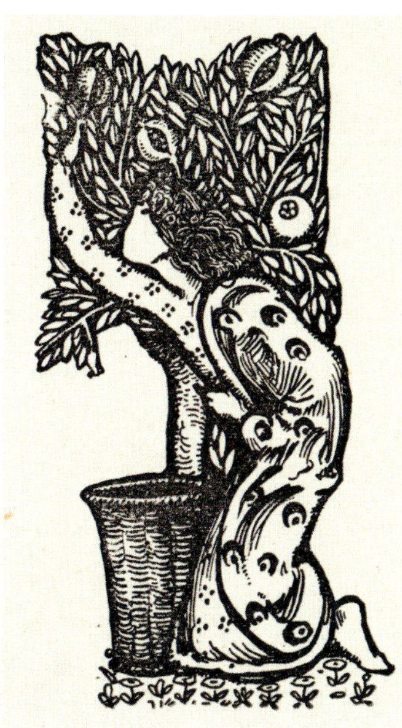

115 Charles Ricketts
Illustration from
A House of Pomegranates
by Oscar Wilde, London 1891
Tate Library and Archive

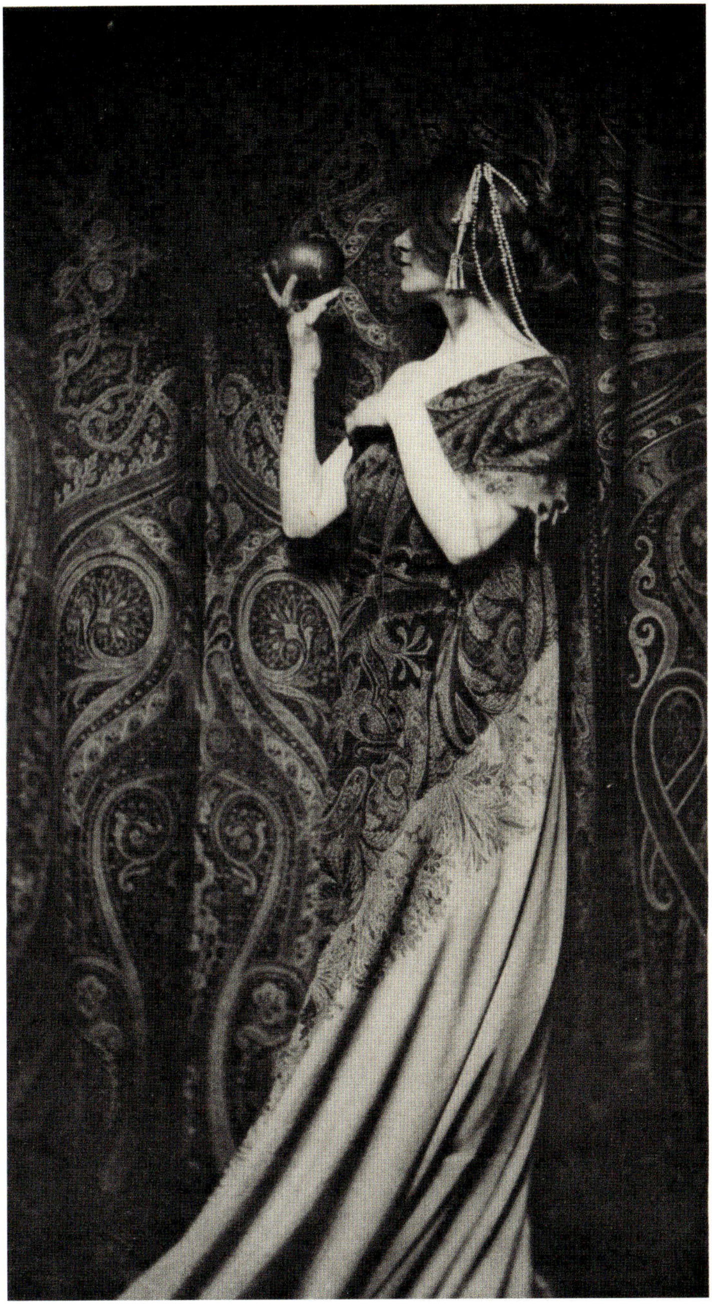

116 Zaida Ben-Yusuf
***The Odor of Pomegranates* 1899**
published in 1901
Photogravure on paper 19.4 x 10.8
Tate

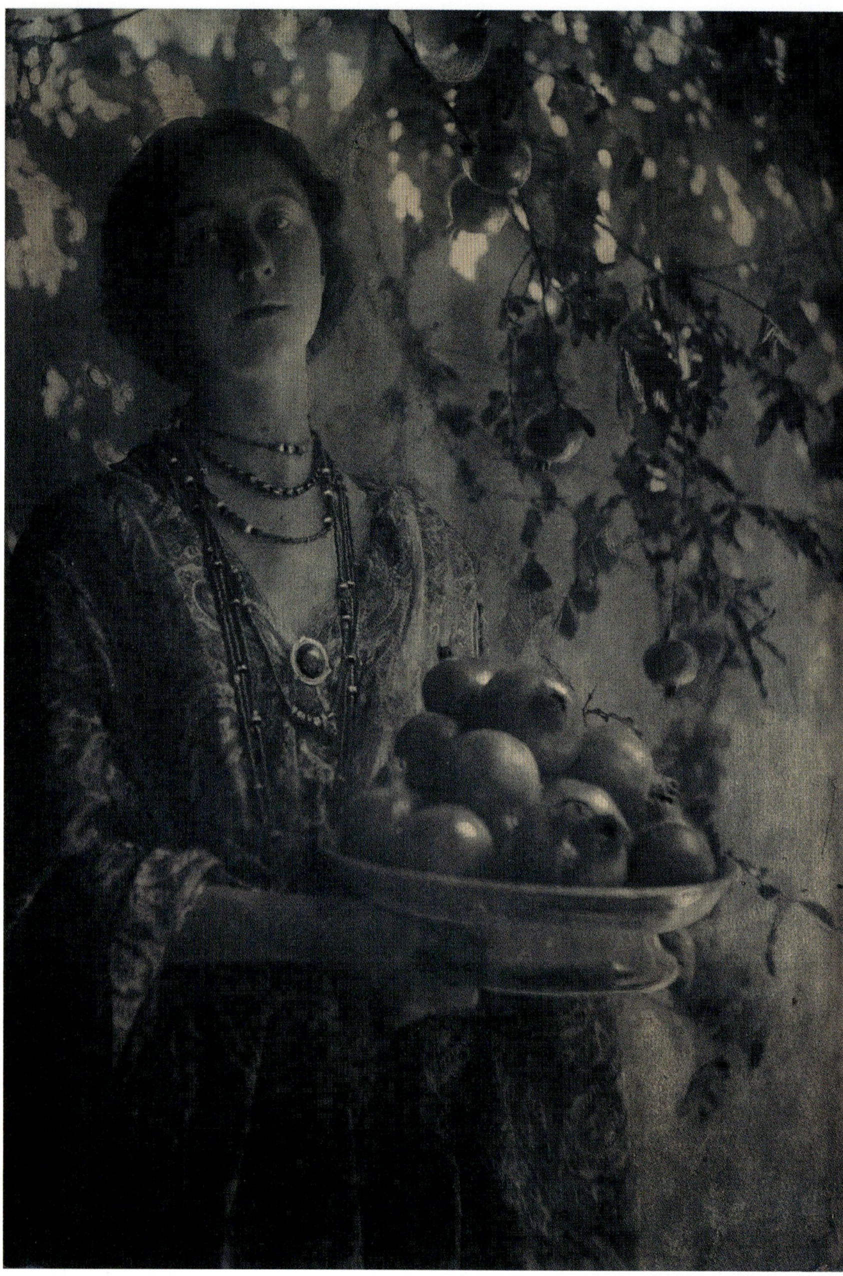

In 1906 another Pictorialist photographer, Minna Keene, exhibited *Decorative Study* representing her daughter, Violet, bearing a plate of pomegranates. The print was worked on by hand, with highlights added to the fruit and colour removed from background areas. Again affinity with Rossetti's famous work *Proserpine* is expressed in the formal qualities of the photograph, in this case soft modelling, a blue cast and filtered light from above. The image has a modern air, however: unlike Jane Morris in *Proserpine*, the model here, who was also a photographer, regards the viewer with a confident gaze. CJ & HK

117 Minna Keene
***Decorative Study* c.1906**
Photograph, carbon print on paper 48.3 x 33.7
The Royal Photographic Society Collection
at the National Media Museum, Bradford

Notes

1 D.S. MacColl, 'Photography and Drawing' (1902), in *Confessions of a Keeper and Other Papers*, London 1931, p.164. MacColl's provocation was a book by the British journalist Charles Caffin: *Photography as a Fine Art*, New York 1901.
2 MacColl 1931. Dugald Sutherland MacColl was Keeper of the Tate Gallery from 1907 to 1911.
3 H.P. Robinson, 'Composition NOT Patchwork', *British Journal of Photography*, vol.7, no.121 (2 July 1860), p.190.
4 [Elizabeth, Lady Eastlake] 'Photography', *Quarterly Review*, vol.101, no.202 (1857), p.442.
5 [Coventry Patmore] 'Mrs. Cameron's Photographs', *Macmillan's Magazine*, vol.13 (Jan. 1866), p.231.
6 Eustace Calland, 'The Influence of Painters on Photography. Whistler, Monet and Manet', *Practical Photographer*, vol.8, no. 88 (April 1897), p.104.
7 George Davison, 'Our Printing Processes', *Photography*, vol.3, no.157 (12 Nov. 1891), p.721.
8 A.C.R. Carter, 'The Two Great Exhibitions. The Photographic Salon', *Photograms of the Year 1900*, London 1900, p.109.
9 Charles Hastings, 'Pictorial Photography at Charing Cross Road: The Camera Club "Invitation Exhibition"', *Amateur Photographer*, vol.16, no.420 (21 Oct. 1892), p.281.
10 George Davison, 'Printing and Printing Methods. - III', *Photography*, vol.6, no.285 (26 April 1894), p.259.
11 Dixon Scott, 'Colour Photography', in *Colour Photography: And Other Recent Developments of the Art of the Camera*, ed. Charles Holme, *The Studio*, Special Number, 1908, p.2.
12 Scott 1908, p.1.
13 P.H. Emerson, 'Mrs. Julia Margaret Cameron', *Sun Artists*, no.5 (Oct. 1890), p.42.
14 J.C. Annan 'Collection of Work by the Late D.O. Hill, R.S.A. (1802–1870)', *Catalogue of the Seventeenth Annual Exhibition of the Photographic Salon 1909*, p.17.
15 Ibid.
16 Hugh Miller, 'The Two Prints' and 'The Calotype', *The Witness*, 24 June 1843 and 12 July 1843; Eastlake 1857, pp.442–68.
17 Quoted in John Ward and Sara Stevenson, *Printed Light: Scientific Art of William Henry Fox Talbot and David Octavius Hill with Robert Adamson*, Edinburgh 1986, p.36.
18 'Euphranor' [J.B. Manson], review of 'The Exhibition of 1864', quoted in Sara Stevenson, *The Personal Art of David Octavius Hill*, London and New Haven 2002, p.156.
19 Quoted in Stevenson 2002, p.148.
20 John Seward (Frederick Stephens), 'The Purpose and Tendency of Early Italian Art', *The Germ*, Feb. 1850, p.61.
21 John Ruskin, *Praeterita* (1885), in E.T. Cook and A. Wedderburn (eds.), *The Works of John Ruskin*, London 1903–12, vol.35, p.372; Ford Madox Brown, *The Diary of Ford Madox Brown*, ed. Virginia Surtees, New Haven and London 1981, p.14 (12 Nov. 1847).
22 'The Photographic Club', *Art-Journal*, no.11, 1 Aug. 1849, p.262.
23 Brown 1981, p.31 (25 Feb. 1858).
24 John Ruskin, 'On Turnerian Mystery', *Modern Painters 4* (1856), in Cook and Wedderburn 1903–12, vol.4, pp.75–6, 81.
25 William Holman Hunt, *Pre-Raphaelitism and the Pre-Raphaelite Brotherhood*, London 1905–6, vol.1, p.91.
26 Philip Hamerton, 'The Relationship between Photography and Painting', *Thoughts about Art*, London 1873, pp.58–9.
27 Quoted in Cook and Wedderburn 1903–12, vol.3, p.210 (7 Oct. 1845).
28 John Ruskin, *Modern Painters 4* (1856), Cook and Wedderburn 1903–12, vol.5, p. 333.
29 John Ruskin, 'Notes by Mr. Ruskin on Samuel Prout and William Hunt', in Cook and Wedderburn 1903–12, vol.14, p.389.
30 John Ruskin, manuscript catalogue, 1878, Ashmolean Museum, Edu. 62 289.
31 Laura Savage (Frederick Stephens), 'Modern Giants', *The Germ*, vol.1, no.4 (April 1850), p.173.
32 John Guille Millais, *The Life and Letters of Sir John Everett Millais*, London 1899, pp.109–10.
33 William Bell Scott, *Autobiographical Notes*, London 1892, vol.1, p.251.
34 John Tupper, 'The Subject in Art', *The Germ*, vol.1, no.1 (Jan. 1850), p.11.
35 William Henry Fox Talbot, *The Pencil of Nature*, 6 vols., London 1844–6, vol.2, pl.4.
36 Roger Fenton, 'On the Present Position and Future of the Art of Photography', *Journal of the Society of Arts*, 24 Dec. 1852, pp.50–53.
37 *Reports by the Juries on the Subjects in the Thirty Classes Into which the Exhibition was Divided*, London, 1851, vol. 1, p. 244
38 Hamerton 1873, pp.54–5.
39 Brown 1981, p.90 (5 Sept. 1854).
40 'Theta', *Photographic Journal*, vol.3, 21 May 1856, p.54.
41 Hamerton 1873, pp.58, 59.
42 Oscar Gustav Rejlander, 'Apology for Art Photography', *Photographic News*, 20 Feb. 1863, p.89.
43 Antoine Claudet, 'figures from the living model' advertisement, *Art Union*, vol.24, p.2 (15 Jan. 1841).
44 *Photographic Journal* (21 Jan. 1859), quoted in Gordon Baldwin, *Roger Fenton: Pasha and Bayadère*, Los Angeles 1996, p.89.
45 Samuel Butler, *Samuel Butler, Author of Erewhon (1835–1902): A Memoir*, London 1919, vol.1, p.41.
46 John Brown, Review of the Royal Society of Arts, *The Witness*, 22 April 1846, p.11.
47 'The Arundel Society', *Athenaeum*, 31 Oct. 1863, pp.576–7.
48 Virginia Dodier, *Lady Hawarden: Studies from Life 1857–1864*, New York 1999, p.101.
49 Sir David Brewster, *The Stereoscope, its History, Theory and Construction with its Application to the Fine and Useful Arts and to Education*, London 1856, p.204.
50 Oliver Wendell Holmes, 'The Stereoscope and the Stereograph', *Atlantic Monthly*, vol.3, June 1859, pp. 3, 744–5.
51 Ibid.
52 Julia M. Cameron, 'Preface', *Leonora*, London 1847, p.vi.
53 Cameron 1847, p.vii.
54 R.A.S. (A.J. Wall), *British Journal of Photography*, vol.9, no.168 (16 June 1862), p.233.
55 Wall 1862, p.234.
56 H.P. Robinson, 'Mr. H.P. Robinson's Pictures at the Club', *Journal of the Camera Club*, vol.3, no.37 (Oct. 1889), p.173.
57 Walter Crane, 'Of the Progress in Taste and Dress, in Relation to Art Education', *Aglaia*, vol.3 (Autumn 1894), p.8.
58 Charles Baudelaire, 'The Salon of 1846', *Oeuvres complètes*, ed. Claude Pichois and Jean Ziegler, Paris 1975–6, vol.2, pp.421–2.
59 Thomas Maitland (Robert Buchanan), 'The Fleshly School of Poetry: Mr. D.G. Rossetti', *Contemporary Review*, vol.18 (Aug.–Nov. 1871), pp.334–50.
60 Quoted in Colin Ford and Julian Cox, *Julia Margaret Cameron: The Complete Photographs*, Los Angeles 2003, p.19.
61 Quoted in Mark Bills and Barbara Bryant, *G.F. Watts: Victorian Visionary*, New Haven and London 2008, p.172.
62 Patmore, p.230.
63 Dante Gabriel Rossetti, *The Correspondence of Dante Gabriel Rossetti: The Formative Years*, ed. William Fredeman, London 2002, 60.38.
64 William Morris, 'The Blue Closet', in *The Defence of Guenevere, and Other Poems*, London 1858, p.195.
65 William Rossetti and Algernon Swinburne, *Notes on the Royal Academy Exhibition*, London 1868, p.48.
66 Ernest Chesneau, *English School of Painting*, trans. L.N. Etherington, London 1885, pp.252, 257.
67 Frederick Evans, 'Some Notes on Interior Work: Part VI - Choice of Subject', *Amateur Photographer*, vol.39, no.1023 (May 1904), p.372.
68 George Clausen, *Royal Academy Lectures on Painting*, London 1913, pp.43–4.
69 George Clausen, 'Autobiographical Notes', *Artwork*, no.7, 1931, p.19.
70 T.F. Goodall, 'Landscape', in P.H. Emerson and T.F. Goodall, *Life and Landscape on the Norfolk Broads*, London 1887, p.46.
71 Emerson and Goodall 1887, p.11.
72 Katherine A. Lochnan, *The Etchings of James McNeill Whistler*, New Haven and London 1984, p.178, figs.214, 215.
73 Margaret F. Macdonald, Grischka Petri, Meg Hausberg and Joanna Meacock, *James McNeill Whistler: The Etchings, a Catalogue Raisonné*, University of Glasgow, 2012, on-line at http://etchings.arts.gla.ac.uk: entry for *The 'Adam and Eve', Old Chelsea*, no.182.
74 P.H. Emerson, *Wild Life on a Tidal Water: The Adventures of a House-Boat and Her Crew*, London 1890, pp.1–2.
75 P.H. Emerson, *Naturalistic Photography for Students of the Art*, London 1889, p.78.
76 Quoted in Fiona Pearson, 'The Correspondence between P.H. Emerson and J. Harvard Thomas', *British Photography in the Nineteenth Century: The Fine Art Tradition*, ed. Mike Weaver, Cambridge 1989, p.201.
77 P.H. Emerson, 'A Nocturne', *Marsh Leaves*, London 1895, p.111.
78 Quoted in William Buchanan (ed.), *James Craig Annan: Selected Texts and Bibliography*, Oxford 1994, p.96.
79 James McNeill Whistler letter to James Craig Annan, 26 May 1893, University of Glasgow, no.8991.
80 Quoted in Buchanan 1994, p.102.
81 [George Davison], text to pl.13, *Kodak Portfolio, Souvenir of the Eastman Photographic Exhibition 1897, A Collection of Kodak Film Pictures by Eminent Photographers*, London 1897.
82 Arthur Symons, *London: A Book of Aspects*, Minneapolis 1909, pp.51, 60.
83 Symons 1909, p.24.
84 Davison, 'Figures in Landscape', *Photography*, vol.1, no.33 (27 June 1889), p.385.
85 Bertram Cox, *Pictorial Photography 1905–1940 by J. Dudley Johnston*, London 1952, n.p.
86 Henry Peach Robinson, 'Figures in the Landscape', *Letters in Landscape Photography*, London 1888, p.49.
87 George Meredith, 'In the Woods', published 1870, reprinted in *Catalogue of the Seventeenth Annual Exhibition of the Photographic Salon 1909*, p.12.
88 Walter Pater, *The Renaissance: Studies in Art and Literature*, London 1873, p.x.
89 Scott 1908, p.3.
90 *Art Journal*, 1888, facing p.65.
91 Scott 1908, p.2.
92 Scott 1908, p.1.
93 J. Page Croft, 'A Plea for Motive', *Photographic Art Journal*, vol.2, no.15 (15 May 1902), p.70.
94 George Edgerton, 'An Empty Frame', in *Keynotes*, Boston and London 1894, p.125. *Keynotes* was Edgerton's first short-story collection, published by Mathews & Lane in 1893. It was immediately successful and notorious on both sides of the Atlantic.
95 Scott 1908, p.9.
96 *The Morning Post* (2 Feb. 1907), quoted in Pamela Roberts, *Alvin Langdon Coburn*, Madrid 2014, p.33.
97 George Bernard Shaw, 'Some Criticisms of the Exhibitions', *Amateur Photographer*, vol.36, no.941 (16 Oct. 1902), p.305.
98 F.H. Day, 'Is photography an art?', unpublished typescript, c.1900, quoted in Patricia G. Berman, 'F. Holland Day and His "Classical" Models: Summer Camp', *History of Photography*, vol.18, no.4 (Winter 1994), p.349.
99 Frederick Stephens, 'Pictures by Mr. Rossetti', *The Athenaeum*, 14 Aug. 1875, pp.219–21; Dante Gabriel Rossetti, 'Sonnets for Pictures', *The Athenaeum*, 28 Aug. 1875, p.273.
100 Henry Marillier, *Dante Gabriel Rossetti: An Illustrated Memorial*, London 1899, pp.169–70.

Acknowledgements

This book could not have been written without the pioneering scholarship of the past few decades and we are especially grateful for the advice and moral support provided by Antonia Laurence-Allen, Gordon Baldwin, Patrizia di Bello, Barbara Bryant, William Buchanan, Caroline Corbeau-Parsons, Virginia Dodier, Elizabeth Edwards, Colin Ford, Clare Freestone, Sarah Hepworth, Ken and Jenny Jacobson, Pete James, Elaine Kilmurray, Brian Liddy, Anne Lyden, Kenneth McConkey, Margaret MacDonald, Brian May, Kevin Moore, Colin Morrison, Lynn Nead, Shirley Nicholson, Richard Ormond, Christiana Payne, Denis Pellerin, Terrence Pepper, Elizabeth Prettejohn, Pamela Roberts, Roddy Simpson, Alison Smith, Lindsey Stewart, Mercè Giralt Sos, Sara Stevenson, Mike and Debra Stutters, Clare Willsdon and especially Roger Taylor.

We would also like to thank Tim Batchelor, Alice Chasey, Colin Grant, Roanne Marner, Emma O'Neill and Maggi Smith.

This exhibition has been made possible by the provision of insurance through the Government Indemnity Scheme. Tate Britain would like to thank HM Government for providing Government Indemnity and the Department for Culture, Media and Sport and Arts Council England for arranging the indemnity.